The Reformation in Eastern and Central Europe

St Andrews Studies in Reformation History

Editorial Board:

Andrew Pettegree, Bruce Gordon and John Guy

Titles in this series include:

The Shaping of a Community: The Rise and Reformation of the English Parish c. 1400–1560
Beat Kümin

Seminary or University? The Genevan Academy and Reformed Higher Education, 1560–1620
Karin Maag

Marian Protestantism: Six Studies
Andrew Pettegree

Protestant History and Identity in Sixteenth-Century Europe
(2 volumes)
edited by Bruce Gordon

Antifraternalism and Anticlericalism in the German Reformation: Johann Eberlin von Günzburg and the Campaign against the Friars
Geoffrey Dipple

Piety and the People: Religious Printing in French, 1511–1551
Francis M. Higman

Reformations Old and New: Essays on the Socio-Economic Impact of Religious Change c. 1470–1630
edited by Beat Kümin

John Foxe and the English Reformation
edited by David Loades

The Reformation in Eastern
and Central Europe

Edited by

KARIN MAAG

Published by
SCOLAR PRESS
Gower House
Croft Road
Aldershot
Hants GU11 3HR
England

Ashgate Publishing Company
Old Post Road
Brookfield
Vermont 05036–9704
USA

British Library Cataloguing in Publication Data

The Reformation in Eastern and Central Europe.
  (St Andrews Studies in Reformation History)
  1. Reformation—Europe, Central.   2. Reformation—Europe,
  Eastern.   3. Protestantism—History.   4. Church history—16th
  century.
  I. Maag, Karin.
  940. 2'3

  ISBN 1–85928–358–6

Library of Congress Cataloging-in-Publication Data

The Reformation in Eastern and Central Europe/edited by Karin Maag.
    p.   cm.
  (St Andrews Studies in Reformation History)
  Includes index.
  ISBN 1–85928–358–6 (cloth : alk. paper)
  1. Reformation—Europe, Eastern—Congresses.   2. Reformation—
  Europe, Central—Congresses.   3. Europe, Eastern—Church
  history—16th century—Congresses.   4. Europe, Central—Church
  history—16th century—Congresses.   I. Maag, Karin.   II. Series.
  BR300.R425   1997
  274.3'06—dc20   96–41760
                                                             CIP

ISBN 1 85928 358 6

Typeset in Sabon by Manton Typesetters, 5–7 Eastfield Road, Louth, Lincolnshire, LN11 7AJ and printed in Great Britain by The Ipswich Book Company, Suffolk

Contents

List of figures

Notes on contributors

Joachim Bahlcke is on the staff of the Centre for the History and Culture of East Central Europe in Leipzig, and an associate lecturer at the Humboldt University in Berlin. His publications include *Regionalismus und Staatsintegration im Widerstreit. Die Länder der Böhmischen Krone im ersten Jahrhundert der Habsburgerherrschaft (1526–1619)* (1994), and as co-editor, *Ständische Strukturen in Ostmitteleuropa* (1996) and *Handbuch der historischen Stätten Böhmen und Mähren* (1996).

Maria Crăciun is a lecturer in the department of Mediaeval History, Babeş-Bolyai University of Cluj, Romania. She has completed a doctoral dissertation on 'Protestantism and Orthodoxy in 16th century Moldavia', and published several articles on different aspects of the subject. She is the editor of a conference volume on *Ethnicity and Religion in Central and Eastern Europe* (1995).

Rona Johnston Gordon is an honorary lecturer in the department of Modern History at the University of St Andrews and a fellow of the Reformation Studies Institute. She is the author of various articles on recatholicization in Austria.

Norbert Kersken is a member of staff at the Herder-Institut, Marburg. His monograph, *Geschichtsschreibung um Europa der 'nationes'. Nationalgeschichtliche Gesamtdarstellungen im Mittelalter* was published in 1995.

Karin Maag is a Research Fellow of the Social Sciences and Humanities Research Council of Canada, and an Honorary Lecturer in Modern History at the University of St Andrews. Her monograph, *Seminary or University? The Genevan Academy and Reformed Higher Education 1560–1620* was published in the St Andrews Studies in Reformation History in 1995.

Janusz Mallek is Professor in Modern History at the Copernicus University in Torun, Poland, and Dean of the Faculty of History. His publications include *Ustawa o rzadzie Prus Ksiazeych z r. 1542* [The Constitution of Ducal Prussia in 1542] (1967), *Prusyksiazece a Prusy Krolewskie w 1. 1525–1548* [Ducal Prussia and Royal Prussia in the years 1525–1548] (1976), and *Preussen und Polen. Politik, Stande Kirche und Kultur vom 16. bis 18. Jahrhundert* (1992).

Sergiusz Michalski is a visiting Professor at several Swiss and German universities. His publications include *The Reformation and the Visual Arts* (1993) and *New Objectivity. Painting, Graphic Art and Photography in Weimar Germany, 1919–1933* (1994), and as editor, *Les Iconoclasmes* (1992).

Michael G. Müller is professor in the department of History and Civilization at the European University Institute in Florence. He is currently completing his monograph *Zweite Reformation und städtische Autonomie im Königlichen Preussen, Danzig, Elbing und Thorn in der Epoche der Konfessionalisierung.* He is also the author of several articles on Royal Prussia.

Graeme Murdock is lecturer in Modern History at the University of Birmingham. He is also currently completing a thesis at Brasenose College, Oxford on 'International Calvinism and the Reformed Church of Hungary and Transylvania, 1613–1658'.

Jiří Pešek is Professor of History at the Charles University, Prague. He is the author of *Mestanská vzdelanost a kultura v predbelohorskych Cechách 1547–1620 – vsední dny kulturního zivota* [Burgher education and culture in the pre-White Mountain Bohemia of 1547–1620 – everday cultural life] and numerous articles on book culture and libraries in sixteenth-century Bohemia.

Christine Peters is lecturer in Early Modern History at the Queen's College, Oxford. She works on the social context of religion, devotional patterns, and the process of the Reformation in England and Romania.

Andrew Pettegree is Reader in Modern History at the University of St Andrews and Director of the St Andrews Reformation Studies Institute. His publications include *Emden and the Dutch Revolt* (1992), *The Early Reformation in Europe* (1992) and (with Alaistair Duke and Gillian Lewis) *Calvinism in Europe 1540–1620* (1994). He is an editor of the St Andrews Studies in Reformation History.

Valery Rees teaches history at St James School in London, and is a member of the group in the Renaissance Department at the School of Economic Science translating the *Letters of Marsilio Ficino*. She is currently researching the connection between Renaissance Florence and Hungary, and has published articles in *History Today* (1994), *Hungarian Quarterly* (1995), and *The European Legacy* (1996).

Heinrich Richard Schmidt is Honorary Lecturer in Modern History at the University of Berne, and Research Fellow of the Swiss National Science Foundation. His publications include *Reichstädte und Reforma-*

tion (1986), *Konfessionalisierung im 16. Jahrhundert* (1992), and *Dorf und Religion* (1995).

Preface

The papers that form the basis for the essays in this volume were first given at an international conference sponsored by the newly reformed British National Committee (BNC) of the International Commission of Historical Sciences at St Andrews in April 1995. The conference was made possible by additional generous financial support from the British Academy, and the University of St Andrews. The decision to offer the conference proceedings as a volume in the St Andrews Studies in Reformation History was warmly encouragaed by the editors of the series, and I would also like to acknowledge the very helpful spirit with which contributors have received my editorial suggestions.

Ventures of this sort are always a team effort, and that this has been both enjoyable and intellectually stimulating I owe to the generosity of many who have contributed their time and intellectual insights. David Watson acted as a highly efficient conference organizer, and the conference would hardly have been possible without the initial encouragement and support of Professor John Guy. Professor Heinz Schilling of the University of Berlin and Professor Robert Evans of the University of Oxford both gave valuable advice as to whom should be approached to contribute. Tom Scott, Ole Grell and Bruce Gordon all offered helpful insights at a final workshop session of the conference, all of which inform the remarks in the introduction. Julian Crowe of the St Andrews Computing Laboratory once again patiently assisted the process of rendering computer discs into a compatible format. Ian Johnston kindly agreed to provide a map for the volume. Rona Johnston provided helpful comments on earlier drafts of the introduction. Above all, my thanks go to Andrew Pettegree, the Director of the Reformation Studies Institute, who has collaborated with me to bring this project to fruition. His enthusiasm, organizational skills and intellectual contribution have made the process all the more rewarding. To all of them, and to my colleagues in the Reformation Studies Institute, I am extremely grateful.

Karin Maag
St Andrews
1996

Abbreviations

ADB	Allgemeine Deutsche Biographie
ARG	Archiv für Reformationsgeschichte
DAW	Diözesanarchiv Vienna
DBI	Dizzionario biographico degli Italiani
DBL	Dansk Biografisk Leksikon
Decades	Rerum Ungaricum Decades
DHGE	Dictionnaire d'Histoire et de Géographie Ecclesiastique
DNB	Dictionary of National Biography
DREL/Pápa	Dunánlál Református Egyház Levéltár
EHR	English Historical Review
LexMA	Lexikon des Mittelalters
MPEIF	Magyar Protestáns Egyházi és Iskolai Figyelmező
Opera	Opera Omnia
PSB	Polski Slownik biograficzny
RESEE	Revue des Etudes Sud-Est Européenes
SCJ	Sixteenth Century Journal
TT	Törtenelmi Tár
ZEP	Zempléni egyházmegye protocolluma

CHAPTER ONE

The Reformation in Eastern and Central Europe

Andrew Pettegree and Karin Maag

It is a curious fact that one can read most general histories of the Reformation without being strongly aware that there *was* a Reformation in Eastern Europe. To be more precise, one would say that the impact of the sixteenth-century Reformation goes largely unnoticed: all general surveys, of course, will refer to the Bohemian Hussite movement of the fifteenth century, though often in the context of an 'incomplete' or 'premature' Reformation; the success of this movement in establishing an enduring counter-Church a century before Luther is still barely recognized.[1] Otherwise Eastern Europe is largely confined to the margins, described mostly as a haven for dissident groups of various complexions as the century wore on, the home of Schwenkenfeldians and Antitrinitarians.[2] The astonishing impact of mainstream Protestantism, both Lutheranism and Calvinism, throughout this region, particularly in the first generation of reform, is barely realized.

One can postulate three main reasons for this curious, and in many ways very distorted perception. Firstly, the success of the Counter-Reformation in recapturing many of these lands for Catholicism in the seventeenth century has obscured the considerable impact of Protestantism in the earlier period. Conversion and military activity together made this one of the Counter-Reformation's most successful regions. In some parts, such as Bohemia, a previously healthy Protestant tradition was all but obliterated.[3] Secondly, linguistic barriers continue to be a powerful impediment to studying these events. The complicated ethnic and linguistic patchwork of Central and Eastern Europe means that a scholar often needs to master several languages as a basic tool of

---

[1] See Frederick G. Heymann, 'The Hussite-Utraquist Church in the fifteenth and sixteenth centuries', *ARG*, 52 (1961), 1–2.

[2] See Róbert Dán and Antal Pirnát (eds), *Antitrinitarianism in the Second Half of the 16th Century* (Budapest, 1982), and Mihály Balázs, *Early Transylvanian Antitrinitarianism (1566–1571)* (Baden-Baden, 1996).

[3] František Kavka, 'Bohemia', in Bob Scribner, Roy Porter and Mikulas Teich (eds), *The Reformation in National Context* (Cambridge, 1994).

research. This can be a compelling disincentive to all but the most persistent and linguistically gifted. But undoubtedly the most powerful reason for the neglect of Eastern Europe has been the troubled history of this region in the twentieth century. The almost total exclusion of lands such as Hungary, Czechoslovakia (as it then was) and Poland from free cultural and political interchange with neighbouring lands to the west for 45 years from 1945 had a hugely distorting effect. To those of us brought up in these post-war generations these lands seemed almost impenetrably foreign: part of an 'Eastern bloc' behind the 'Iron Curtain'. Cultural intercourse with these countries was almost completely suspended. Travel, even for tourism, was arduous and complicated, and invariably expensive; scholarly archives could seldom be accessed. Nor, of course, were scholars in these lands invariably free to choose the subject or intellectual direction of their work. The study of religious movements such as the Reformation was particularly affected by an intellectual environment strongly hostile to truly independent research in these fields.[4]

This modern perspective is clearly extremely misleading. The tragedy of war in our own century obscures the sixteenth-century reality, when lands such as Bohemia and Hungary were fully a part of the Central European economic and cultural system, linked by a dense and intricate system of trade routes and intellectual connections to lands west and south. In intellectual terms these lands sometimes gave the lead to Germany and the Empire, rather than vice versa (take for instance the extraordinary influence and vitality of the University of Prague in the later Middle Ages); economically these lands possessed some of the most developed urban cultures, and provided much of Europe's supply of precious metals before the discovery of the gold and silver mines of the New World.[5] This was not a faraway land, and clearly no backwater; cities such as Prague and Cracow would have been more familiar, and played a more important role in European society, than the remote and relatively underpopulated lands on the northern and western periphery.[6]

---

[4] See for instance Hermann Barge, *Luther und der Frühkapitalismus* (Gütersloh, 1951) or Bernd Moeller (ed.), *Luther in der Neuzeit* (Gütersloh, 1983), especially Günter Vogler's article, 'Martin Luther und die Reformation im Frühwerk von Karl Marx'.

[5] On the importance of mining, see Ward Barrett, 'World bullion flows, 1250–1800' and Herman van der Wee, 'Structural changes in European long-distance trade, and particularly in the re-export trade from south to north, 1350–1750', in James D. Tracy (ed.), *The Rise of Merchant Empires: Long-Distance Trade in the Early Modern World, 1350–1750* (Cambridge, 1990), pp. 21, 245.

[6] The city of Prague flourished especially in the mid-fourteenth century. See Elizabeth Wiskemann, *Czechs and Germans: A Study of the Struggle in the Historic Provinces of Bohemia and Moravia* (London, 1967), p. 6.

It is only with the recent political transformation of Eastern Europe that we can fully realize this, and recognize the vigour and subtlety with which the populations of this region reacted to the new cultural and religious movements emanating from Germany and Italy from the fifteenth century.

Of course, even with the more open frontiers established in the last few years, the problems of studying the Reformation in these lands remain formidable. Chronologically, one could justifiably begin with Jan Hus and his early fifteenth-century movement for reform. At the other end, it seems equally important not to omit the impact of the Catholic Reformation which began to be felt at the end of the sixteenth century and continued through the seventeenth. Indeed, the term 'Reformation' is perhaps inadequate for a movement which subsumed such a variety of confessional approaches from Catholicism, Utraquism, Lutheranism and Calvinism through Mennonites, Hutterites, Unitarians and other groups.

Furthermore, research into confessional struggles in the sixteenth and early seventeenth centuries is complicated by the shifting political, ethnic and religious map of East-Central Europe at the time. Figure 1.1 and the following geographical overview may help to set the scene.

Beginning in the north, the kingdom of Poland-Lithuania was ruled by the Jagiellon dynasty until 1572, after which the royal family died out, and successive monarchs were hence elected by the noble estates. In 1466, the Polish crown incorporated Western Prussia, henceforth known as Royal Prussia. Eastern Prussia, ruled by the Teutonic knights, became a vassal of the Polish crown, but preserved some measure of independence and was known as Ducal Prussia. In 1525, Albert of Hohenzollern, the last Teutonic knight to be Duke, secularized the Duchy, thus creating a hereditary possession for his own family.

Moving southwards, the lands of the crown of Bohemia were constituted by Bohemia, Moravia, Silesia and Lusatia. Although these four lands had been incorporated for the first time in 1348, the political overlordship remained in flux over the next 200 years. Thus while Moravia and Bohemia formed a close unit, Silesia was ruled directly by Hungary between 1469 and 1490 before rejoining Bohemia after the death of the powerful Hungarian king, Matthias Corvinus.

Between 1490 and 1526, the four lands were ruled by Ladislas II Jagiellon, succeeded by his son, Louis II Jagiellon, members of the Polish royal house. As in Poland after 1572, the Bohemian lands placed a strong emphasis on the right of the estates gathered in the Diet to elect their monarch. After the death of the childless Louis II at the battle of Mohács in 1526, the Bohemian crown lands recognized the Habsburg Ferdinand I as their ruler, with varying degrees of enthusiasm in the

1.1 Map of Eastern and Central Europe

different lands.[7] Thus by 1526, the Bohemian crown lands formed part of the Habsburg Empire.

To the south-east of Bohemia lay the kingdom of Hungary. After the strong rule of Matthias Corvinus, the Hungarian estates joined with the Bohemian lands in recognizing Ladislas II Jagiellon as their king. In order to prepare for a Habsburg claim to the Hungarian throne, the Emperor Maximilian organized the marriage of his grandson, Ferdinand, to Louis II Jagiellon's sister, while Louis himself married a granddaughter of Maximilian. Consequently, after Louis II's early death in 1526, Ferdinand claimed the Hungarian throne. However, Ferdinand was challenged by John Zapolya, who was the preferred candidate of the Hungarian nationalists. In the end, the pressures of the Turkish advance led to a three-way partition of the country, with Royal Hungary, ruled by the Habsburgs, in the west, the central part of Hungary governed directly by the Turks, and eastern Hungary, known as Transylvania, ruled by Zapolya and his heirs, under the overlordship of the Ottomans.

To the east of Hungary lay Moldavia, a tribute-paying vassal of the Ottoman Empire. Thus, the Moldavian princes, although preserving some measure of autonomy, were under the control of the Turks.

Finally, to the south of Bohemia lay the Austrian lands, hereditary possessions of the Habsburgs. The Austrian lands were split into four parts, three of which concern us here: Upper and Lower Austria, separated by the Enns river, and Inner Austria, constituted by the southern provinces of Styria, Carinthia, Gorizia and Carniola.

Hence by 1526, there were three spheres of influence: the lands controlled by Poland–Lithuania in the north, the Habsburg possessions in the centre and south, and the lands under direct or indirect Ottoman control to the east.

While political borders generally achieved some measure of recognition by the middle of the sixteenth century, the distribution of different ethnic groups did not neatly match political boundaries. The most numerous ethnic group throughout Eastern Europe were the Slavs, especially in the Bohemian lands and in Poland. In Hungary, the dominant ethnic group were the Magyars, whose language distinguished them from their Slav neighbours. In Ducal Prussia, Silesia, parts of the other Bohemian lands, Hungary and especially in Austria, German-speakers, generally known as Saxons, were in the majority. Other smaller groups in eastern Hungary included the Romanians and the Szeklers, who were related to the Magyars, while communities of Jews settled throughout Eastern European towns and cities.

---

[7] On Bohemia and Ferdinand I, see Kenneth J. Dillon, *Kings and Estates in the Bohemian Lands 1526–1564* (Brussels, 1976).

Prior to the Protestant Reformation, the confessional picture across Eastern Europe was largely uniform. In Poland, Ducal Prussia, most of the Bohemian lands, Hungary and the Austrian lands, the over-whelming majority of the population was Catholic. Eastern areas in many of these lands had a certain number of Orthodox communities. Further east, in Moldavia, the Orthodox formed the majority. Groups of Jews and Muslims made up the rest of the religious mosaic. The major division in confessional terms in the decades preceding the Reformation was in Bohemia, where the Utraquist church, following the practices and theology of Jan Hus, existed in parallel with the Catholic church.

The confessional and ethnic diversity of Eastern Europe, even prior to the first signs of interest in the Reformation, serves to show that an overarching explanation for the course of the Reformation in this area would not encompass this variety in a satisfactory way. Nevertheless, the Eastern European context does display some common features in the different lands, of particular interest to scholars familiar with the often very contrasting contemporaneous situation in Western Europe. In comparison with much of Western Europe, Eastern Europe was sparsely populated, and largely remained so throughout the sixteenth century. In the fourteenth century, most of East-Central Europe only had two to ten inhabitants per square kilometre, as compared with more than 20 per square kilometre in the more populated areas of the west, including Italy, the Netherlands, and parts of France and the German Empire.[8] The majority of the population in Eastern Europe was rural, with only a small proportion of inhabitants living in urban areas. Poland was the most highly urbanized of the Eastern European lands, as by the end of the fifteenth century, there were 600 Polish towns, of which five or six had more than 10 000 inhabitants, although Danzig had reached 50 000 inhabitants by the end of the sixteenth century.[9] Hungary and Bohemia had both fewer and smaller towns. Apart from Prague, which had a population of 50 000 by 1600, the other Bohemian towns averaged 3 000 inhabitants, a similar size of population to the Hungarian towns.[10] In Hungary, the noble landowners created a specific system of small semi-rural towns entirely under their control, known as *Oppida*. As these towns had no independent existence, they

---

[8]   Henryck Samsonowicz and Anton Maczak, 'Feudalism and capitalism: a balance of changes in east-central Europe', in Anton Maczak, Henryck Samsonowicz and Peter Burke (eds), *East-Central Europe in Transition* (Cambridge, 1985), p. 8.

[9]   Philip Longworth, *The Making of Eastern Europe* (Basingstoke, 1992), p. 192.

[10]   Maria Bogucka, 'The towns of East-Central Europe from the fourteenth to the seventeenth century', in Maczak et al., *East-Central Europe in Transition*, pp. 97–101.

could not assist in providing a counterweight to the decision-making powers of the nobility, including in matters of religion. By the end of the sixteenth century, an average of 20 per cent of Poles lived in urban settings, and this proportion did not change much within the next 100 years. Overall, therefore, it seems that in contrast to the development of urban centres in Western Europe at the time, both the rate of urbanization and the percentage of the population of eastern and central areas living in cities were more modest.

The more minor importance of towns and of economic activity centred on the cities had a lasting impact on the course of the Reformation as, in most cases, the cities were not strong enough to create a powerful alliance on a par with the noble estates. Indeed, the economic activity of the Eastern European cities confirms their less-powerful status, as the cities' merchants were primarily engaged in exporting raw produce, including timber, grain and metals, in return for the importation of finished products from the west.[11] This trading pattern meant that the towns and cities of Eastern Europe did not become large production centres, and that the artisans constituted a more limited group within the cities. Exceptions to this included the large port city of Danzig, which exported finished goods such as glassware, weapons and furniture to the rest of Poland and Scandinavia.[12] Furthermore, the merchants themselves often originated from elsewhere, especially from Germany. In some areas, the presence of German merchants was of long standing, and their settlements had been encouraged by the nobility.[13] Thus the merchant élites of the larger Eastern European cities were in a sense peripheral to the processes of political power in Eastern Europe, both through their own ethnic origin and the geographical location of the merchant cities on the western fringes of these eastern lands. The Bohemian and Hungarian cities had only limited representation in the national Diets.[14] For instance, the Hungarian towns sent representatives to the lower chamber of Hungary's Diet, but only had one vote between them, and so held little influence.[15] In Poland by the first years of the sixteenth century, the Diet

---

[11] Ibid., pp. 102–3.

[12] Ibid., p. 102.

[13] Ibid., p. 104, and see also Norman J. G. Pounds, 'The urbanization of East-Central and South-East Europe: an historical perspective', in George W. Hoffmann (ed.), *Eastern Europe: Essays in Geographical Problems* (London, 1971), p. 59.

[14] Bogucka, 'The towns of East-Central Europe', p. 107

[15] László Makkai, 'The Crown and the Diets of Hungary and Transylvania in the sixteenth century', in R. J. W. Evans and T. V. Thomas (eds), *Crown, Church and Estates: Central European Politics in the Sixteenth and Seventeenth Centuries* (Basingstoke, 1991), p. 82.

was constituted by 40 to 45 deputies, 80 to 90 senators and two delegates representing the city of Cracow.[16]

The more minor role played by the towns and cities on the political scene left the stage open for the nobility to consolidate their position as the largest power-block facing the monarch, a situation common to all of Eastern Europe. The peasants, although numerically strong, were often reduced to serfdom and had no legitimate political voice,[17] as any peasant revolts were rapidly suppressed by the nobles. The noble estates were commonly divided between the gentry, or lower nobility and the more powerful magnates, who controlled large tracts of land. The other potential political force was the Catholic Church, recognized solely, or jointly in the case of Bohemia with Utraquism, as the legitimate confession in the Eastern European lands. However, while the bishops and other prelates sat in the upper chamber of the Diets, and often combined their ecclesiastical position with their role as secular lords,[18] their number and power could not match that of the nobility, a tension heightened when a majority of the latter became Protestant.

The role of the monarchy in the gradual definition of the nobles' power was a crucial one. When the monarchy was strong, as had been the case in the reign of King Matthias Corvinus in Hungary in the fifteenth century, noble factions were kept in check. The king's court also played a vital role in bringing to Eastern Europe both the new learning and some of its Italian exponents.[19] The royal court of Matthias provided a focal point for cultural and political life, one which was lost when his weaker heirs succeeded him and noble powers increased again.

Both before and during the Reformation, the nobility's main source of influence was that their agreement in the Diets was needed before the monarch could set any taxes. In most instances, the ruler would present a proposal to raise taxes before the assembly of the noble estates each year. Without their agreement and co-operation, the monarch could not legitimately raise the funds he required from his subjects to administer

---

[16]   Andrzej Wyczanski, 'The system of power in Poland 1370–1648', in Maczak et al., *East-Central Europe in Transition*, pp. 142–3.

[17]   See Kálmán Benda, 'Habsburg absolutism and the resistance of the Hungarian estates in the sixteenth and seventeenth centuries', in Evans and Thomas, *Crown, Church and Estates*, p. 124; Georg Heilingsetzer, 'The Austrian nobility 1600–1650: between court and estates' in Evans and Thomas, *Crown, Church and Estates*, p. 82.

[18]   In Poland, the bishops formed part of the Royal Council, or senate. See Wyczanski, 'The System of Power in Poland', in Maczak et al., *East-Central Europe in Transition*, p. 142. In Hungary, the bishops and other prelates also took their seats in the Royal Council. See Makkai, 'The Crown and Diets of Hungary' in Evans and Thomas, *Crown, Church and Estates*, pp. 81–2.

[19]   See Chapter 2 in this volume.

his realm and do battle against his enemies, in most cases the Turks.[20] The constant threat posed by the military pressure of the Ottoman Empire on the lands of Eastern and Central Europe made it imperative in the rulers' eyes to have sufficient forces to repel the Ottomans or at least maintain the *status quo*. As the estates were themselves aware of the danger posed by the Ottomans, the monarch's appeal for funds was often successful. Yet this tense military situation provided the noble estates with one of their most favourable opportunities to negotiate terms with their rulers, as the latter were forced to agree to concessions in return for the estates' agreement to the raising of taxes.[21]

Although the main concessions sought by the nobility in the course of the sixteenth century were tied to the recognition by the monarch of the legitimacy of various forms of Protestantism,[22] the fragmentation of confessional unity in Eastern Europe did not begin with the advent of Lutheranism. Jan Hus's movement in Bohemia in the fifteenth century had split into two factions after his execution in 1415. The more conservative group, known as the Utraquists because of their demand for the sacrament of communion in both kinds (*sub utraque specie*), split from the more radical Taborites, who reduced the number of sacraments and did without consecrated bishops.[23] By the 1540s, the Taborites' importance had dwindled, and they were replaced on the left wing by the Bohemian Unity of Brethren, who advocated strict discipline and rejected oaths, focusing on the importance of faith, but placing equal stress on the role of works.[24] Reconciliation proved difficult between the Brethren and the Utraquists, especially as the latter held an advantage as they benefited from legal recognition in the Compactata of Basle of 1436. Although the Utraquists profited both from the support of significant sections of the nobility and from the institutional backing of Prague University, the ecclesiastical structures of Utraquism remained close to Catholicism, so that the Reformation message coming from the west had a greater impact on the Bohemian Brethren than on the more established Utraquist Church.[25]

---

[20] This was the case in the Habsburg lands: see Alfred Kohler, 'Ferdinand I and the estates: between confrontation and cooperation, 1521–1564', in Evans and Thomas, *Crown, Church and Estates*, p. 48, and Günther R. Burkert, 'Protestantism and the defence of liberties in the Austrian lands under Ferdinand I', in Evans and Thomas, *Crown, Church and Estates*, p. 58.

[21] Burkert, 'Protestantism and defence of liberties', in Evans and Thomas, *Crown, Church and Estates*, p. 64.

[22] Ibid., pp. 60–1 and see Chapter 13 in this volume.

[23] František Kavka, 'Bohemia', in Scribner et al., *The Reformation in National Context*, pp. 131–4.

[24] Ibid., pp. 137–9.

[25] Heymann, 'The Hussite-Utraquist Church', 1–15.

Outside Bohemia, the main impetus for religious change came from beyond the borders of Eastern and Central Europe in the sixteenth century. In this context, the role of the cities with their settlements of German merchants was crucial, as it was here among the Saxon communities that Luther's influence was first felt. For instance, already by the 1520s, Lutheranism was spreading among the Saxon population of Ducal Prussia.[26] In general, Lutheranism tended to dominate in areas where there was a majority of German-speakers, as in Prussia and the Austrian lands, or in ethnically diverse areas. Thus, the German-speakers in Royal Hungary, ruled by the Habsburgs, tended to opt for Lutheranism in contrast to the Magyars who generally became Reformed.[27] The growing influence of Lutheranism was also due to the number of young men from Eastern Europe who studied in Wittenberg in the first half of the sixteenth century.[28] However, the association of Lutheranism and German-speaking areas was not automatic everywhere. In Royal Prussia, the magistrates and ministers of the leading cities of Danzig, Elbing and Thorn unofficially adopted a moderate confessional outlook, and strengthened their links with the Reformed in Poland–Lithuania. These cities only moved to an explicitly Lutheran position after 1600, due to increasing pressure from the more strongly Lutheran elements of the population.[29]

The influence of the Reformed, rather than Lutheran faith in certain areas and for certain ethnic groups had a variety of causes. In Royal Hungary, for instance, Magyar resentment of the growing advancement and influence of the German-speaking sectors of the population[30] may have translated itself into support for non-Lutheran Protestantism, although according to some scholars, this schema does not hold true in other areas, such as Transylvania.[31] In Bohemia and Moravia, the Bohemian Brethren found that their own confessional approach more closely matched the Reformed rather than the Lutheran faith.[32] In Poland,

---

[26] Janusz Tazbir, 'Poland', in Scribner et al., *The Reformation in National Context*, p. 168. See also Chapter 11 in this volume.

[27] David P. Daniel, 'Calvinism in Hungary: the theological and ecclesiastical transition to the Reformed faith', in Andrew Pettegree, Alastair Duke and Gillian Lewis (eds), *Calvinism in Europe, 1540–1620* (Cambridge, 1994), p. 229.

[28] Ibid., p. 215; and see Chapter 11 in this volume.

[29] See Chapter 12 in this volume.

[30] Makkai, 'The Crown and Diets of Hungary' in Evans and Thomas, *Crown, Church and Estates*, pp. 83–4.

[31] See Chapter 6 in this volume.

[32] R. J. W. Evans, 'Calvinism in East-Central Europe: Hungary and her neighbours', in Menna Prestwich (ed.), *International Calvinism 1541–1715* (Oxford, 1985), pp. 169–71.

where established Protestantism made fewer inroads, although barely a fifth of the gentry became Protestant, most of these adopted Calvinism.[33] Indeed, the increasingly precarious situation of Protestantism in the Polish kingdom by the last quarter of the sixteenth century was mainly due to the varying degrees of support provided by its rulers and to the lack of co-ordinated church structures among the Protestants.[34]

One further cause for the general preference for the Reformed approach among non-German speaking populations was simply that the period of time it took for the Reformation message to spread from the German-speaking community to those speaking very different languages corresponded to the growing international influence of Reformed Protestantism at the expense of earlier Lutheranism.[35] Similarly, the academic travels of young Eastern Europeans also shifted, from Wittenberg to Reformed centres of learning, including Heidelberg, Basle and, sometimes, Geneva.[36] Ethnic differences alone, however, cannot be taken as the sole basis for confessional choices. Indeed, Christine Peters in her article in this volume suggests that the confessional paths followed by different communities were shaped more by medieval traditions of piety than by ethnic origin alone. This more long-range view emphasizes the survival of liturgical practices over time, even in changed confessional settings, and was particularly true in Transylvania, where the influence of humanism led to the toleration of a wide range of devotional forms.[37]

Yet Lutheranism and Calvinism were not the only confessions to find adherents among the inhabitants of Central and Eastern Europe. Eastern Hungary, and Transylvania in particular, as well as Bohemia, Moravia and Poland, also attracted members of more radical groups, including Unitarians or Antitrinitarians, and Anabaptists, among them communities of Hutterites. The first Anabaptists appeared in Moravia and Silesia, coming from the West in the late 1520s. Generalized concern about Anabaptist practices and their radical split from the rest of society led to several royal decrees expelling them from the Bohemian lands, as for instance in 1530 and 1534.[38] In 1529, Jakob Hutter's arrival in Moravia led to the first settlements of his followers on noble estates. Many of the Hutterite communities were created when inhabit-

---

[33] Tazbir, 'Poland', in Scribner et al., *The Reformation in National Context*, p. 170.

[34] See Chapter 11 in this volume.

[35] Evans, 'Calvinism in East-Central Europe', p. 167.

[36] R. J. W. Evans, *The Making of the Habsburg Monarchy 1550–1700* (Oxford, 1979), pp. 27–8, and see Chapter 4 in this volume.

[37] See Chapter 6 in this volume.

[38] George Williams, *The Radical Reformation* (Kirksville, 3rd edn, 1992), pp. 624, 639.

ants of other areas, such as the Tyrol, left their homelands to avoid persecution.[39] However, the decrees published by Ferdinand I against Anabaptists of all kinds in the Bohemian lands led to the dispersal of these communities, with some making their way northwards into Poland. Contact between the Anabaptists and the native Bohemian Brethren, who might seem to share broadly similar theological views, was surprisingly limited, apart from a number of colloquies, in 1528, 1543, 1559 and 1565. The Brethren, too, migrated to Poland after an edict banning them from the Bohemian lands in 1548.[40]

The second significant Radical group was the Antitrinitarians, whose main period of influence began in the 1560s, primarily in Poland and Transylvania. Between 1563 and 1565, the Polish Protestants divided into the Major (Reformed) Church and the Minor (Antitrinitarian) Church. In Transylvania, an edict of toleration was promulgated in 1568, leading to a period of expansion among Transylvanian Antitrinitarians, especially as they had the support of the king, John Sigismund, and many of the nobility.[41]

In certain areas these groups could benefit from a degree of toleration: for instance, in Transylvania Unitarians were officially recognized by 1571.[42] The protection of sympathetic or interested magnates provided essential political support. The Hutterites, in particular, were valued for their strong work ethic and careful craftsmanship.[43] Other religious communities coexisted alongside these nascent Protestant groups, including Orthodox Christians, Jews and Muslims, although toleration of these groups fluctuated.[44]

The development of Protestantism in Eastern Europe took place mainly at the expense of Catholicism, as the Orthodox Church was largely left to its own devices and thus remained unaffected.[45] Indeed, the contacts between the Orthodox faith and Protestantism were limited, apart from short-lived attempts to bring the latter to the attention of the Orthodox,

---

[39]   Williams, *The Radical Reformation*, pp. 638–9.

[40]   Williams, *The Radical Reformation*, pp. 624, 1001, and Jarold Knox Zeman, *The Anabaptists and the Czech Brethren in Moravia 1526–1628: A Study in Origins and Contacts* (The Hague, 1969), p. 311.

[41]   Williams, *The Radical Reformation*, pp. 997, 1113, 1115.

[42]   Peter Sugar, *Southeastern Europe Under Ottoman Rule, 1354–1804* (Seattle, 1977), p. 154.

[43]   Claus-Peter Clasen, *Anabaptism: A Social History, 1525–1618* (Ithaca, 1972), p. 289, and George Williams, *The Radical Reformation* (London, 1962), p. 672.

[44]   Sugar, *Southeastern Europe*, p. 155. Sugar points out that there was no official toleration of the Orthodox in Transylvania, for instance.

[45]   Tazbir, 'Poland', in Scribner et al., *The Reformation in National Context*, pp. 173–4.

either through written works or through political pressure. The relationship between the Orthodox and the brief rule of Jacob Basilicos Heraclides, known as Despot, in Moldavia is a case in point. His efforts to bring the Orthodox communities to Protestantism through schooling and the confiscation of sacred objects only increased his unpopularity among the Orthodox, and led to his assassination in 1563.[46] Over the longer term, theological debates between Protestants and Orthodox did take place, although the positions of each group did not alter to any significant degree.[47]

In a sense, it seems that the rise of Protestantism caught the Catholic Church in Eastern Europe off guard. The lack of priests was acute, and contributed further to the disaffection of the population.[48] The Protestants also proved more adept at getting their message across, particularly through the medium of preaching and printing. In Hungary, the first Catholic press was established only in 1578, as compared with seven Protestant presses already in operation at the time.[49] By 1600, 29 of the 30 printing presses in Hungary produced Protestant works.[50] The production of Protestant literature is reflected in the surviving inventories of books held in personal libraries across Eastern Europe. While some of these were printed locally, others were brought in from the main western printing centres, and the inventories reflect this eclecticism.[51] Ambitious international projects were launched by Protestants outside Eastern Europe to provide works in the local vernacular destined to strengthen believers and potentially attract even more interest in the new faith. The impact of these projects is, however, more doubtful given the large proportion of non-urban, and thus often mainly non-literate, population in Eastern Europe.[52]

---

[46] See Chapter 8 in this volume, and Gedeon Borsa, 'Le livre et les débuts de la Réforme en Hongrie', in Jean-François Gilmont (ed.), La Réforme et le Livre (Paris, 1990), pp. 387–8.

[47] See Chapter 7 in this volume.

[48] See Winfried Eberhard, 'Bohemia, Moravia and Austria', in Andrew Pettegree (ed.), The Early Reformation in Europe, (Cambridge, 1992), p. 34, and István Bitskey, 'The Collegium Germanicum Hungaricum and the beginning of Counter Reformation in Hungary', in Evans and Thomas, Crown, Church and Estates, p. 110. See also Evans, The Making of the Habsburg Monarchy, pp. 3–4.

[49] Katalin Peter, 'Hungary', in Scribner et al., The Reformation in National Context, p. 163.

[50] See Chapter 4 in this volume.

[51] See Chapter 3 in this volume.

[52] See Chapter 8 in this volume. The ongoing importance of the oral transmission of ideas is stressed in Alodia Kawecka-Gryczowa and Janusz Tazbir, 'Le Livre et la Réforme en Pologne', in Gilmont, La Réforme et le Livre, p. 429.

The wide variety of Protestant confessions in Eastern and Central Europe by the sixteenth century was a result both of religious toleration and of the balance of power between political forces in Eastern Europe, which favoured the growth of diverse confessional groups. On the other hand, the absence of religious cohesion among the different Protestant groups made it difficult to present a unified front against the combined onslaught of a determined monarch and a rejuvenated Catholicism.[53] Indeed, official acts of union among the Protestants, such as the Union of Sandomierz in 1570, foundered both because there was no overall political power with a vested interest in seeing the union work, and because there was no agreement on how inclusive the confessional alliance ought to be.[54] The same was true after 1608 in the Habsburg lands, when the Protestants had their best chance to form alliances to resist the Habsburg pressure for catholicization. Their alliances were weakened by the lack of an agreed aim and by confessional and ethnic divides.[55] One way in which attempts were made to build up a sense of unity among Protestant populations was the writing of national histories, which sought to legitimize Protestantism by stressing its historical roots. This strategy had a more minor immediate impact, but could prove effective over the long term, as it enabled Protestants to respond to Catholic challenges by pointing to their past.[56]

By the end of the sixteenth century, the confessional map of the Eastern European lands had become far more complex. The inhabitants of the towns and a certain proportion of the nobility were Protestant. Other features of Protestant communities began to develop as these communities took root. In Reformed areas, one of the key features indicating the growing confidence of the Church was the establishment of corporate discipline. This was no easy or straightforward task, as the ecclesiastical authorities often found they could make only slow progress in imposing standards of conduct and matching punishments. They were resisted largely by village communities, more accustomed to dealing with social disorder in a case-by-case fashion. In this regard Chapter 9, on church discipline in Hungary and Transylvania, provides a helpful contrast to Chapter 10 which presents a longer-term analysis of the

---

[53]   See Gernot Heiss, 'Princes, Jesuits and the origins of Counter-Reformation in the Habsburg lands', in Evans and Thomas, *Crown, Church and Estates*, p. 93; Robert Birely, 'Ferdinand II: founder of the Habsburg monarchy', in Evans and Thomas, *Crown, Church and Estates*, p. 234; Evans, *The Making of the Habsburg Monarchy*, p. xxiii.

[54]   Tazbir, 'Poland', in Scribner et al., *The Reformation in National Context*, p. 173.

[55]   Evans, *The Making of the Habsburg Monarchy*, pp. 55–7.

[56]   See Chapter 5 in this volume and Bruce Gordon (ed.), *Protestant History and Identity in Sixteenth-Century Europe* (2 vols, Aldershot, 1996).

work of the Bernese moral courts.[57] The growing pressure of the Catholic revival which cut short the expansion of the Reformed Church in Hungary and elsewhere in Eastern Europe highlights the difficulties inherent in effecting more than a surface transformation in liturgies and beliefs over a relatively limited time span. Yet by the end of the sixteenth century, in Hungary, for instance, Protestants constituted 90 per cent of the population.[58] At the same time, although the influence of the Catholic Church had waned in these areas, the hierarchy of the Church had survived. Furthermore, in nearly every instance, the ruling monarchs of these lands had remained loyal to Catholicism.[59] The restoration of the Catholic Church following the Council of Trent and, in particular, the arrival of the Jesuits in Eastern Europe signalled a sea change in the balance of power between Catholics and Protestants.[60] However, the transformation in the Eastern European lands of the Protestant majority into Catholic predominance did not happen overnight, nor did it happen everywhere at the same rate or with the same outcome.

Politically, the factors in the defeat of the Protestant forces were varied. In some areas, such as Poland and Austria, the conversion of the nobility from Protestantism to Catholicism went relatively smoothly, if slowly. Significantly, the nobles in both these countries had never actively considered relinquishing their loyalty to their sovereign, apart from the Upper Austrian and some of the Lower Austrian nobility during the final stages of the Bohemian uprising in 1619.[61] Over time, many nobles became convinced that it was both right and in their best interests to revert to Catholicism, and were aided in this decision by the Jesuit centres of learning for boys and young men, competing with Protestant institutions,[62] and political incentives to convert, including access to royal patronage and posts in the royal administration.[63] Furthermore, the mon-

---

[57]   See Chapters 9 and 10 in this volume.

[58]   Makkai, 'The Crown and Diets of Hungary', in Evans and Thomas, Crown, Church and Estates, p. 86.

[59]   See for instance Sergij Vilfan, 'Crown, estates and the financing of defence in Inner Austria, 1500–1630', in Evans and Thomas, Crown, Church and Estates, p. 72.

[60]   The Jesuits arrived in the Austrian lands in 1550, in Bohemia in 1551, in Poland in 1560 and in Hungary in 1565. Longworth, The Making of Eastern Europe, p. 193.

[61]   For Austria, see Vilfan, 'Crown, Estates', in Evans and Thomas, Crown, Church and Estates, p. 77, and Gottfried Schramm, 'Armed conflict in East-Central Europe: Protestant noble opposition and Catholic royalist factions, 1604–1620', in Evans and Thomas, Crown, Church and Estates, p. 193.

[62]   Gernot Heiss, 'Princes, Jesuits', in Evans and Thomas, Crown, Church and Estates, p. 93.

[63]   Gottfried Schramm, 'Armed Conflict', in Evans and Thomas, Crown, Church and Estates, p. 179.

archies ruling Austria and Poland (the Habsburgs in the Austrian lands and the Vasas in Poland after 1586, respectively) were not considered alien by the nobility, taking away one of the causes of resentment allied to the ongoing strength of Protestantism in other areas of Eastern Europe.[64] The monarchs themselves contributed actively to the revival of Catholicism, as did Emperor Ferdinand II for instance, when he provided full or partial endowments for Jesuit colleges across his territory.[65] Some nobles who did not choose to convert to Catholicism went into exile instead, settling in Germany or in Hungary.[66]

Hungary became one of the few places of refuge for Protestants, as the recatholicization organized by the Habsburgs had a more muted impact in this area, largely because of the confessional counterweight provided by Transylvania, which lay outside Habsburg control. Furthermore, at the Hungarian Diet of 1608, the Habsburg rulers had been forced to agree to the legalization of Protestantism in Royal Hungary, following the defeat of the Habsburg forces by a Transylvanian army led by Istvan Bocskai.[67] The renewal of Catholicism and the simultaneous increase in pressure and control by the Habsburg ruler also led to opposition in Bohemia and Moravia. Hungary, Bohemia and Moravia had several features in common making them more resistant to Catholic and royal inroads. The language and ethnic background of the nobility was different from that of the ruler, and they were among the most Protestant of the Eastern European populations. The impact of international Calvinism in particular, brought to these areas by returning students and academics who had spent time in the Palatinate and elsewhere, strengthened the nobles' intent to defend their prerogatives against royal powers.[68] In the end, Bohemian opposition to the growing Habsburg domination led to the Defenestration of Prague in 1618, the short-lived Protestant rule of the Elector Palatine Frederick V, and the wholesale defeat of the Protestant nobility at the hands of the Habsburg army in 1620 at the Battle of the White Mountain. The Habsburg victory led to the dispossession and exile of committed Protestants and, thus, to the rapid disappearance of Protestantism in Bohemia.[69]

---

[64]   Ibid., p. 192.
[65]   Robert Birely, 'Ferdinand II', in Evans and Thomas, *Crown, Church and Estates*, p. 239.
[66]   Georg Helingsetzer, 'The Austrian nobility 1600–1650', in Evans and Thomas, *Crown, Church and Estates*, p. 251.
[67]   Evans, *The Making of the Habsburg Monarchy*, pp. 52, 71–2.
[68]   See Chapter 4 in this volume.
[69]   Jaroslav Pánek, 'The religious question and the political system of Bohemia before and after the Battle of the White Mountain', in Evans and Thomas, *Crown, Church and Estates*, p. 144.

By contrast, in Hungary both the resistance to the pro-Catholic Habsburgs and the outcome of the conflict were less violent. The growing impetus of the Catholic Church did have an impact, especially with the establishment of a training college in Rome, the Collegium Germanicum Hungaricum, run by the Jesuits. The Hungarians who attended the college went on to become leading figures in the Hungarian Catholic Church hierarchy. Even though the college's enrolment was small, (45 Hungarian students between 1580 and 1600), its impact was considerable, largely because of the calibre of the pivotal posts in the Church structure filled by its graduates.[70] And yet in spite of the growing power of the Catholic Church, the Hungarian nobility did not convert as readily as elsewhere, chiefly due to the tolerance granted to Protestants in neighbouring Transylvania.[71] Furthermore, the nobles had gained in political strength at the expense of the Habsburgs thanks to the resolutions of the Diet of Pozsony in 1608; for instance, the monarch could not declare war without the agreement of the noble estates.[72] Thus, Protestantism in Hungary retreated eastwards, and continued to survive, albeit in a reduced form.

The rise and decline of Protestantism in its various forms in Central and Eastern Europe had several root causes, chief of which was the ongoing power struggle between the noble élites and the monarchies. The nobles who became Protestant added the new faith to the list of privileges to be defended against any encroachment by the monarchy. By associating political and religious issues, the survival of Protestantism was thus tied to the survival of noble as against royal powers. The lack of any broader political movement, namely any significant alliance among nobles or with other sectors of society such as the cities, to provide support to the nobles meant that Protestantism became less and less popular, as the strength of royal power and Catholic resurgence came together as an increasingly potent force.

Over the course of two centuries, therefore, the Catholic Church in many parts of Eastern Europe recovered to an extraordinary extent. From a position of unchallenged eminence but underlying structural weakness, Catholicism in these parts appeared first in danger of being swept away, then rallied to achieve an impressive supremacy in lands which had once seemed destined to fall victim to the German heresies. But none of this was uniform, or consistent throughout the region. The

---

[70] István Bitskey, 'The Collegium Germanicum Hungaricum in Rome', in Evans and Thomas, *Crown, Church and Estates*, pp. 111–15.

[71] Evans, 'Calvinism in East-Central Europe', p. 181.

[72] Kálmán Benda, 'Habsburg Absolutism', in Evans and Thomas, *Crown, Church and Estates*, p. 127.

patchwork quilt of Eastern Europe, with its complicated political, ethnic and social make-up, meant that religious unity, once breached,
could never again effectively be restored, unlike in many of the more
uniform and centralized Western European states. Local ethnic and
political rivalries provided plentiful scope for continuing division, as
well as protection for different religious minorities which in many cases
found in Eastern Europe their most congenial and permanent home.

The essays presented in this volume are in some respects a celebration
of the sheer richness of this diversity. Our intention here is to offer a
range of specialized studies drawn from many parts of Eastern and
Central Europe, all of which are based on a mastery of incredibly
diverse research materials. Scholars of the Western European Reformation will be immediately struck by how different the resource base is in
many of these writings. Without the extraordinarily detailed parish
registers which students of the English Reformation use, for instance, or
the rich civil archives of the German towns, scholars of these eastern
lands must look to other types of resource: chronicle sources, or the
elusive remains of the pictorial wealth of many eastern Christian cultures.

In many cases, even these studies can only scratch the surface of areas
of scholarship crying out for further investigation. The relationship
between ethnic background and confessional choice is by no means
clear or obvious, as several of our contributors make clear. The fasci-
nating triangular engagement between eastern churches, Catholicism
and the Protestant challenge would also repay further investigation. But
to the extent that this collection may make western scholars aware of
these questions, it will have served a useful purpose; if it encourages
some younger scholars to make this their field of work, it will have
fulfilled the original hopes of those who first persuaded contributors to
take part in this project.

CHAPTER TWO

Pre-Reformation changes in Hungary at the end of the fifteenth century

Valery Rees

The roots of the developing reform movement in Hungary lay in the preceding period of change, the Renaissance, which found a home in Hungary as early as the 1470s. To explore these roots will be well worth the effort for any scholar of the Reformation. At the outset we must acknowledge the many difficulties involved: Hungarian source material of the fifteenth and early sixteenth century is often fragmentary. Much has not survived,[1] and many areas of research have therefore been neglected. But if we are prepared to gather clues from many sources and try to piece together a picture of what was happening, we will find at least some outlines will appear, and will enhance our understanding of the period of early Reform.

This chapter attempts to sketch some general developments in outlook in the decades prior to the Reformation, and against this background it presents King Matthias Corvinus and the circle of humanists around him. In considering these early humanists one must also examine what they thought their task was, and here our trail goes back to Florence, to the Platonic Academy and Marsilio Ficino.

A particular feature of Renaissance thought is the sense of conscious experiment. In the Italian city states changes in economic circumstance led to changing social and political needs. The great expansion of trade in Italy, especially in Venice and Florence from the thirteenth century onwards, increased wealth and power to the point where what had been minor city states now seemed to rival the great kingdoms in power and prestige. By the middle of the fifteenth century new ideas about society

---

[1] There was widespread destruction in Hungary both when the Turks invaded, and when they were driven out, besides subsequent losses in later centuries. In addition to losses caused by fire and devastation, a barge full of royal archives sank in the Danube while being 'rescued' from Buda in 1526. See Shayne Mitchell, 'The image of Hungary and Hungarians in Italy, 1437–1526', (PhD dissertation, Warburg Institute, London, 1994).

were of great practical interest to anyone involved in the running of a city state.[2] Ancient Roman literature was suddenly of very topical interest because of its republican tendencies. Some of the literature was already well known but some texts, known only through quotations in the writings of others, were now coming to light in their entirety: Poggio Bracciolini travelling to the Council of Constance ferreted out the dusty texts of Lucretius and Silius Italicus from a rubble filled tower in St Gallen.[3] Texts of Livy, Tacitus and numerous lost Cicero orations were also newly available. When King Alfonso of Naples thought he had discovered Ovid's house in Sulmona and the villa where Cicero died at Gaeta, he was immensely excited.[4] In Rome many antique statues were unearthed during building projects in the city.[5] Never before had people felt closer to the golden age of Rome, and never before had interest in the classical past reached such a fever pitch. The supply of copies of the new texts could hardly keep up with the demand, and literary education took on a new significance.

The debate on values that this brought about was linked directly with Reformation. For some time there had been a rising tide of dissatisfaction with the tone of public life in both Church and State, an awareness of corruption. There were men in high office who had no corresponding sense of public duty. Promotion was according to birth and family influence: to be a bishop was a political post, unconnected with spiritual leadership or Christian teaching. By the later part of the fifteenth century there were many flagrantly unsuitable characters in charge of the Church, including the Pope and many cardinals.[6] When outbreaks of plague or war threatened the community, it was often felt to be divine punishment. This applied especially to incursions by the Moslem Turks, who had been expanding steadily at the expense of Christendom.

---

[2] See P. O. Kristeller, *Renaissance Thought* (New York and London, 1965), *passim* and *Eight Philosophers of the Italian Renaissance* (London, 1965); also Shayne Mitchell, *The De Comparatione Rei Publicae et Regni of Aurelio Lippo Brandolini* (London, 1985).

[3] The excitement of these discoveries is best conveyed in Poggio Bracciolini's correspondence, translated by P. W. G. Gordon in *Two Renaissance Book Hunters* (New York, 1974), esp. pp. 193–6.

[4] Alan Ryder, *Alfonso the Magnanimous, King of Aragon, Naples and Sicily* (Oxford, 1990), p. 314.

[5] A visit to the Vatican Museum's sculpture galleries conveys a sense of the effects of renewed contact with the relics of antiquity. Many of the works displayed there were found in the Renaissance period, e.g. the Laocoon in 1506, the Apollo Belvedere and the Venus Felix in 1509.

[6] Popes Sixtus IV and Alexander VI are just two among many notorious examples.

Turkish expansion had also brought a new intensity to the contacts developing between Italy and Byzantium.[7] In 1439, the Emperor of Byzantium had come to Italy to seek help in fighting the Turks. He brought with him the Patriarch of the Eastern Orthodox Church and numerous dignitaries. Because of the gravity of the political crisis, reconciliation with the Church of Rome looked more attractive than it had before, after centuries of doctrinal difference and mutual loathing. A council was convened in Ferrara, and the next year moved to Florence. Amid the meetings and dialogue, the Italian representatives could not fail to be impressed by the magnificent books the Eastern representatives carried with them (whether for consultation or display is not always clear). It was here that Cosimo de' Medici acquired the famous copy of the complete works of Plato which he handed over to Ficino for translation into Latin. The main aim of the conference was not achieved: the rescue operation did not actually happen. But, as often happens at conferences, the contacts brought about between the participants produced the most remarkable effects.

In 1453 Constantinople fell to the Turks. It is hard for us now to appreciate the sense of shock and loss this entailed. The reputation of Byzantium had stood high, even though internal decay had been eating away at the substance of the Empire for a long time. Now refugees who could do so were coming to Italy. Greek scholars found they could support themselves by teaching Greek and lecturing on philosophy. Among these scholars were the great controversialist George Trapezuntius,[8] and the more widely celebrated John Argyropoulos.[9] Italians were keen to hear their lectures and began to compete with each other to build up libraries of the books that were coming out of Greece. Greek texts that had been known of in the West but never studied were received with great enthusiasm, and the Byzantine scholars themselves benefited from making available what had become for them a somewhat arid academic tradition. It was thus an invigorating experience for both sides.

The intensive study of Greek seems to have sparked off more critical study of Latin,[10] and interest was also revived in Dante and Petrarch's

---

[7] These are explored in full in N. G. Wilson, *From Byzantium to Italy* (London, 1992), and K. M. Setton, 'The Byzantine background to the Italian Renaissance', in *Proceedings of the American Philosophical Society*, (Philadelphia, 1956) also reprinted with other papers in *Europe and the Levant in the Middle Ages and the Renaissance* (London, 1974), pp. 1–76.

[8] Setton, 'Byzantine Background', pp. 74–5, and Wilson, *Byzantium*, pp. 76–8.

[9] Wilson, *Byzantium* , pp. 86–90.

[10] For comment on the linguistic exercises of various Italian Renaissance schools, see C. Marchesi, *Bartolomeo della Fonte* (Catania, 1900).

development of Italian as a serious literary language.[11] Great store was set by language itself as a tool of exploration. What distinguishes Renaissance Latin from earlier Medieval Latin is a preoccupation with style. Sometimes this produced a rather florid prose and *orotunditas* [12] but in general the aim was to convey accurately and clearly to others what one had just discovered for oneself. Consequently one finds a playful dabbling in the styles of the great masters accompanied by a sense of having something new to say and the need to say it.[13] Cicero and Livy were taken as models of fine prose style and many of the language changes that had established themselves during the medieval period were now swept away in pursuit of elegance. Parallel developments in the vernacular languages were to be of the greatest significance in allowing the new learning to spread beyond the narrow confines of the scholarly world, and the broadsheet polemics of the high Reformation years would have been unthinkable without it.

A main centre of classical studies was the academy established in Florence by Cosimo de' Medici, under the direction of Marsilio Ficino. It was a loose assembly of scholars drawn together by their mutual love of enquiry after truth. They met on an informal basis, by invitation, as and when they were able to. The correspondence between Ficino and his many followers, which he himself gathered together for publication, presents a very vivid picture of their concerns.[14]

Ficino was the son of Cosimo's physician. He was picked out by Cosimo at an early age to study Greek, and he soon learned enough to start translating the new texts Cosimo was busy acquiring. He had not long embarked on translating Plato's dialogues when fresh instructions came to him from Cosimo to lay Plato aside and work instead on some new writings that had just come to light, the works of Hermes

---

11   Landino's major commentary on Dante was published in 1481. See also Ficino's celebration of Dante, *The Letters of Marsilio Ficino* , translated by the Language Department of the School of Economic Science (London, 1975–), 5, pp. 79–80.

12   Implying empty magniloquence as in Horace, *Ars Poetica*, Fairclough (ed.) (London, 1991), p. 476, lines 322–3.

13   For examples concerning Hungary, read Janus Pannonius' satires modelled on Martial, in Anthony A. Barrett, *Janus Pannonius Epigrammata* (Budapest, 1985) or Stephen Broderics' opening words echoing Livy's Preface, P. Kulcsar (ed.), *Stephanus Brodericus, De Conflictu Hungarorum cum Solymano Turcarum Imperatore ad Mohach Historia Verissima* (Budapest, 1985), p. 21.

14   The literature on Ficino is enormous. P. O. Kristeller's studies lead the field, but Ficino's own correspondence also speaks for itself. See *The Letters of Marsilio Ficino* , which includes full bibliographical information. Ficino's *Opera Omnia* are most readily available in the Basle edition of 1576 which was reprinted in Turin 1959 and this will henceforth be referred to simply as *Opera* .

Trismegistus.[15] Following St Augustine, Ficino believed that the early Greek philosophers had been deeply influenced by their studies of the Egyptian tradition of priestly knowledge, and that they also came into contact in Egypt with the Hebrew teachings. Hermes Trismegistus was the greatest exponent of the Egyptian tradition and was thought to have been a contemporary of Moses.[16] A link was thus provided between the classical world of Greece and Rome and the world of the Bible. Through this rediscovered missing link could be traced an unbroken chain of teachings, like a golden thread, uniting all the ancient philosophies. The Bible was already being studied afresh in newly learned Greek, with some surprising changes of emphasis. Any obscurities that remained could be subjected to comment in the light of the non-Christian philosophers. Legitimate interest could be expressed in the teachings of Zoroaster, the Persian tradition, the teachings of Orpheus, of Pythagoras and, of course, of Plato, the great publicist of Socrates' method of rational enquiry.

A few of Plato's dialogues had been transmitted through Christian writers, especially St Augustine and Thomas Aquinas.[17] Some of the dialogues were quoted in Cicero and other Roman writers, but these had not been widely popularized in education. This was partly because they were presented through the filter of Roman republicanism, and were therefore unattractive to the Church, the arbiter of education. From the 1420s, more Platonic dialogues became available in translation through the work of Collucio Salutati and Leonardo Bruni.[18] By the mid-fifteenth century, with republican forms of government gaining precedence in the city states of Italy, everything connected with ancient city states seemed to hold advice worth considering.

Political and philosophical issues went hand in hand. Attempts to utilize Greek political thought for the solution of contemporary political problems were accompanied by attempts to bring Platonic philosophy to bear on contemporary moral problems.[19] One might summarize much of Ficino's writing as an effort to reinterpret Christian teachings from the standpoint of Greek ideas, and to apply the findings precisely to the needs of the day. Those who followed Plato's

---

[15] See Corsi's *Life of Marsilio Ficino* (Florence 1506) translated in *The Letters of Marsilio Ficino*, 3, p. 138. For Ficino's translations of Hermes, see *Opera*, p. 1836 ff.

[16] Ficino, *Opera*, p. 1836; St Augustine, *City of God*, VIII, xi–xxiii, tr. H. Bettenson (London, 1984), pp. 314–33.

[17] See P. O. Kristeller, *Renaissance Thought and its Sources* (New York, 1979), ch. 6.

[18] Several of these works are discussed in Hans Baron, *Humanistic and Political Literature in Florence and Venice at the Beginning of the Quattrocento* (Cambridge, MA, 1955), and *The Crisis of the Early Renaissance* (Princeton, 1955), *passim*.

[19] See footnote 2 in this chapter.

method of rational examination, of Socratic dialectic, could hardly help developing an independence of outlook. Pursuing their search for universal rational laws, some were led into conflict with received religious teachings.[20] The entire universe was being studied in relation to eternal principles of harmony, mathematics and motion. Foundations were being laid for scientific investigation of every kind. It was the self-appointed task of Renaissance scholars to show that these principles were not in conflict with essential Christian belief. This is a theme returned to again and again in Ficino's letters, and forms the direction of his two large works, *Platonic Theology* and *De Religione Christiana*.

These developments in Italy had a direct bearing on pre-Reformation changes in Hungary because it was towards this scene that King Matthias deliberately turned, not simply because it was Italian, as has sometimes been suggested,[21] but because it was at the forefront of modern thinking. Matthias's father, János Hunyadi had been inspired by Renaissance ideas at the court of Milan where he served the Visconti and met the Sforzas.[22] His tutor and Chancellor, János Vitéz, had pursued every aspect of Renaissance learning and practice with great zeal and enthusiasm.[23] Under Vitéz's tuition Matthias had received a thoroughly humanist schooling, covering Latin, history, mathematics and astronomy, as well as the practical aspects of diplomacy, and it appears that Matthias was a very willing and able pupil. His favourite reading as a boy was Quintus Curtius's lively biography in Latin of Alexander the Great and Silius Italicus's epic of the Punic wars.[24] These works were among the

---

[20]   Ficino himself escaped persecution by the authorities, although it was a matter of concern to him. See *Opera*, pp. 907, 909, 910–12 and the *Apologia* to the *De Vita*, in Marsilio Ficino, *Three Books on Life*, C. V. Kaske and J. R. Clark (eds) (New York, 1989), pp. 394–401. The Roman Academy of Pomponius Laetus fared less well. Several of its members were imprisoned in 1468, and Philippo Buonaccorsi was obliged to flee to Poland. Ficino's pupil Pico della Mirandola was also pursued by the Church for his views.

[21]   Antonio Bonfini presented this view as early as 1486 in the *Symposion de virginitate et pudicitia coniugali*, S. Apró (ed.) (Budapest, 1943), and elaborated it in the *Rerum Ungaricum Decades* (Basle, 1568), referred to henceforth as *Decades*. 'Pannoniam alteram Italiam reddere conabatur', *Decades* IV, vii, 87, I. Fógel, B. Iványi and L. Juhász (eds) (Budapest, 1941), p. 135.

[22]   Joseph Held, *Hunyadi: Legend and Reality* (New York, 1985), p. 11. Bonfini, *Decades* III, iv, 448.

[23]   Klára Csapodi-Gárdonyi, *Die Bibliothek des Johannes Vitéz* (Budapest, 1984) presents a dazzling list of books known to have belonged to Vitéz, and from the marginal notations in his own hand it is fair to assume he was thoroughly familiar with their contents.

[24]   Jóasef Teleki, *Hunyadiak kora magyarországon*, (Budapest, 1855), XI, p. 454–5.

exciting new 'finds' of recent years.[25] Matthias modelled himself on the
ancient heroes of Greece and Rome. In 1458 Pope Calixtus III had
called him 'the man sent by God'. He was certainly conscious of his
providential role as defender of Christendom against the Turks, but he
looked to the classics, to the ancient world, for his inspiration.

Matthias's great talent was to put what he learned from the classics
to practical effect in the everyday affairs of his kingdom. It is interesting
to consider how his studies of the Greek philosophers may have enhanced his understanding of the need for high standards of moral and
ethical conduct in the everyday affairs of the kingdom.[26] He certainly
earned a reputation for probity and justice. Tales grew up about the
king who liked to go about in disguise to find out what was really
happening among his subjects.[27] Many of these stories may be embel-
lishment and legend, but he certainly gained a place in folklore as
Matthias the Just, which must surely be at least a reflection of a devotion to his subjects' welfare.

Better documented is the influence on him of the Roman historians,
especially Caesar.[28] Through studying Caesar's extraordinary successes,
and through the intelligent analysis of his own practical experience in
the field, Matthias became fully committed to the idea of a highly
trained army. Such an army required a different administrative basis
from the old feudal levy, so laws to permit the raising and funding of
such troops were a priority measure. A special tax[29] was introduced in
Matthias's first parliament, and renewed every year thereafter. Thus a
substantial force of quality troops moving under his own banner, rather

---

[25] Silius Italicus's text was discovered by Poggio Bracciolini in 1416 or 1417, and
first printed in 1471. Matthias received a manuscript copy for his library in the 1460s as
well as a printed copy from Pomponius Laetus in 1471. Quintus Curtius's *Life of
Alexander* copied in 1467 was in Matthias's library, but again he knew the work earlier,
perhaps through Vitéz who owned a copy. Cs. Csapodi, *The Corvinian Library History
and Stock* (Budapest, 1973), pp. 196 and 354; K. Csapodi Gárdonyi, ibid., p. 98.

[26] See Huszti, 'Tendenze Platonizzanti alla Corte di Mattia Corvino', in *Giornale
critico della Filosofia Italiana* (Rome, 1930), p. 136 ff. Matthias received all Ficino's
translations of Plato. See Jolán Balogh, *A Müvészet Mátyás Király Udvarában* (Budapest,
1966), I, p. 332.

[27] Ildikó Kriza, *The Good Leader According to Hungarian Folklore* (Budapest,
1992) and *Mátyás az Igazságos* (Budapest, 1990).

[28] I am indebted to discussions with Professor Gyula Rázsó for this insight. See also
his article 'The mercenary army of King Matthias Corvinus', in B. Király and J. Bak
(eds), *War and Society in Medieval and Early Modern Hungary* (New York, 1982), pp.
125–40.

[29] 9 October 1458, a levy of 1 golden florin per hearth was raised, specifically for
the Turkish war. For its continuation see János Bak, 'The Late-Medieval Period, 1382–
1526', in P. Sugar (ed.), *A History of Hungary* (London and New York, 1990), p. 71.

than those of his feudal warlords, became available to respond to the country's pressing defence needs, and was later supplemented with a standing army of Hussite and Polish mercenaries.

In addition to the special tax, a number of other reforms of financial administration were implemented. The details of these changes have been described and discussed in a wealth of publications by János Bak, Erik Fügedi and András Kubinyi.[30] The importance of the changes lies not only in the extra revenue they brought in, but equally in the two lines of change they generated in their wake. The first of these was the centralizing tendency characteristic of the 'new' monarchies of the six-teenth century. Medieval tax systems operated on a local basis whereby both the funds for raising the militia and the command over it went to the local count or castellan. Now the king had increasing control over both money and troops. Legislation enabling these changes had to be passed by the estates, which began to meet more regularly and to enjoy more power. Through these parliaments the lesser nobility helped the king reduce the might of the great barons by a series of modest but steady changes, not unlike Tudor reforms in England.[31]

The second effect was a social one. Matthias made a deliberate policy of selecting for service in his administration young men of peasant origin who had entered the Church for their basic education.[32] Selection on the basis of merit alone opened a career path for able individuals to rise to positions previously reserved for the nobility. Education also opened the door to later reform because of its humanist nature.

Most of the nobility remained illiterate, though this by no means implies a lack of culture. We should not be lulled by the self-propa-ganda of the humanists into underestimating the fine oral culture of Hungarian family traditions, of epics and religious ballads. To do so would be to overlook the fact that, for a real Hungarian renaissance to

[30] See especially János Bak, 'The kingship of Matthias Corvinus: a Renaissance state?', in *Matthias Corvinus and the Humanism in Central Europe* (Budapest, 1994), pp. 40–5; Eric Fügedi, Pal Engel and András Kubinyi, 'Monarchie im Wellental: Materielle Grundlagen des Ungarischen Königtums im 15. Jahrhundert', in R. Schneider (ed.), *Spätmittelalterliches Königtum in Europäischem Vergleich* (Sigmaringen, 1987), pp. 347–84; also András Kubinyi, 'The road to defeat: Hungarian politics and defense in the Jagiellonian period', in B. Király and J. Bak (eds), *War and Society in Medieval and Early Modern Hungary* (New York, 1982), pp. 160–1.

[31] This is a large subject, but one with which many readers may be familiar. Its outlines are most clearly set out in G. R. Elton, *The Tudor Revolution in Government*, (Cambridge, 1953), and summarized in G. R. Elton, *England under the Tudors* (London, 1962), pp. 54–69, 180–4.

[32] E. Fügedi, 'Hungarian bishops in the 15th century', in J. M. Bak (ed.), *Kings, Bishops, Nobles and Burghers in Medieval Hungary*, esp. p. 384.

arise, both elements would be required, that is to say a marriage of tradition and reason. Recognizing that the pursuit of reason was the domain of classical culture, Matthias took on the ambitious idea of making his nation the new home of classical learning, and he was ready to promote any who showed talent in this direction. However, he never forgot that he represented all the traditional values of Hungarian manliness and courage, and he managed to combine in himself the best of both cultures.

While new men were rising up in the king's service to create a new social challenge, the economic importance of the barons was also being eroded by the growth of towns and cities, encouraged by royal edicts and laws.[33] Tenants who wished to leave their lord's land and build new homes in the cities and towns were permitted to do so. Royal charters gave cities exemption from the legal jurisdiction of the landed aristocracy and city taxes were payable directly to the king. As customs duties also contributed a sizeable portion of the royal revenues the king had a direct financial interest in fostering trade.[34] Indeed, when Matthias's war efforts began to turn away from the Turks and towards Vienna, it was partly in order to stem the flow of the profits of trade into the hands of German merchants or Italian bankers by recapturing the main commercial centres.

To what extent the Church was an extension of royal government is an interesting issue. The Hungarian Church was for the most part the king's dependable ally. The Hungarian Crown had considerable influence in the matter of church appointments.[35] One might well expect to see a common aim and common policies between church and crown. The appointment of Janus Pannonius to the lucrative Bishopric of Pécs is a case in point: an ecclesiastical benefice given to a committed politi-

---

[33] János Bak, 'The Late-Medieval Period, 1382–1526', in P. Sugar (ed.) *A History of Hungary* (London and New York, 1990), pp. 57–60. Also László Makkai, 'The Emergence of the Estates', in G. Barta, I. Bona, B. Köpeczi et al. (eds), *History of Transylvania*, pp. 231–5.

[34] While economic statistics are hard to evaluate for this period, customs duties as a proportion of Hungarian revenue rose to 6 per cent or more by 1470, as estimated by Ferenc Szakály, 'Mecenatismo Regio e Finanze Pubbliche in Ungheria sotto Mattia Corvino', in Carlo Vecce (ed.), *Rivista di Studi Ungheresi*, (Rome, 1989), vol. 4, pp. 19–35. Diomede Carafa's influence was also felt in Hungary, through his influence on Beatrix. His advice to her father, Ferrante, included encouraging trade to promote the economic welfare of his subjects. See David Abulafia, 'Crown and economy under Ferrante I of Naples', in T. Dean and C. Wickham (eds), *City and Countryside in Late Medieval and Renaissance Italy* (London, 1990), p. 130.

[35] The *placetum regium* of 1404, and negotiations between the Pope and Sigismund at the Council of Constance secured power over Church appointments for the Crown. Though abrogated by a later Pope, the powers continued to be used.

cal and cultural ally who had no religious leanings whatsoever.[36] But even this did not imply submission. When Matthias's tax-raising ventures began to require sizeable contributions from Church property, he met fierce opposition led by Pannonius and his uncle Vitéz, both of whom hitherto had been the king's most loyal supporters. The conflict led to armed uprising in 1471, and a showdown in which Vitéz was imprisoned and disgraced, dying shortly afterwards, and Pannonius fled, succumbing in his difficulties to the consumption that had plagued him for so long. It also led to disillusionment on Matthias's part for a time with all things Italian and humanist.

However this disillusionment did not last long, and by 1476 Italian emissaries were again very much in favour at court. Matthias had for some time been contemplating an Italian marriage. After the death of his first wife in 1464 he had opened negotiations with the Sforza family, but in 1465 Ippolita Sforza was married to the Duke of Calabria, eldest son of the King of Naples. The kingdom of Naples offered a glorious example of Renaissance court life, and soon Matthias was exploring the possibilities of marriage there.

It seems as if he had formed a clear idea of what he wanted from a wife, very much related to his own ideals of the role of a king. Through Janus Pannonius, Matthias had become interested in the teachings of Marsilio Ficino, and the potential for a ruler to bring about a transformation in his country. The essential aspect of Plato's teaching which inspired much of the work of his later years was Plato's maxim that until philosophers be kings or kings philosophers, there would be no true justice or happiness on earth.[37]

There is also a crucial passage in Ficino's commentaries on Plato, describing the goddess of Philosophy, that holds the key to Matthias's search for an ideal queen consort. After describing her sheer physical beauty, Ficino says:

> She delights in encouraging all who wish to learn and to live a good life to enter the Platonic Academy ... In the gardens of the Academy, poets will hear Apollo singing beneath his laurel tree. At the entrance to the Academy, orators will behold Mercury declaiming. Under the portico and in the hall, lawyers and rulers of the people will listen to Jove himself, ordaining laws, pronouncing justice and governing empires. Finally, within the inner-most sanctuary, philosophers will acknowledge their Saturn, contemplating the hidden mysteries of the heavens ...

---

[36] For a detailed assessment of this important figure in Hungarian politics, see Marianna Birnbaum, *Janus Pannonius – Poet and Politician* (Zagreb, 1981) and Bak's introduction to Pannonius's *Epigrammata*, tr. Anthony A. Barrett (Budapest, 1985).

[37] Plato, *Republic*, V, 473.

This is the path, he says, for all 'who pursue the ways of liberation, for here you will achieve your aims and attain freedom of life'.[38]

It does appear that Matthias took this to heart, and decided to find a bride both beautiful enough and intelligent enough to play this part. It took him more than ten years. In 1476, he married Beatrix of Aragon, younger daughter of the King of Naples. Though only 19, her beauty and accomplishments were as striking as her courage, and the magnificence of the wedding celebrations, of which we have an eye-witness account, was symbolic of their importance.[39]

An extremely interesting figure entered Hungarian history at this point, about whom we know tantalizingly little. Francesco Bandini was appointed by King Ferrante of Naples to look after his daughter on her marriage to the Hungarian king. Bandini had entered Ferrante's service after spending some years with Ficino in Florence, at the very heart of the Platonic Academy. He had left Florence for Naples against his will, when his brother brought the family into political disgrace. Now he was coming to Hungary against his will too, but once there he rapidly became King Matthias's friend and closest advisor. It was Bandini who advised the king in matters of taste and style, and, more important, became the living link between the king and Ficino.[40]

Another influential Italian humanist particularly associated with the queen (though he did not come to Hungary until the mid-1480s) was Antonio Bonfini. His *Symposium*, while not strictly a factual account of court life, none the less gives a clear indication of the tenor of discussion in which the king loved to engage, and in which Beatrix was able to play a part.[41]

From the late 1470s classical learning began to blossom in Hungary. The new queen appears to have acted entirely according to the quotation from Ficino: she made beautiful gardens in Hungary with fountains and fruit trees not previously known. She took on enthusiastically the task of redecorating the palace at Buda, and of turning the summer palace of Visegrád into a haven of beauty and tranquillity described

---

[38] Marsilio Ficino, Proem to the commentaries on Plato, *Opera*, pp. 1129–30.

[39] *Nuptia et Coronatio Reginae atque illorum postea ingressus in Budam*, written by the envoy of the Count Palatine in 1476, and published in *Rerum Hungaricum Scriptores Varii*, J. G. Schwandtner (ed.) (Vienna, 1746), 1, pp. 519–27.

[40] See *Letters of Marsilio Ficino* , *passim* , and especially Book VIII of the letters (not yet translated) in *Opera*, pp. 864–92; Rozsa Feuer-Toth, *Art and Humanism in Hungary in the Age of Matthias Corvinus* (Budapest, 1990), p. 56 ff., and P. O. Kristeller, *Studies in Renaissance Thought and Letters* (Rome, 1956), pp. 411–35.

[41] Antonio Bonfini, *Symposion de virginitate et pudicitia coniugali*, ed. S. Apró (Budapest, 1943).

even by a sophisticated Roman observer as *'paradiso terrestri'*.[42] She gathered to the court the finest musicians in Europe. And through her protégés, Bandini and Bonfini, and possibly her own contribution, she promoted the arts of eloquence and informed debate. Her husband was free to concentrate on the duties of Ficino's portico and hall: 'ordaining laws' and 'governing empires' and, increasingly through the 1480s, he was attracted to the work of the innermost sanctum, the 'mysteries of the heavens', pursuing both astronomy and spiritual work. As Ficino wrote in a letter to the king,

> What doth it profit a man if he gain the whole world but suffers the loss of his own soul. You labour in vain, O philosopher, while you are trying to grasp all things if you do not take hold of the soul, for through that you will be ready to take hold of the rest.[43]

Matthias did increasingly turn towards things of the soul, and Ficino dedicated to him the third book of the *De Vita*, 'On obtaining the life of the heavens'. This does not mean that Matthias abandoned his passionate interest in the world: the two were seen as entirely compatible. Indeed according to the humanist view the one is a reflection of the other. Therefore the later years of his reign saw building, diplomacy, learning, letters and the arts all in full flood of development supported by most generous patronage from the king. But the spiritual aspect of the work does seem to have exerted a powerful influence on him.[44]

After Beatrix's arrival there was an ever-increasing flow of visitors from Italy; not only her personal guests, but merchants and adventurers and also Renaissance scholars, writers, artists, stonemasons and architects, all looking to the king for patronage and work. The style of architecture Matthias favoured was fully intended to be a revival of the aesthetic principles of ancient Greece and Rome. The governing idea, as expressed in Filarete, was that a prince may lawfully engage in works of public *magnificentia* for the greater glory of his nation or of God, without incurring penalty for the sin of pride or lavish excess.[45] Likewise, the great Corvina library, filled with every available text of Latin and Greek, many of them beautifully copied out and illuminated at the great Italian manuscript houses, was intended not only for the king's personal delight but to encourage both nobility and church to take an active interest in intellectual pursuits and to make use of this wonderful

---

[42] Bartolommeo de Maraschi in a letter to Pope Sixtus IV, 25 October 1483, quoted in Jolán Balogh, *A Müvészet Mátyás Király Udvarában*, I, p. 224.

[43] Marsilio Ficino, *Opera*, p. 885.

[44] For the text of the remarkable *De Vita* see Marsilio Ficino, *Three Books on Life*, C. V. Kaske and J. R. Clark (eds) (New York, 1989).

[45] Feuer-Toth, *Art and Humanism*, pp. 35–45.

collection.[46] Matthias wished to establish Buda as a centre of European learning. The university he founded at Pozsony under Vitéz had rather faded away after Vitéz's death, but during the 1480s he tried to persuade Ficino to come in person and set up a Platonic Cloisters with plans for an impressive expansion.[47] Though Ficino never came, he certainly endorsed the academy, sent newly translated philosophical works as soon as they were ready, and wrote in 1481 of the citadels of Pallas at last rising again in the court of Matthias.[48] Thus, the royal court was not so much a second Italy, but a revival of ancient Greece.

The work of this Dominican Academy is of great interest in terms of pre-Reformation changes, for it was here that the preachers of the next generation received their basic education, and any work which is able to throw light on its activities will be of enormous value to students of the Renaissance and the Reformation alike.[49] It appears that after Bandini, the next leader of studies here was a certain Petrus Niger. While the name could be interpreted as Peter the Black, namely a Black friar or Dominican and impossible to identify, it could equally be the Latinized version of Pietro Nero, Ficino's close friend and collaborator, mentioned in the Apology to the *De Vita*, and charged by Ficino with its defence should it run into difficulties with the Church authorities.[50]

By 1485 Matthias's prowess in government and war had enabled him to expand his territory into Silesia, Bohemia and part of Austria. For the last five years of his reign, Vienna became his capital and it seems highly likely that his aim was not just a Danubian empire but election to the Holy Roman Empire itself. By all accounts he kept his affection for Buda, his new Athens, to the end, and the expansion of the Dominican Academy into a full-scale university, housed in magnificent style and spreading enlightenment to all, failed to be fulfilled only on account of his death.[51]

In many ways, Matthias behaved as a model Renaissance prince. Plato's philosopher king was the ideal held out to him by Ficino, and clearly it was a vision that appealed to him. Nevertheless the Renaissance kingship did not survive him. This was partly for lack of a legitimate heir and the resultant rivalries between widow, natural son

---

[46]   Cs. Csapodi, *Bibliotheca Corviniana* (English edn, Budapest, 1981), p. 29.

[47]   Tibor Klaniczay, 'Egyetem Magyarországon Mátyás Korában', *Irodalomtörténeti Közlemények*, (1990), XCIV, 5–6, pp. 575–612.

[48]   *Letters of Marsilio Ficino*, vol. 3, p. 78.

[49]   See Tibor Klaniczay, 'La Corte di Mattia Corvino e il pensiero accademico' and Klára Pajorin, 'L'educazione umanistica e Mattia Corvino', in *Matthias Corvinus and the Humanism in Central Europe* (Budapest, 1994), pp. 165–74, 185–92.

[50]   Ficino, *Three Books on Life*, pp. 395–7; *Opera*, p. 572.

[51]   K. Pajorin, 'L'educazione umanistica', p. 189.

and foreign contenders,[52] and partly for other reasons. For example, the very nature of Matthias's administrative reforms contributed to their overthrow. Resentment ran deep among the old baronial families whose powers had steadily diminished. They seized upon the first opportunity to reverse some of the changes by deliberately electing a weak king after Matthias's death.[53] Even the new nobles, those faithful servants whom Matthias had used to control the old barons, and had rewarded with grants of land and power, deserted the royal cause. The very bishops whom Matthias had raised from humble origins deserted his natural son and became the princely prelates of the Jagiellonian period. Besides, having made large grants of land, Matthias passed on a far smaller power base to his successor than he had inherited from his own father.

The deliberate undoing of much of Matthias's work is a complex story, which can only be followed in part, where sources permit.[54] The disintegration was perhaps less complete than we have been inclined to think; if we are to believe Stephen Broderics, Chancellor at the time of Mohács, Louis II still had some hope of defeating the Turks in 1526.[55] However once battle was joined, the outcome was disastrous for the kingdom of Hungary. In spite of astonishing acts of bravery from individual sections of the Hungarian army, they were annihilated. What followed is well known: king, bishops, leaders and the flower of the Hungarian forces were killed on the battlefield; the kingdom was divided, one part seized by the Habsburgs, one part under Turkish occupation and one part struggling to preserve its heritage under Turkish suzerainty. Much was lost, but much survived too. While administrative reforms were swept away or carefully unravelled, the humanist teachings Matthias had done so much to foster had their effect, especially in the principality of Transylvania. Far more was involved in the Hungarian Renaissance than a simple importation of foreign culture by a court élite. We must guard against being misled by the polemicists of either side. Hungary did not become a second Italy, as Bonfini would have had us believe,[56] nor was the bitter resentment against preferment of foreigners always justified. Even Beatrix and her nephew Ippolito d'Este,

[52] A. de Berzeviczy, *Beatrice d'Aragona* (French edn, n.p., 1911), 2, ch. v.

[53] His successor Ulászló was given the derisive title *dobje* for his propensity to agree to whatever decision was put before him.

[54] András Kubinyi, 'The road to defeat: Hungarian politics and defense in the Jagiellonian period', in B. Király and J. Bak (eds), *War and Society in Medieval and Early Modern Hungary* (New York, 1982) p. 159–77.

[55] Stephanus Brodaricus, *De Conflictu Hungarorum cum Solymano Turcarum Imperatore ad Mohach Historia Verissima*, ed. P. Kulcsar (Budapest, 1985), pp. 46, 149–51.

[56] *Decades* IV, vii, 87.

who have both had a particularly bad press, may yet have their reputations restored when new researches yield their full results.[57]

More research may also yield further information on key figures whose influence bridged the uneasy transition from Hunyadi to Jagiellonian reigns; figures such as Bandini's noble friend and protector, Nicholas Báthory, who played a leading role at court and was also a keen follower of Ficino. The contributions of János Filipecs and Peter Váradi need further investigation, as well as the generation of students at the Dominican Academy in Buda. Hungarian historians at the turn of the century made thorough searches in Italian archives to supplement the resources available on Hungarian soil. P. O. Kristeller's *Iter Italicum* also unearthed valuable documents including such writings as we have from Bandini. It may well be that the gaps in documentary evidence cannot be filled, but Jolán Balogh and Rozsa Feuer Toth both pointed the way to a thorough reanalysis of documentary sources in the light of archaeological evidence and works of art. The first fruits of the joint evaluation of written sources and archaeological evidence can be found in the recently published account of medieval Visegrád,[58] which clearly demonstrates the validity of this approach. For example it confirms, in a way that documentary evidence alone could not, that royal patronage did not cease under the Jagiellonians. Ulászló's hold on policy and expenditure was tenuous, but building at Visegrád continued on a princely scale in the friary alongside Matthias's splendid palace complex, by workmen also associated with Renaissance additions to the royal palace of Prague.

Furthermore, patronage of education and the arts was also actively supported by the prelates. Ulászló's chancellor Thomas Bakócz was dedicated to Renaissance aspirations, aiming for the papacy for himself and bequeathing a magnificent chapel of pure Renaissance style in Esztergom.[59] His was not the only humanist household among the bishops of this later generation, nor was he the only prelate of humble birth. The path of promotion through education was now established, and the Franciscan preachers who brought a simple religious message to the people in Hungarian did much to foster attitudes that would become receptive to Reform. This is borne out by evidence from 1514, the last attempt at a crusade against the Turks, which turned into a social

---

[57] On Ippolito d'Este, see Shayne Mitchell, 'The image of Hungary and Hungarians in Italy', ch. vii. On Beatrix, there has been no serious assessment since Berzeviczy's biography in 1911.

[58] József Laszlovszky (ed.), *Medieval Visegrád* (Budapest, 1995), esp. pp. 19–25.

[59] See Vilmos Fraknói's biography of 1889 or, in English, Miklós Horler, *The Bakócz Chapel of Esztergom Cathedral* (Budapest, 1987).

uprising. Reports of the time show how closely interwoven political and economic issues were with the religious fervour deliberately engendered by the preachers in their crusading sermons.[60] The seeds of the Reformation were in the Renaissance. The questions asked by one generation of humanists produced the answers found by the next. The presence of German humanists at the court of Louis II and his queen, Mary of Habsburg, introduced Lutheran ideas early to Hungary.[61] They were taken up enthusiastically by the Saxon burghers of Transylvania. Many Franciscan preachers became Lutherans and the new ideas soon spread to the Hungarian section of the community too. The practical, rational reorganization of the Church by reforming pastors met the needs of communities struggling for survival after 1526.[62] Furthermore, the earlier development of Hungarian as a preaching language by the Franciscans began to blossom into Bible translation. Although Gáspár Károli's full translation did not appear until 1590, János Sylvester's New Testament was printed in 1541, the first book printed in Hungarian, and Gáspár Heltai followed with further translations in the 1550s.[63] The translation of the Bible into Hungarian and the flowering of Reform in Transylvania can certainly be linked back to the developments of Matthias's reign.

To conclude, let us reflect upon a letter from 1480, which foreshadows a theme familiar in Reformation writing – the reaction against the abuse of high office. The letter was written by Ficino in 1480. Philosophy is addressing Cardinal Giovanni of Aragon, who has just been appointed Archbishop of Esztergom:

> Almost all mortals, dearest son, appear to me so blind as to seem sometimes to behave rather like night-loving owls. For the present I shall not mention the many other signs of human blindness, but since I am addressing a man established in the highest office, I shall simply reveal how blindly people get involved in these dignities.
>
> In the first place they put a false limit on dignity, as if it consisted only in attaining high public office. But I define true dignity as to be deserving of high public office.
>
> Secondly, they look forward to being masters, and men at peace, only when they are engaged in controlling great numbers of men and events. But I consider them, as the outcome plainly shows, to be the slaves of all and to be oppressed by every perturbation from

---

[60] Documents relating to the disastrous Peasants' War of 1514 have been gathered together by Antonius Fekete Nagy and others in *Monumenta Rusticorum in Hungaria Rebellium anno MDXIV* (Budapest, 1979).

[61] B. J. Spruyt, '"En bruit d'estre bonne luteriene": Mary of Hungary (1505–58) and religious reform' *EHR*, 109 (1994), 275–307.

[62] Gábor Barta, 'The Emergence of the Principality and its first crises: 1526–1606', in G. Barta, I. Bona, B. Köpeczi et al. (eds), *History of Transylvania*, pp. 287–93.

[63] Péter Hanák (ed.), *The Corvina History of Hungary*, (Budapest, 1991) p. 51.

the very moment they rashly subject their backs to the burden of sustaining all public affairs. Likewise, I deem that to be true mastery which serves no slave; which, if ever it does serve, serves only that one which is the slave of none. Again, I observe that that is true peace which is so established that no perturbations touch it; or if by chance they do touch it, they serve it inasmuch as they rule everything else.

Besides, mortals are so devoid of reason that when, either by destiny or by villainy, they have obtained great positions, they consider that they themselves have all at once become great; like someone who is so mentally enslaved that, putting on a longer garment or entering a large palace, he prides himself that he has become taller and larger. On the contrary, I affirm that only those men are truly great who carry high office with equally high virtue and are not overcome by high office but surpass it or at least equal it ... [64]

Ficino's letters are full of reminders on many themes that were elaborated later. In considering how Renaissance changes paved the way for reform, we must consider changes in kingship, administration, and power politics. But we should never forget that at the heart of Renaissance teaching, especially as propounded by Ficino, is a powerful moral direction, to bring human behaviour into line with dictates of both Reason and Love, into harmony with the Divine. This surely was a foundation for the Reformation.

---

[64] *The Letters of Marsilio Ficino*, 5, p. 57.

CHAPTER THREE

Protestant literature in Bohemian private libraries *circa* 1600

Jiří Pešek

During the last three decades of the sixteenth and the first two decades of the seventeenth centuries, until the imperial forces crushed the revolt of the Bohemian estates in the Battle of the White Mountain and made possible the reconquest of Bohemia for Catholicism, the religious situation in Bohemia was in many ways complicated if not confusing. Yet a genuine religious tolerance unique in contemporary Europe flourished in Bohemia, due to the earlier recognition of two national confessions – Catholicism and Utraquism – based on the incorporation of the Compactata of Basel in the law of the land and the acceptance of the Kutná Hora agreement on religious tolerance of 1485 (peace in land).[1]

Although the above agreements did not apply to the independent *Unitas Fratrum* nor to confessions founded during the Reformation in the sixteenth century, the tradition of 'tolerance of necessity' and respect paid to peace in land made their continued development and relatively peaceful coexistence possible. Lutheranism had spread to almost all border and other German-speaking regions and before long found its way also to the Czech-speaking regions of Bohemia and Moravia. There it helped to revive the Utraquist religion which a century after the Hussite wars had been ideologically frozen: its religious practices were hardly distinguishable from lukewarm Catholicism. It is well known that attempts had been made to effect its quiet return to the Roman Church. After some delay, Calvinism also found devoted followers in the Czech lands. In the last quarter of the sixteenth century the new reformist trend attracted part of the Utraquists and from the 1580s onwards it won over most of the members of the *Unitas Fratrum*.[2]

---

[1] Josef Janáček reviews religious development in sixteenth-century Czech lands in Jaroslav Purš and Miroslav Kropilák (eds), *Přehled dějin Československa* [Outline of the History of Czechoslovakia] 1/2, pp. 56–69. Of the older literature, Zikmund Winter, *Život církevní v Čechách. Kulturně historický obraz XV. a XVI. století* [Religious life in Bohemia. Cultural and Historical Picture of the Fifteenth and Sixteenth Centuries], (2 vols, Prague, 1895–96), is still of value.

[2] Ferdinand Hrejsa, *Česká reformace* [Bohemian Reformation] (Prague, 1914); František Hrubý, 'Luterství a kalvinismus na Moravě před Bílou horou' [Lutheranism

The Protestant Churches joined forces in 1575 while preparing the so-called Bohemian Confession, a joint declaration of the Church and the estates, calling upon the Bohemian King and Roman Emperor Maximilian II to declare freedom of confession. Though the emperor had refused to sign it and even to permit its printing, and the alliance of the Protestant Churches soon broke up, this joint action became a starting-point at the beginning of the seventeenth century. In 1609 Emperor Rudolf II was forced to reward the Bohemian Estates for their support in the conflicts within the Habsburg dynasty by the Letter of Majesty granting them freedom of religion. The Utraquist consistory, the supreme governing body of the Utraquist Church, a body hitherto much too conservative, which often sided with Catholicism in times of Catholic offensives, became then a joint Protestant consistory composed of representatives of all non-Catholic churches in the land.[3]

However, these were only the main events in the history of religious development in Bohemia before the Thirty Years War. A burgher of Prague, Eger or Kutná Hora, a country nobleman or an ordinary farmer, saw events in a simpler way. *Cuius regio, eius religio* applied to selected Estates and with some exceptions involved only the official church practice, that is the confessional allegiance of the parish clergy, who were few in number and poorly educated, both formally and morally.[4] Few, if any, church or secular authorities had the means to examine let alone influence the religious interests of their parishioners. This was even more true as regards the religious supervision of burghers in the 32

and Calvinism in Moravia before the Battle of the White Mountain], *Český časopis historický*, 40 (1934), 265–309, 41 (1935), 1–40, 237–68. František Hrubý, 'Luterství a novoutrakvismus v českých zemích v 16. a 17. století' [Lutheranism and Neo-Utraquism in the Czech Lands in the Sixteenth and Seventeenth Centuries], *Český časopis historický*, 45 (1939), 31–44. On the conversion of the *Unitas fratrum* to Calvinism: Rudolf Říčan, *Dějiny Jednoty bratrské* [History of the *Unitas fratrum*] (Prague, 1957), pp. 273–88.

3   Ferdinand Hrejsa, *Česká konfese, její vznik, podstata a dějiny* [The Bohemian Confession, its Emergence, Principles and History] (Prague, 1912); Kamil Krofta, 'Nový názor na český vývoj náboženský v době předbělohorské' [New view on the Bohemian religious development before the Battle of the White Mountain], *Český časopis historický*, 20 (1914), 1–19; Alois Míka, 'Z bojů o náboženskou toleranci v 16. století' [The struggle for religious tolerance in the sixteenth century], *Československý časopis historický*, 18 (1970), 371–82. The most recent study of this attempt by the estates to form a common Protestant confession is Jaroslav Pánek, *Poslední Rožmberkové. Velmoži české renesance* [The Last Rosenbergs. The Aristocrats of the Bohemian Renaissance] (Prague, 1989), pp. 148–60. For the struggle for religious freedom at the beginning of the seventeenth century, Kamil Krofta, *Majestát Rudolfa II* [The Letter of Majesty of Rudolf II] (Prague, 1909) and J. B. Novák, *Rudolf II. a jeho pád* [Rudolf II and his Fall], (Prague, 1935).

4   See Heinrich Richard Schmidt, *Konfessionalisierung im 16. Jahrhundert* (Munich, 1992), pp. 60–75, esp. p. 69.

royal towns. Preserved catalogues of their private libraries and the places they sent their sons to study bear witness to this fact.[5]

In Bohemia and Moravia in the late sixteenth and early seventeenth centuries it was a matter of prestige and common practice for burghers' sons to study not only at town Latin schools administered by the Prague Protestant University, but also at an urban Latin school in one of the German-speaking border regions or in nearby Saxony or Franconia, at Prague University or a foreign one. In the latter half of the sixteenth century the majority of burghers were literate and at least capable of understanding Latin and German texts.[6] Prominent burghers of towns of any size considered education a matter of prestige and self-identification. Their attitude to books was similar. During the period under review books were the attribute of the scholar. Mass production of books, and the book trade in particular, turned now relatively cheap books into objects of daily common use ordinarily found in homes of burghers of lesser means and lower social standing. Interestingly, books tend to be rather rare in probate inventories of the richest representatives of business and food-making. But all in all, during the period under review one-third to one-half of all burghers held books in high regard. There is also reasonable evidence that many burghers' wives were literate in spite of the absence of formal or informal education.

The sources of our research are catalogues of the libraries of burghers of free royal towns in Bohemia. These catalogues have been preserved in the town records of the civil judiciary as part of probate inventories, testaments or protocols on estate division, orphan property and so on.[7]

---

[5]   For the studies of young burghers abroad, Jiří Pešek and David Šaman, 'Les étudiants de Bohème dans les universités et les académies d'Europe centrale et occidentale entre 1596 et 1620', in Dominique Julia, Jacques Revel and Roger Chartier (eds), *Les universités européennes du XVIe au XVIIIe siècle. Histoire sociale des populations étudiantes* (Paris, 1986), I, pp. 89–111; Jiří Pešek and Michal Svatoš, 'Die sozialen Folgen der akademischen Peregrination in den Böhmischen Ländern in den zweiten Hälfte des 16. Jahrhunderts', *Zeszyty naukowe Uniwersytetu Jagiellonskiego*, 870 (1989), 51–4.

[6]   Frantisek Palacký, 'Obyvatelstvo českých mest a skolní vzdelání v 16. a na začátku 17. století' [Inhabitants of Czech towns and school education in the sixteenth and the beginning of the seventeenth centuries], *Československý časopis historický*, 18 (1970), 345–70. Palacký's research indicates that besides attending the school in their birthplace, three-quarters of town-school pupils in the towns of north-western Bohemia enrolled in two to four other municipal Latin schools. Compare Jiří Pešek, 'The University of Prague, Czech Latin schools, and social mobility 1570–1620', *History of Universities*, 10 (1991), 117–36; Jiří Pešek and Michal Svatoš, 'The Czech education before White Mountain and Comenius's didactics', in *Homage to J. A. Comenius* (Prague, 1991), pp. 73–80.

[7]   For further information see Jiří Pešek, 'Pražské knihy kšaftů a inventářů pozůstalostí – příspěvek k jejich struktuře a vývoji v době předbělohorské' (Prague records of testaments and probate inventories – contribution on their structure and development in the

A complete set of inventories including almost all the series of volumes from the 1570s until 1784, and a smaller but very interesting series of catalogues, are found in the northern Bohemian town of Louny and in the central Bohemian town of Beroun, to name one of the smaller sets. Large sets of estate inventories have been preserved in the northern Moravian town of Olomouc. In addition, numerous isolated catalogues of burgher libraries in smaller Bohemian and Moravian towns have survived.[8] Research into burgher libraries carried out in Silesian Wroclaw, Polish Cracow or the German mining towns of Upper Hungary can be used for comparison.[9] However, relevant information of greater than

---

period before the Battle of the White Mountain), *Pražský sborník historický*, 15 (1982), 63–92. His analysis is based on the study of manuscripts in the Archives of the City of Prague: Archives of the City of Prague, 1173–1175, 1208–1214, 1217, 2209, 2210.

[8] For a general review see Jiří Pešek, *Měšťanská vzdělanost a kultura v předbělohorských Čechách 1547–1620 – všední dny kulturního života* [Burgher Education and Culture in the Pre-White Mountain Bohemia of 1547–1620 – Everyday Cultural Life] (Prague, 1993), pp. 64–103; Zikmund Winter, 'Měšťanské libráře v XV. a XVI. věku' [Burgher libraries in the fifteenth and sixteenth centuries], *Časopis Českého musea*, 66 (1892), 65–79, 281–92; Josef Vávra, 'O držbe knih v Berouně 1537–1619' [On ownership of books in Beroun 1537–1619], *Časopis Českého musea*, 65 (1891), 89–94; Jiří Pešek, 'Knihy a knihovny v kšaftech a inventářích pozůstalostí Nového Města pražského v letech 1576–1620' [Books and libraries in the probate inventories in the New Town of Prague in 1576–1620], *Folia Bohemica Historica*, 2 (1980), 247–82; Olga Fejtová, 'Lounské měšťanské knihovny v dobe předbělohorské' [Burgher libraries in Louny during the pre-White Mountain period], *Sborník okresního archivu v Lounech*, IV (1991), 3–23; Oldřich Kašpar, 'Z knihoven kolínskych humanistů' [From libraries of Kolín humanists], *Práce muzea v Kolíně*, 2 (1982), 69–75; Oldřich Kašpar and Zdenek Kašpar, 'Knihovna prostějovského písaře Mauricia. Příspěvek ke kulturním dejinám města v 16. století' [The library of Prostejov scribe Mauritius. Contribution to the cultural history of the town in the sixteenth century], *Zpravodaj muzea Prostějovska*, (1982), 19–23; Petr Voit, 'Kniha a knihtisk u olomouckých měšťanů před Bílou horou' [The book and printing by Olomouc burghers before the Battle of the White Mountain], *Vlastivědný věstník moravský*, 32 (1980), 312–20; Petr Voit, 'Měšťanské knihovny v Olomouci před Bílou horou' [Burgher libraries in Olomouc in the pre-White Mountain period], *Vlastivědný věstník moravský*, 33 (1981), 197–202; Jiří Pešek, 'Ke srovnání kulturního vývoje Olomouce a Prahy před Bílou horou' [Comparison of the cultural life of Olomouc and Prague during the pre-White Mountain period], *Historická Olomouc a její současné problémy*, 4 (1983), 293–303.

[9] Kazimiera Maleczynska, *Zainteresowania czytelnicze mieszczan dolnoslaskich okresu Renesansu* [Reading Interests of Lower Silesian Burghers in the Renaissance] (Wroclaw, 1982); Renata Zurek, 'Ksiegozbiory mieszczan Krakowskich XVII wieku' [Book collections of Cracow burghers of the seventeenth century], *rozcnik Biblioteki PAN w Krakowie*, 13 (1967), 21–51; Michal Rozek, *Mecenat artystyczny mieszczanstwa krakowskiego w XVII wieku* [Art Patronage Among Burghers of Cracow in the Seventeenth Century] (Cracow, 1986); Viliam Čičaj, *Knizná kultúra na strednom Slovensku v 16.–18. storočí* [Book Culture in Central Slovakia Between the Sixteenth and Eighteenth Centuries] (Bratislava, 1985). The author studied burgher libraries in the towns of Banská Bystrica, Banská Stiavnica and Kremnica. Austria only provides a study by Roman Sandgruber,

merely illustrative value can be obtained only from the analysis of a homogeneous set of library catalogues.

The following section presents the results of an analysis of 1 041 probate inventories of Prague burghers' possessions from 1570 to 1620. These contained 469 entries concerning books or library catalogues comprising a total of 13 000 volumes. Of these it was possible to identify roughly one-third of the books thanks to their more detailed description (name of the author or title of the book if not its complete title). Most of them were large or expensive volumes. Books in smaller formats, many being religious books not considered by town officials to be worth listing separately, were recorded as 'in octauo et sedecimo libri viginti' owing to their minimal monetary value. Yet, according to H. J. Martin, 70 to 80 per cent of all books printed in France at the beginning of the seventeenth century were octavo or smaller formats.[10] This was overwhelmingly true for everyday religious literature such as homilies, prayers, moralist works and so on.

The conclusions drawn by O. Fejtová from her analysis in Louny are helpful in evaluating the results of research in Prague. Fejtová's sale-record for the period 1552–1612 contains 323 inventories with 50 entries for books and libraries, comprising 700 books in all. Research in the northern Moravian town of Olomouc also produced valuable information. There P. Voit and J. Pešek found lists of preserved inventories for 1579–85 and 1617–20 which included books totalling 3 400 copies in 123 libraries.

Analysis of the material collected shows that despite the admirably high quality of Bohemian and Moravian book-printing, particularly in Prague, domestically produced books in Bohemian and Moravian burgher libraries, even in towns with an overwhelmingly Czech-speaking population, lagged far behind imported books. Before and after 1500 the most prestigious publishers and booksellers had been in Speyer, Nuremberg and Leipzig. These were later replaced by the Frankfurt and Leipzig book fairs, by dealers who offered books at local town fairs and by agents who were buying books on order for their important customers. An investigation of preserved libraries and library catalogues reveals that large quantities of books in Bohemia came from Venice, Geneva, Lyon, Paris and other Western European book publishing centres. But by far the greatest number of books reaching Bohemia had been pub-

---

Alltag und materielle Kultur. Städtischer Lebensstil und bürgerliche Wohnkultur am Beispiel zweier oberösterreichischer Städte des 16. Jahrhunderts, (Wiener Beiträge zur Geschichte der Neuzeit, 14, 1987), pp. 23–44.

[10] H. J. Martin, *Livre pouvoirs et societé à Paris au XVII^esiécle (1598–1701)* (Paris, 1969), p. 1064.

lished in Germany – from Basle and Strasbourg to Frankfurt am Main, Nuremberg or Wittenberg, and Leipzig or Cologne. An analysis of Silesian libraries by Maleczynska produced similar results. Even though most of the books (25 per cent) were printed in Paris and Lyon, books printed in Basle, Frankfurt am Main, Wittenberg, Cologne, Leipzig, Heidelberg or Strasbourg made up 50 per cent of the total. Silesian book production was totally absent.[11] Polish and Slovak researchers also confirm the predominant role of book imports from German, French and Italian centres.[12]

The German book market, in which religious literature was well represented, was the chief source of Bohemian religious book imports. Appendices in Kapp's classical work give us a general idea of the range of books of the German wholesale market.[13] Between 1571 and 1620 religious literature (the Bible and its books, theological works, homilies, prayers, lives of the Saints, collections of sermons and so on) represented an impressive 40 to 46 per cent of the volume of titles offered and sold at German book fairs. Roughly one-third of these were Catholic writings with the ratio of Catholic to Protestant literature changing moderately in favour of non-Catholic books. Since the number of copies of religious books tended to exceed the number of copies of legal or medical books for instance, the proportion of the former sold on the market probably exceeded 45 per cent, while the volume of books sold during the period under review continued to grow rapidly.

We have selected a small sample of seven catalogues of clerical libraries from the Prague burgher inventories. This selection, of course, might influence the overall picture, but it reveals that religious books amounted to nearly 60 per cent of the identifiable titles.[14] This is a higher proportion than in Silesian libraries (30 per cent); the portion of religious literature in the other towns being studied is approximately 50 per cent of the identifiable books. One must also bear in mind the social background of the sources – in places such as Prague, where we find many estates of

---

[11] Maleczynska, *Zainteresowania czytelnicze*, pp. 26–9.

[12] Alodia Kawecka-Gryczowa, *Drukarze dawnej Polski od XV do XVIII wieku* [Bookprinters of Old Poland from the Fifteenth to the Eighteenth Centuries] (Wroclaw, 1983), p. 108; Jozef Kuzmík, *Knižná kultúra na Slovensku v stredoveku a renesancii* [Book Culture in Slovakia in the Middle Ages and Renaissance], (Martin, 1987), p. 64. Internalization of readers' interests and the book market are also addressed in Zdenek Šimeček, 'K problematice knižního obchodu na sklonku 15. a v 16. století' [On issues of the book market at the close of the fifteenth and in the sixteenth centuries], in *Knihtisk v Brne a na Morave* (Brno, 1987), p. 154.

[13] Ferdinand Kapp, *Geschichte des deutschen Buchhandels bis in das 17. Jahrhundert* (Leipzig, 1886), pp. 786–8.

[14] Pešek, *Měšt'anská vzdělanost*, p. 80.

tradespeople including only small amounts of religious literature, this nucleus of every library often exceeds two-thirds of the total number of books. On the other hand in the libraries of the estates of leading citizens with a higher formal education the share of religious literature drops to 30 per cent in favour of books devoted to scholarly subjects.[15]

Prague, extraordinarily abundant in sources, has been the focus of our research. However, it should be noted that Prague in the decades around 1600 was in many ways an extraordinary town composed in fact of four independent royal towns. For many reasons it enjoyed a highly exceptional freedom of confession, especially as regards private confessional views. Unlike the relatively homogeneous confessional structure of burgher libraries in the previously examined towns, and the libraries of dissenters, as in Lutheran Olomouc in Moravia which experienced a forceful advance of the Counter-Reformation, Prague libraries, particularly the medium-sized and large ones, displayed confessionally diversified characters. Occasionally one library contains volumes linked with the tradition of the fifteenth-century Bohemian Reformation and the works of Jan Hus and Petr Chelčický, a fifteenth-century unorthodox religious thinker, next to the works of later Bohemian Reformed authors and preachers (Martin Philadelph Zámrský of Opava, to name the most prominent), numerous German Lutheran works from the Empire and Bohemian border regions, and works by John Calvin and Theodore Beza. The writings of Erasmus of Rotterdam, regarded as a Protestant author in post-1550 Bohemia rank among the most common and popular works.

The Bible or its books was the basic and most frequently occurring book in all European burgher libraries of the Reformation. This was true also of Prague in that period. The reason for the frequent presence of the Bible in burghers' catalogues can be attributed to the fact that Bibles were usually large and well-printed books. In addition, most copies were also abundantly illustrated. Thus its layout and price alone made it worth recording in the estate inventory even when the Council commission put all the remaining books under one entry. In Prague, biblical literature as a whole (without psalms and apocryphal writings) represented over 10 per cent of identifiable book titles. In Olomouc, the Bible can be found in about half of the libraries identified, and was also prominent in the libraries of Louny.

Even though the Bohemian tradition of Bible printing centred on Prague goes far back into the fifteenth century, Prague libraries contained many copies printed in German (especially the Luther edition) and in Latin.

---

[15] Maleczynska, *Zainteresowania czytelnicze*, pp. 37, 38, 73.

Besides the most frequently recorded complete sets of biblical texts, burghers also possessed separate editions of the New Testament, again in Czech, Latin, German and, occasionally, in Greek. In contrast, separate editions of the Old Testament were to be found comparatively rarely; virtually only in its Czech edition. Books of psalms were also popular. We often come across separate editions of the prophecies of Jesus Syrach, whose text was included in some Bohemian editions of the Bible.

Homilies made up the second large group of religious literature. In Prague we have documented about 30 per cent fewer copies compared with the Bible; in the German-speaking, predominantly Lutheran Olomouc their number was double that of the Bible. In general, Bohemian editions of the homilies predominated in the Czech-speaking towns (Spangenberg, Hus, the repeatedly banned Philadelphus Zámrský and Chelčický) over the wide spectrum of German homilies. Martin Luther dominated in the German-speaking towns of the Bohemian border regions, in the German Olomouc and the German mining towns of Upper Hungary.

Strangely, *circa* 1600, Martin Luther rather than the Bohemian reformer and martyr Jan Hus was the most widely read author of religious literature in Prague, the seat of the Bohemian archbishop and of the conservative Utraquist consistory. The second most popular was the Lutheran preacher and author Johann Spangenberg. Philipp Melanchthon seems to have been more popular in Bohemia in that period as an author of philological, philosophical and pedagogic works than as a theologian and religious writer. Yet many libraries had copies of his *Corpus doctrinae christianae*. Interpretations of the Gospel, the homilies or prayers of Urbanus Rhegius, Simon Paul, Eobanus Hessius, Wolfgangus Musculus, Johannes Habermann or Christoph Vischer also found their readers.

Thus the writings of Lutheran authors represented the core of religious literature in the Protestant libraries of Prague. There, as in most Bohemian, Moravian, Silesian and other neighbouring towns, the work of Martin Luther encompasses the widest range of titles. In the Prague material his works occurred 152 times. Surprisingly, only a few of his books had been translated into Czech and his Prague readers read most of them in German. Seventeen copies of Luther's translation of the Bible have been found in Prague, but his homilies were the most frequent, with a minimum of 41 documented copies, despite their relatively high price. In 1594, the first and second editions in the estate of Old Town burgher Ambrosius Netter of Glouchov were valued at 1.5 and 2 thaler respectively.[16]

---

[16]   Archives of the City of Prague, Manuscript 1173, f. 276a.

Luther's sermons, and editions of his Song (*Cythara Lutheri*) can be found in Prague fairly frequently; three collected editions of Luther's works have been documented in the Prague Old Town – not an inexpensive matter. In 1587, Bernhard Mon possessed an eight-volume set, in 1594 the library of Ambrosius Netter of Glouchov took pride in a folio 14-volume edition of Luther's works valued at 22 thaler; in the same year an inventory commission discovered 12 folio volumes of the *Opera Lutheri* in the estate of Ruprecht Pichler.[17] With the exception of the more common Book of Psalms, we find only isolated pieces of his work such as *On Jews and their Lies* or his *Tischreden*. An entry in the estate inventory of Old Town ironware businesswoman Kateřina Mildbergerová (hence not a specialized bookseller) reflects the amount of Luther's writings imported to Prague. In 1606, she offered among other goods also '25 New Testaments in German by Dr Martin Luther in white leather binding' (charging one gulden for four copies), 192 German books of prayers and five copies of the German psalms.[18]

Prague burghers seem to have read Luther almost exclusively in German or Latin. On the other hand, judging by the list of books printed in Czech between the sixteenth and eighteenth centuries, Johann Spangenberg was the most translated author in sixteenth-century Bohemia.[19] His 'Homilies', which some Prague citizens read also in German, was published in seven Czech editions over the period 1546–66. Our study of that period has documented them occurring in Prague libraries even more often than the *Homilies* of Luther. (The third most popular Lutheran homily in Prague, published only in German, was the *Homily of Simon Paul*.) Occasionally we can also find isolated copies of Spangenberg's *Epistolae dominicales* and *On the Order of Marriage*.

Urbanus Rhegius, a favourite of the most prominent sixteenth-century Prague printer Jiří Melantrich of Aventinum, was another author frequently translated into Czech. The first Czech edition of his *Medicine of the Soul* appeared as early as 1539 and was re-edited five times before 1608; his *Sermons* had three Czech editions. Prague burghers read his works also in German and Latin, as for instance his German *Dialogus*.

One of the great Lutheran writers active in Bohemia, whose work we occasionally come upon in Prague libraries, is the author of the famous

---

17   Archives of the City of Prague, Manuscript 1173, f. 174a, 276a, 292a.

18   Archives of the City of Prague, Manuscript 1174, f. 221a.

19   See Z. V. Tobolka and F. Horák, *Knihopis českých a slovenských tisků od doby nejstarší do konce XVIII. století. Díl II. tisky z let 1501–1800* [Catalogue of Czech and Slovak Prints from the Earliest Period to the End of the Eighteenth Century. Vol. II, prints from 1501 to 1800] (Prague, 1939–67).

Bergpostill Sarepta, the priest and school governor Johann Mathesius of Joachimsthal. In 1589 Tomáš Řešátko translated into Czech the *Kinderpostill* [Children's Homily] by Mathesius's pupil Christopher Vischer, later superintendent of Braunschweig.[20]

The literature of the Czech Reformation ranks second behind Lutheran writings. Not surprisingly, the reformer and Utraquist saint Jan Hus takes first position, mainly as the author of one of the permanently popular homilies. In contrast, his *Exegesis of the Twelve Articles of the Christian Creed* and the collected *Opera Hussii* are found only exceptionally, although Hus's works had been well received and much studied from the very beginning of the Reformation in the sixteenth century, both by Luther and later also by other Protestant theologians. Hus's popularity with the burgher readers of that time depended on what the market had to offer. The principle of market availability also restricted the distribution and influence of the work of Petr Chelčický, the spiritual father of the *Unitas fratrum*. Around 1600 his homily was a rarity and more readers were likely to have had *The Net of the Creed*. On the other hand, the Czech homily of Opava clergyman Martin Philadelph Zámrský had found its way to vast numbers of Czech readers despite the massive supply of homily literature on the market.

Books of hymns form a special chapter of the burgher book culture in Bohemia in the sixteenth century. The hymn books by authors of the *Unitas fratrum*, dating from the first half of the sixteenth century, were widely popular. These books, often referring only to a known melody instead of notes, maintained high artistic standards and were used by virtually all confessional groups in the country far into the seventeenth century. Editions in German spread into the Lutheran environment beyond Bohemian borders.

Calvinist and Utraquist–Calvinist literature found its way mostly into major Prague libraries, where Calvin's *Institutes* is seen standing next to the works of Luther, Melanchthon, Bullinger, Erasmus or even next to the lives of Church Fathers and writings of some Catholic authors. Calvin's *Institutes*, probably in its Latin edition, outnumbered the whole of the rest of his writings. Surprisingly, this key work of the Reformed faith was translated into Czech, but at the beginning of the seventeenth century failed to find a publisher. The remainder of Calvin's works are recorded only as isolated entries. The same is true of the work of Theodore Beza, who had maintained relatively extensive contacts with the Czech lands; after his death his library was passed on to the *Unitas*

---

[20] Compare Jarmila Pešková, 'Postila dítek Božích Tomáše Řešátka Soběslavského z r. 1589' [Homily of the children of God by Tomáš Řešátko of Soběslav from 1589], *Studia Comeniana et Historica*, 21 (44), (1991), 107–11, which includes also other literature.

fratrum. The isolated copies of Beza's writings documented in Prague include the Book of Psalms, Catechism, and homilies or writings such as *De predestinatione* or *De coena*. The presence of Calvin's books in Prague is not remarkable for their number (even though seven copies of his *Institutes* is not an insignificant number), but indicate that Calvin and his fellow theologians captured the interest of manneristic Prague to a degree definitely exceeding that of Catholic authors.

The Catholic homily of Jan Fer appears to have been the foremost Catholic book, published by Jiří Melantrich (a printer with moderate Lutheran leanings and a good businessman) thanks to a commission by archbishop Brus in 1575. It could not be reliably documented in the material under study, but it may be included in many of the entries under 'Bohemian homily' or simply 'homily'. Other Catholic-orientated publications which appear repeatedly in the documentation are the *Examen consilii Tridentini*, *Cathechesis Jesuitarum*, *Doctrina Jesuitica* or *Petri Foncecae Dialectica Jesuitarum*. Of the earlier book production we can identify 'Following Jesus Christ', the work of Gerson, the medieval Paris philosopher and theologian. It is difficult to decide how to classify the confessional orientation of Savonarola's *Meditationes*.

We should also mention the books published by the various confessions dealing with confessional policy rather than pure religion. The highest number of documented copies include the *Concordia Confessionis Augustanae Augspurgensis*, the Bohemian Confession of 1575, the Saxon Confession, Utraquist Confession, but also the *Confessio fidei Ferdinando regi Ungarise et Bohemise oblate*.

In general, the Prague literature of the period can be characterized as a combination of the earlier Bohemian Reformation tradition with the powerful stream of Lutheranism. The remaining religious literature simply added colour to bigger libraries reflecting the diversified interests of burgher intellectuals.

The analysis of the libraries of Louny by O. Fejtová has produced a picture similar to Prague, yet somewhat simpler and relatively more influenced by Lutheranism. However, unlike Prague, where readers among the intelligentsia had no problem reading Latin and Greek writings, citizens of this lesser royal town bordering on the German-speaking region were reading most of the religious books in Czech (with the exception of leading intellectuals) or in German, namely Luther's works and Lutheran literature in general. There is also sporadic evidence of Calvinist and Utraquist literature, particularly in mainly Lutheran book collections (see the library of Ondřej Cholossius of Pelhřinmov).[21]

---

[21]   The analysis is part of an earlier descriptive study by Antonín Kamiš, 'Knihovny lounskych měšťanů v 16. a na začátku 17. století' [Libraries of the burghers of Louny in

The inventories of libraries of the Protestant clergy in Prague preserved from the period 1584–1617 bear witness to the varied confessional composition of religious literature in Bohemian and especially Prague Protestant libraries.[22] Burghers, mainly the educated ones, added Bohemian Brethren, Calvinist and Zwinglian works to their initially Utraquist and Lutheran libraries. Surprisingly, these inventories, six altogether, have been preserved in the town records. Since the libraries in question belonged to prominent clergymen this minor sample provides interesting information even in the absence of other data. There is only general data available on the biggest clerical library of the time, amassed by the former consistory administrator *sub utraque* (1594–1604) Václav Dačický (+1607). It contained 349 printed books, manuscripts, collections of sermons, and so on. On the other hand, Dačický is known to have held very liberal views on the attempts of Catholics at reintegrating Utraquism, on the other, he is known to have been very close to Lutheranism. The probate inventory, dating from 1584, of a little-known priest, Jindřich of the St Michal's church also supplies only general data.

More satisfactory is the library of Mikuláš Rejský of Heřmanův Městec, clergyman of the Old Town Church of Egidins. Rejský, who was involved in many conflicts with the consistory as a result of his attempts to introduce Calvinist practices, amassed a library of 302 volumes including the collected works of John Calvin, which he bought in 1602 for 24 gulden, together with works of other Reformed theologians, but mainly of Martin Luther and other Lutheran authors. He also had the *Monumenta* of Jan Hus and even Catholic homilies of Jan Fer and Tomáš Bavorovský.

The town records contain only part of the library of the prolific writer and clergyman of St Hastalus's church, Jiřík Tomáš Mošovský (the part inherited by his orphaned grandson). Mošovský, head of the Reformed consistory (1614–17), had owned a library with a distinctly Lutheran orientation, but it also contained a work by the Polish Calvinist Gregor of Zarnowce. The traditionalist library of the Utraquist clergyman Pavel Kamil (+1585) included two Lutheran catechisms (by Luther and Rhegius) and one Catholic homily. The last library in our series was the property of Jachym Balken Dakos, murdered in the Prague New Town in 1590. His 66 books in German were distinctly

---

the sixteenth and the beginning of the seventeenth centuries], *Listy filologické*, 85 (1962), 297–307.

[22]   See Jiří Pešek, 'Knihovny pražských předbělohorských farářů' [Libraries of Prague clergymen prior to the Battle of the White Mountain], *Documenta Pragensia*, IX (1991), 417–38. This study also includes the edition of catalogues of six individual libraries.

Lutheran, but the inventory commission also found a volume of *Examen tridentini*. To sum up, Prague clerical libraries as a whole document the key role of Lutheran literature printed in German.

The German city of Olomouc, strictly Lutheran over a long period, saw the start of recatholicization very soon, as early as the 1580s. This process manifested itself in newly emerging Catholic libraries or, more accurately, through the appearance of Catholic, primarily Jesuit, literature in otherwise Lutheran burgher libraries containing writings by Martin Luther, Philipp Melanchthon, Johann Spangenberg, Simon Paul, Christopher Vischer and others. In the period under study Silesia was part of the Czech lands. The libraries of Wroclaw and Swidnice burghers were as a rule strictly Lutheran. Leading intellectuals educated abroad (as in distant Danzig) were fervent adherents of Calvinism. These conflicts were reflected for instance in the catalogue of the Wroclaw town (Lutheran) school, which lists scores of Calvin's and Calvinist works, obviously donations which the school dared not refuse.

The libraries of citizens of the Upper Hungarian mining towns were almost entirely Lutheran. In contrast, Cracow was wholly Catholic as early as the beginning of the seventeenth century after the Protestants had been pitilessly expelled from this seat of Polish kings during the 1590s. The profound change in the town's atmosphere was also confirmed by the burghers' libraries whose catalogues contain only Catholic or neutral literature.

As yet, Prague is the only example one can use to assess the effect of recatholicization following the uprising of the Estates during 1618–20. Even though the wave of repressions, enforced exiles or conversion had soon changed the religious character of Prague, Protestant literature survived in private libraries well into the eighteenth century. Recently, O. Fejtová has presented the results of her analysis of seventeenth-century libraries in the New Town.[23] According to her findings, Utraquist and Lutheran literature prevailed unequivocally throughout the century; Catholic writings were finding their way to private libraries only sporadically as late as the latter half of the seventeenth century.

These conclusions confirm the results of research into Prague Catholic clerical libraries from the period *circa* 1700, whose catalogues have been preserved in the books of inventories of the archiepiscopal archives.[24] Eight of the 23 clergymen serving prominent parishes in the

---

23   Olga Fejtová, Zum Vergleich der bürgerlichen Privatbibliotheken in Prager Neustadt und Heilbronn im 17. Jahrhundert, Paper presented at the symposium on the history of book culture [Bürgerliche Kultur im Vergleich] (1995), Szeged, in press.

24   Milada Svobodová, 'Knihovny pražských kněží 1671–1713' [Libraries of Prague clergymen 1671–1713], *Documenta Pragensia*, **IX** (1991), 489–517.

capital and having private libraries, owned Protestant literature (Luther, Buenting, Moller, Rhegius, Bugenhagen, Gerhard, Melanchthon but also John Calvin or Philipp de Mornay). In addition to the 19 heretical books, these Catholic clergymen also owned earlier Bohemian reformed literature. A massive survival of literature from the sixteenth century is also demonstrated by analyses of the catalogues of Prague burgher libraries dating from the eighteenth century by J. Pokorný.[25]

These findings should not be overestimated, nor should they be ignored. They bear witness to the lasting close ties of part of the intellectual élite of Bohemian society to Protestant literature (above all German literature) which played a key role in the lives of the people of the Czech lands between 1520 and 1620.

---

[25] Jiří Pokorný, 'Knihy a knihovny v inventářích pražských měšťanů v 18. století 1700–1784' [Books and libraries in the probate inventories of Prague burghers in the eighteenth century 1700–1784], *Acta Universitatis Carolinae – Historia Universitatis Carolinae Pragensis*, **28/1** (1988), pp. 56–8. According to these findings 42 per cent of books printed in Czech and 22 per cent of books in other languages in Prague in the eighteenth century dated from the period before 1620. Unlike clergymen, burghers did not as a rule keep Protestant books in their private libraries.

CHAPTER FOUR

Reformation and the writing of national history in East-Central and Northern Europe

Norbert Kersken

In the sixteenth century, especially after 1550, the processes of early modern state-building and of confessionalization accelerated within European societies. These tendencies strengthened the formation of identities in the new national states.[1] These developments found expression in their respective views of history, a trend which can often be traced back to lines of development stemming from the Middle Ages and which now showed an unmistakably national character.

Such a view of history finds its most distinct mark in the individual expression of specific historical cultures, by which I mean complete surveys of national history. In these texts the problems of actual politics are separated from their contexts and embedded in greater historical contexts.

In the following chapter I offer a survey of the national historiographic texts of Northern and East-Central Europe, to be followed by a summary of the backgrounds of the formation of these texts. A concluding section reflects on the significance of these texts in the context of the history of historiography and the history of the Reformation.

The historiographical cultures of the regions to the north and east of the former *Romania* can be regarded as typologically connected in a number of ways. The relevant traditions were developed in two stages: first, in the first quarter of the twelfth century in Poland, Bohemia and the Kievan Rus' and (with restrictions) in Hungary and, at the turn of the thirteenth century, in Norway and Denmark; second, as late develop-

---

[1]   See Heinz Schilling, 'Nationale Identität und Konfession in der europäischen Neuzeit', in Bernhard Giesen (ed.), *Nationale und kulturelle Identität. Studien zur Entwicklung des kollektiven Bewußtseins in der Neuzeit* (Frankfurt am Main, 1991), pp. 192–252.

ments, at the end of the fourteenth century in Scotland and at the end of the fifteenth century in Sweden.[2]

These developments were clearly distinct from the historiographical cultures in the lands of the *Romania* in two ways: there does not seem to have been any 'pre-national' stage of historiographical development; and only a small historiographical production existed, not bound to the developing high medieval powers on a national basis. All these outlines of national history matched the relative stability of these medieval states on a national basis; this seems to be a self-evident statement, which nevertheless is not applicable to a number of other countries. In Spain, France or England, for instance, the early outlines of national history show a considerable 'Utopian potential', in so far as there were developed conceptions of political-geographical unity which surpassed political reality.[3] In terms of the presentation of prehistory, namely in the passages that describe the beginnings of the connection between people, land and dominion, events which took place before the stage of time that is known and documented in the strictly historical sense, the historiographical conceptions of these countries were much more strongly characterized by autochthonous ideas than in the countries on formerly Roman ground. Here references to the sons of Noah or to the descendants of the great peoples of antiquity (Greeks, Trojans) dominate, conceptions which are not prevalent – perhaps with the exception of Scotland – in the countries of Northern and Eastern Europe.[4]

Without going further back in time, one can state that a tradition of writing national histories had been created across Europe by the end of the Middle Ages.[5] For the countries of the northern and eastern periphery we can name the following texts as the starting-point for sixteenth-century historiography. In Scotland the *Chronica gentis Scotorum* by John Fordun written *circa* 1385–87 was taken up and continued by Walter Bower's *Scotichronicon* in the middle of the fifteenth century. The reference text for Danish history was the great work of Saxo,

---

[2] For this, see in detail Norbert Kersken, *Geschichtsschreibung im Europa der nationes. Nationalgeschichtliche Gesamtdarstellungen im Mittelalter* (Cologne and Vienna, 1995) (Münstersche Historische Forschungen, 8).

[3] See, for instance, *Historia Gothorum, Wandalorum et Suevorum* by Isidor of Sevilla from 619–24 or Bede's *Historia Ecclesiastica gentis Anglorum* from 731–35, who both assume in their historiography a political-geographical unity of Spain and England which in no way corresponds to the political reality of their time.

[4] There are hints of these theories of descent from famous ancestors, but these were of secondary importance, rather than a component of a clearly thought out conception of prehistory.

[5] The most important exceptions are – for different reasons – the *imperium* and Italy and the countries of Southeastern Europe.

summarized and continued in the so-called *Compendium Saxonis* from *circa* 1340. For Sweden the *Chronica regni Gothorum* by Eric Olai was written *circa* 1470 but was not printed until 1615; for Poland the monumental *Annales seu cronicae inclyti regni Polonorum* by Jan Długosz had taken on the role of a historiographical text formerly held by Kadłubek's *Chronica Polonorum* ; in Hungary the medieval tradition of courtly chronicle writing came to an end with the work of János Thuróczy; only Bohemia lacked a national historiographic reference text at the end of the Middle Ages after the chronicle of Cosmas, the Old-Czech 'Dalimil' and new beginnings in this field in the time of Charles IV which had only a minor success.

Summarizing this brief survey one can justifiably speak of a developed text tradition of national histories in all countries of Northern and East-Central Europe at the beginning of the sixteenth century. At this point it must be stressed that most of the texts of the fifteenth century are rather a continuation of the conceptual achievements of medieval historiography than the realization of independent historiographical ideas. This group of sixteenth-century texts are examined in the following sections in the light of the generally epigonal quality of the fifteenth-century outlines of national history.

The difference becomes evident already in the quantitative findings. For the six countries taken into consideration we have no fewer than 32 new outlines: four for Scotland, two each for Denmark and Sweden, fourteen for Poland, and five each for Bohemia and Hungary. The writing of these texts falls into three broad periods: the 1520s, the years around the middle of the century and the last third of the century, with a particular stress on the 1570s and 1580s.

In 1519 in Cracow, Matthias of Miechow (*c.*1457–1523) published his *Chronica Polonorum*. He was a physician, historian and geographer, who laid the foundation of Polish sarmatism in the field of historiography; his Polish history was re-edited in 1521,[6] supplemented by the shorter Polish history by Jost Ludwig Decjus (1485–1545).[7] Matthias had been royal secretary since 1520, visited Martin Luther in 1532, but remained Catholic. In the same year the *Historia Majors*

---

[6]   Mathiae de Mechovia Chronica Polonorum, Cracow 1521; for this see *Bibliografia literatury polskiej. – Nowy Korbut – .* vols 1–3: *Piśmiennictwo staropolskie,* Roman Pollak (ed.), (Warsaw, 1963–65), vol. 2, pp. 518–22; Leszek Hajdukiewicz, 'Maciej z Miechowa', *Polski Słownik Biograficzny* (vols 1–[35], Cracow, 1935–[94], 19 (1974), 28–33.

[7]   His outline consists of three books: De vetvstatibvs Polonorum. Liber I.; De Iagiellonum familia liber II; De Sigismvndi regis temporibvs Liber III. For this see Władysław Pociecha, 'Jost Ludwik Decjusz', *PSB,* 5 (1939–46), 42–6; *Nowy Korbut,* 2 (1964), 120–3.

Britannie quam Anglie tam Scotie by John Major (1467–1550) was published in Paris; here he developed the conception of a common English-Scottish history of Great Britain for the first time.[8] *Circa* 1523 the humanist Danish carmelite Poul Helgesen (*c.*1480–after 1534) wrote his 'Compendiosa et succincta regum Danie historia',[9] while in 1526 the *Scotorum Historiae* by Hector Boethius (*c.*1465–1536) was published[10] and after 1533 Olaus Petri (1493–1552), the leading Swedish

---

[8] *Historia Maioris Britanniæ, tam Anglie quam Scotie, per Ioannem Maiorem, nomine quidem Scotum, professione autem Theologum, e veterum monumentis concinnata* (Paris, 1521) – for this see George Washington Sprott, 'John Major or Mair', *DNB*, 35, 1893, pp. 386–8; William Forbes-Leith, *Pre-Reformation Scholars in Scotland in the XVIth Century. Their Writings and their Public Services with a Bibliography and a List of Graduates from 1500 to 1800* (Glasgow, 1915), pp. 12, 23f., 150–3; Eduard Fueter, *Geschichte der neueren Historiographie* (Munich and Berlin, 1936), p. 171; J. Durkan, 'John Major: after 400 years', *Innes Review*, 1 (1950), 131–9; Anthony Ross, 'Some Scottish Catholic historians', *Innes Review*, 1 (1950), 5–21, here 5–7; John and Winifred MacQueen, 'Latin prose literature', in Cairns Craig (ed.), *The History of Scottish Literature. vol. 1: Origins to 1660 (Medieval and Renaissance)*, (Aberdeen, 1988), pp. 227–43, here pp. 235f.; Ludwig Hödl, 'Johannes Maior(is)', *Lexikon des Mittelalters* 5 (1991), 587f.

[9] Compendiosa et succincta regum Daniæ historia in hoc congesta ut studiosi cuiuspiam memoriam adiuvaret, in Marius Kristensen, Hans Ræder (eds), *Skrifter af Paulus Helie* (Copenhagen, 1937), vol. 6. pp. 1–50; see the commentaries in Marius Kristensen (deceased), Niels-Knud Andersen (eds), *Skrifter af Paulus Helie* (Copenhagen, 1948), 7, pp. 148–53. The better known so-called 'Skibby-chronicle' with a introductory survey of the time since Sven Estridsen (1047–74) is essentially an unfinished history of the time of the Danish Reformation starting with the accession of the first Oldenburgian to the Danish throne, Christian I. (1448) to 1534: for this in general see Ellen Jørgensen, *Historieforskning og historieskrivning i Danmark indtil aar 1800* (Copenhagen, 1931), pp. 75–85; Herluf Nielsen, 'Skibbykrøniken', *Kulturhistorisk leksikon for nordisk middelalder fra vikingetid til reformationstid* (Copenhagen, 1970), 15, p. 476f.; Kai Hørby, 'Paulus Helie', in Sv. Cedergreen Bech (ed.), *Dansk Biografisk Leksikon*, (16 vols, Copenhagen, 1979–84), vol. 6 (1980), pp. 210–12; Mikael Venge in Aksel E. Christensen et al. (eds), *Danmarks Historie*, (10 vols, Copenhagen, 1977–92), 2, 1, (1980), p. 283f. [Lit.]; *Biographisch-Bibliographisches Kirchenlexikon*, Friedrich Wilhelm Bautz and Traugott Bautz (eds), (vols 1–[8], Hertzberg, 1975–[94]), 2 (1990), col. 701f.; Kai Hørby, 'Humanist profiles in the Danish Reform Movement', in Leif Grane, Kai Hørby (eds), *Die dänische Reformation vor ihrem internationalen Hintergrund*, (Göttingen, 1990) (Forschungen zur Kirchen- und Dogmengeschichte, 46), pp. 28–38, here pp. 31–4.

[10] I used the edition published twice in Paris (1574, 1575), with the continuation by Giovanni Ferrerio: *Scotorvm Historiæ a Prima Gentis origine ... Libri XIX. Hectore Boethio Deidonano auctore. Duo postremi huius Historiæ libri nunc primum emittuntur in lucem. Accessit & huic editione eiusdem Scotorum Historiæ continuatio, per Ioannem Ferrerium Pedemontanum, recens & ipsa scripta & edita ...* (Paris, 1575) – for this see Aeneas James George MacKay, 'Hector Boece or Boethius', *DNB*, 2 (1885–86), 759–62; Forbes Leith, *Pre-Reformation Scholars* (1915), pp. 6, 41f.; Fueter, *Geschichte* (1936), pp. 171f.; J. B. Black, 'Boece's *Scotorum Historiae*' in *Quartercentenary of the Death of Hector Boece. First Principal of the University of Aberdeen*, (Aberdeen, 1937), pp. 30–

Reformer, composed the 'Swenska Cröneka'.[11] In the early 1530s, the cartographer and court historiographer to Sigismund I, Bernard Wapowski (c.1450–1535), emulating Długosz, wrote an outline of Polish history up to 1535, but the work never went to press in his lifetime and the part up to 1380 is considered lost.[12] At the same time two attempts were made at writing a Hungarian history: in 1534, Hans Hauge zum Freystein, counsellor to the Habsburg Ferdinand who at that time was working to get his claim to the Hungarian throne accepted, published a Hungarian history in German, based on Thuróczy,[13] while the highly structured Hungarian history by Miklós Oláh, secretary to Mary of Habsburg, widow of Louis II, was not finished.[14] Of these only the Scottish history by Boece had a greater impact, whereas both of the

---

53; Friedrich Brie, *Die nationale Literatur Schottlands. Von den Anfängen bis zur Renaissance* (Halle/Saale, 1937), pp. 329–53; A. de Meyer, 'Hector Boèce', *Dictionnaire d'Histoire et de Géographie Ecclesiastique*, (vols 1–[25], Paris, 1912–[94]), 9 (1937), pp. 383f.; Ross, 'Historians', pp. 7–9; Denys Hay, 'Scotland and the Italian Renaissance', in Jan B. Cowan and Duncan Shaw (eds), *The Renaissance and Reformation in Scotland: Essays in Honour of Gordon Donaldson* (Edinburgh, 1983), pp. 114–24, here pp. 121f.; MacQueen, 'Latin prose literature', pp. 236f.

[11] The text had been printed for the first time as Olai Petri 'Svenska Crónica', in *Scriptores rerum Suecicarum medii aevi*, Erich Michael Fant (ed.), (Uppsala, 1818; reprinted Graz, 1968), 1, 2, pp. 216–348 and is now available in the edition by Jöran Sahlgren: *Samlade Skrifter af Olavus Petri*, vol. 4 (Uppsala, 1917). For this see Conrad Bergendoff, *Olavus Petri and the Ecclesiastical Transformation in Sweden 1521–1552. A Study in the Swedish Reformation* (Philadelphia, 1928) [Repr. 1965], pp. 212–19; Gunnar T. Westin, *Historieskrivaren Olaus Petri. Svenska krönikans källor och krönikeförfattarens metod* (Lund, 1946); J. Svennung, *Zur Geschichte des Goticismus* (Stockholm, 1967) (Skrifter utg. av k. humanistiska vetenskapssamfundet i Uppsala 44, 2 B), pp. 44, 81f.; Gunnar T. Westin, 'Olaus Petris Svenska krönika', *Kulturhist. leks.* 12 (1967), 557–61; W. Johnson, 'Olaus Petri', in Byron J. Nordstrom (ed.), *Dictionary of Scandinavian History* (Westport, CT and London, 1986), pp. 437–39; Christina Söderhjelm McKnight, 'Olavus Petri', in Virpi Zuck (ed.), *Dictionary of Scandinavian Literature* (New York, 1990), pp. 454f.

[12] For this see *Nowy Korbut*, 3 (1965), 373–5; Henryk Barycz, *Szlakami dziejopisarstwa staropolskiego. Studia nad historiografia w. XVI-XVII* (Wrocław, 1981), pp. 35–9.

[13] 'Der Hungern Chronica inhaltend wie sie anfengklich ins land kommen sind, mit anzeygung aller irer könig, ... biß auff König Ludwig, so im 1526. jar bey Mohatz vom Türcken umbkommen ist', (Vienna 1534) – for the otherwise unknown author cf. the remarks of Károly Kertbeny, *Ungarn betreffende deutsche Erstlings-Drucke. 1454–1600* (Budapest, 1880) (Bibliographie der ungarischen nationalen und internationalen Literatur 1), pp. 111f.

[14] Nicolai Oláhi Archiepiscopi Strigoniensis Hvngaria, sive De Originibus Gentis, Regionis Situ, Diuisione, Habitu, atque Opportunitatibus, Liber Singularis, Nunc primum in lucem editus, in Matthias Bel (ed.), *Adparatus ad historiam Hungariae* (Posonii, 1735), pp. 1–41 – for this see Gabriel Adriányi, 'Oláh, Miklós', *Kirchenlexikon*, 6 (1993), col. 1171–4.

Scandinavian national surveys (Helgesen, Petri) were not printed at that time.

In the years around the middle of the century there was a considerable increase in the number of national histories, and only at this point was it possible for Reformation views to manifest themselves in historiography.[15] In this period three outlines of Bohemian history were published, namely the *Kronika o založenj země české* (1539) by the humanist poet Martin Kuthen (*c*.1510–64),[16] then the *Kronika česká* (1541) by Václav Hájek of Libočan (died 1553)[17] and ten years later, in 1552, the *Historia regni Bohemiae* by the Olomouc bishop, Jan Skála z Doubravky, latinized Dubravius (1486–1553).[18] As for the Hungarian view of history, the first, though incomplete, print of the *Rerum Ungaricarum decades* by Antonio Bonfini (1427 or 1434–1502/03 or

---

[15] From the authors of the first third of the century, only the two Scandinavians can be placed in Reformation contexts, but their texts remained unprinted in their time!

[16] The edition of 1539 can be used in a facsimile: Martin Kuthen, *Kronika o založenj země české*, Zdeněk Tobolka (ed.) (Prague, 1929) (Monumenta Bohemiae typographica 7) – for this see František Kutnar, *Přehledné dějiny českého a slovenského dějepisectví*. Vol. 1: *Od počátků národní kultury až po vyznění obrodného úkolu dějepisectví v druhé polovině 19. století* (Prague, 1973), pp. 54; 58f.; Jaroslav Kolár, 'Zur Typologie der tschechischen historischen Prosa in der Epoche des Humanismus', in Hans-Bernd Harder and Hans Rothe (eds), *Studien zum Humanismus in den böhmischen Ländern* (Cologne and Vienna, 1988) (Bausteine zur Geschichte der Literatur bei den Slaven 29; Schriften des Komitees der Bundesrepublik Deutschland zur Förderung der Slawischen Studien 11), pp. 405–24, here pp. 413–15; Jaroslav Kolár, 'Martin Kuthen ze Sprinsberka', in Vladimír Forst (ed.), *Lexikon české literatury. Osobnosti, díla, instituce* (Prague, 1993), 2, 2, pp. 1065f.

[17] Waczlaw Hajek z Libočżan, *Kronyka čzeksá* (Stare Miesto Pražske, 1541) – *Václava Hájka z Libočan Kronika česka*, Václav Flajšhans (ed.), (4 vols, Prague, 1918–33), (Staročeská knihovna 2–5) (text up to the year 1347) – for this see Kutnar, *Přehledné dějiny* (1973), pp. 55–7; Jaroslav Kolár, 'Hájekova kronika a česká kultura', *Václav Hájek z Libočan, Kronika česká. Výbor historického čtení* (Prague, 1981), p. 724; Jaroslav Kadlec, *Přehled církevních českých dějin*, (2 vols, Rome, 1987), I, p. 47; Kolár, 'Zur Typologie' (1988), pp. 413f., 422f.; Jaroslav Kolár, 'Václav Hájek z Libočan', *Lexikon české literatury*, 2, 1, (1993), pp. 33–5.

[18] Johannes Dubravius, *Historiae regni Boiemiae* (Prostannae, 1552); I used the edition *Io. Dvbravii Olomvzensis episcopi Historia Bohemica*, (Hanau, 1602). For this see Josef Hejnic and Jan Martínek (eds), *Rukovět' humanistického básnictví v Čechách a na Moravě*, (5 vols, Prague, 1966–82), II (1966), pp. 74–84; Zdeněk Ticha, 'Jan Dubravius', *Lexicon české literatury*, 1 (1985), pp. 609f.; Peter Wörster, 'Zwei Beiträge zur Geschichtsschreibung in Olmütz in der ersten Hälfte des 16. Jahrhunderts', in Hans-Bernd Harder and Hans Rothe (eds), *Studien zum Humanismus in den böhmischen Ländern*, pt III (Cologne, Weimar and Vienna, 1993) (Schriften des Komitees der Bundesrepublik Deutschland zur Förderung der Slawischen Studien 13), pp. 35–49, here pp. 40–9; idem, *Humanismus in Olmütz. Landesbeschreibung, Stadtlob und Geschichtsschreibung in der ersten Hälfte des 16. Jahrhunderts* (Marburg, 1994) (Kultur- und geistesgeschichtliche Ostmitteleuropa-Studien 5), pp. 155–78.

1505) in 1543, and its first German translation published shortly thereafter, in 1545, were both important.[19] In 1554 the *De omnibus Gothorvm Sveonumque regibus* by the last Swedish archbishop John Magnus (1488–1544) was published, having been completed ten years before[20] and was followed in the next year by the great survey on Polish history, the *De Origine et rebus gestis Polonorum* by Martin Kromer (1512–1589)[21] and in 1556 by the short *Chronologia Rerum Hungaricum* by the Kronstadt jurist and later minister in Stolzenburg (Szelindek), Thomas Bomel (died 1592).[22] One should also mention in this context the *Chronologiae* by the Kronstadt notary and later minister in Gross Scheuren (Nagycsür), Michael Siegler (died 1585). His work was written *circa* 1562 or 1563 and was dedicated to Stephen Báthori, though it

---

[19]   *Antonii Bonfini, Rerum Ungaricarum decades tres, nunc demum industria Martini Brenneri Bistriciensis Transsylvani in lucem editae* (Basle, 1543). For this edition see Antonius de Bonfinis, *Rerum Ungaricarum decades quatuor cum dimidia*, I. Fógel, B. Iványi and L. Juhász (eds), (Leipzig, 1936) (Bibliotheca scriptorum medii recentisque aevorum. Saec. XV. [22] 1) 1, pp. XIV–XVI, XXXIII. For the German translation, see below, note 75.

[20]   'Historia Ioannis Magni Gothi sedis Apostolicae legati Svetiae et Gotiae primatis ac Archiepiscopi Vpsalensis', *De omnibus Gothorvm Sveonumque regibus* (Rome, 1554). Only four years later a second edition was published: *Gothorvm Sveonumqve historia, avtore Io. Magno Gotho, Archiepiscopo Vpsaliensi* (Basle, 1558). For this see Svennung, *Goticismus*, pp. 44, 64, 82f., 85f.; Sten Lindroth, 'Johannes Magnus', *Svenskt biografiskt lexikon*, (vols 1–[27], Stockholm, 1917/18–[1973–75]), vol. XX (1973–75), pp. 220–6; Kurt Johannesson, *Gotisk renässans. Johannes och Olaus Magnus som politiker och historiker* (Stockholm, 1982), esp. ch. 4; Allan Ellenius, 'Wiedergeburt, Erneuerung und die nordische Renaissance', in Georg Kaufmann (ed.), *Die Renaissance im Blick der Nationen Europas* (Wiesbaden, 1991) (Wolfenbütteler Abhandlungen zur Renaissanceforschung 9), pp. 261–77, here pp. 263, 266.

[21]   Martini Cromeri *De Origine et rebus gestis Polonorum libri XXX* (Basle 1555); I used the third, revised edition (Basle, 1568) – for this see *Nowy Korbut*, 2, pp. 412–19; Henryk Barycz, 'Kromer Marcin', *PSB*, 15 (1970), 319–24; *idem, Szlakami*, pp. 83–123; *idem, 'O życiu i twórczości dziejopisarskiej Marcina Kromera', in idem, Między Krakowem a Warmią i Mazurami. Studia i szkice* (Olsztyn, 1987), pp. 272–95; Jerzy Topolski, 'Marcin Kromer', in Lucian Boia (ed.), *Great Historians from Antiquity to 1800. An International Dictionary* (New York, 1989), pp. 305f.

[22]   *Chronologia Rerum Hungaricarum, a primo Unnorum in Pannoniam adventu, ad millesimum quingentesimum sextmum a nato Christo annum, per Thomam Bomelium Coronensem collecta* (Coronae 1556) – for this see Johann Seivert in: Joseph Trausch, *Schriftsteller-Lexikon der Siebenbürger Deutschen* (Kronstadt, 1868), 1 pp. 159–61; [Repr.: Cologne-Vienna, 1983 (Schriften zur Landeskunde Siebenbürgens 7)]; Friedrich Schuler-Lybloi, 'Thomas Bomel', *Allgemeine Deutsche Biographie*, (56 vols, Leipzig, 1875–1912), III (1867), p. 118; Józef Szinnyei, *Magyar írók élete és munkái*, (14 vols, Budapest 1891–1914), I, col. 1205; Béla v. Pukánszky, *Geschichte des deutschen Schrifttums in Ungarn* (Münster, 1931) (Deutschtum und Ausland 34/36), 1, p. 144; Emma Bartoniek, *Fejezetek a XVI–XVII. századi Magyarországi történetírás történetéböl* (Budapest, 1975), pp. 162f.

remained unpublished at the time.[23] This synopsis shows that for Bohemian, Polish and Hungarian history, the production and publication of important new outlines of national history occurred primarily in the period 1540–55.

In this regard the 1570s and 1580s are comparable as a third main period during which these general surveys came into existence. At the beginning of this period there was a short chronological outline of Hungarian history by Abraham Bakschay from Selmecz (Schemnitz, Banská Štiavnica) in Upper Hungary, secretary to the *woiwode* of Sieradz and lord of Késmárk (Kežmarok, Käsmark) in the Zips, Olbracht Laski (1536–1605);[24] next were two new editions of national histories, the first complete edition of Bonfini's 1568 Hungarian history[25] and the second edition of the Bohemian history of Dubravius from 1575;[26] furthermore in this period the *Chronica a Magyaroknac dolgairól* by Gáspár Heltai (*c.*1500–74) from Kolozsvár in Transylvania[27] was pub-

---

[23] Michael Siegler, Chronologiae Regum Hungaricarum, Transilvanicarum, et vicinarum Regionum, Libri duo, in Matthias Bel, *Adparatus*, pp. 43–88 – for this see Johann Seivert in: Trausch, *Schriftsteller-Lexikon*, 3 (1871), pp. 301–3; Szinnyei, *Magyar írók*, 12 (1908), col. 975; Pukánszky, *Geschichte*, pp. 144, 440.

[24] Abrahami Bakschay Scemnicenis Pannonii, ... *Chronologia de regibvs Hungaricis* ... (Cracow, 1567); I used the reimpression in the Bonfini edition by János Zsámboky of 1568 (cf. the following note, pp. 897–920); for this see Szinnyei, *Magyar írók* (1891), pp. 372f.; Bartoniek, *Fejezetek* (1975), p. 128; *Slovenský biografický slovník (od roku 833 do roku 1990)* 6 vols, Martin, 1986–94), vol. 1, p. 112. For Laski see Roman Żelewski, 'Laski, Olbracht', *PSB*, 18 (1973), 246–50.

[25] *Antonii Bonfinii, Rerum Ungaricarum decades quatuor cum dimidia*, excusae Ioan. Sambuci Tirnaviensis, (Basle, 1568). The work is now available in the critical edition: Antonius de Bonfinis, *Rerum ungaricarum decades quatuor cum dimidia*, Margarita and Péter Kulcsár (eds), (vols 1–3, Leipzig, 1936); (vols 4, 1–2, Budapest, 1941, 1976) (Bibliotheca scriptorum medii recentisque aevorum. Saec. XV. [22] 1–4. Series Nova 1) – for this see Péter Kulcsár, *Bonfini magyar törtétének forrásai és keletkezése* (Budapest, 1973) (Humanizmus és reformáció 1); further Gerhard Rill, 'Bonfini, Antonio', *Dizzionario biografico degli Italiani*, ed. Istituto della Enciclopedia italiana, (vols 1–[43], Rome 1960–[93]), XII (1970) col. 28–30; D. Ciurea, 'Sur l'historiographie de la Hongrie au moyen âge', *Le Moyen âge*, 78 (1972), 115–21, here 119–21; Eric Cochrane, *Historians and Historiographers in the Italian Renaissance* (London, 1981), pp. 344–9; Michel Feo, 'Bonfini, Antonio', *LexMA*, 2 (1983), col. 411; Lajos Demény, 'Antonio Bonfini', *Great Historians from Antiquity to 1800. An International Dictionary* (New York, 1989), pp. 203f.

[26] *Io. Dubravii olomuzensis episcopi historia boiemica* ... (Basle, 1575).

[27] Gáspár Heltai, *Chronica a Magyaroknac dolgairól* (Colosvarot, 1575) [Facsimile. with introduction by Péter Kulcsár, Budapest, 1973 (*Bibliotheca Hungarica antiqua* 8)]; for this see Trausch, *Schriftsteller-Lexikon*, 2 (1870), pp. 101–18; vol. 4 by Friedrich Schuller (Hermannstadt, 1902), pp. 181f. [Repr.: Cologne and Vienna, 1983]; Jenö Sólyom, 'Caspar Helth', *Neue Deutsche Biographie*, (vols 1–[17], Berlin, 1953–[1994]), here 8 (1969), p. 508; Emma Bartoniek, *Fejezetek*, pp. 109–17; Oskar Wittstock, 'Kaspar

lished. This was the first Hungarian history in the Hungarian language. It was followed by two Scottish histories by John Leslie (1527–96), the *De origine, moribvs, et rebus gestis Scotorum Libri decem* (1578)[28] and George Buchanan's (1506–82) *Rervm Scoticarvm Historia* (1582)[29] as well as the writing on Hungarian history by the Italian Gian Michele Bruto (1517–92), commissioned by Stephen Báthori and intended as a continuation of Bonfini's *Decades*.[30] National histories for Poland are strikingly numerous in this period. In the years 1571 to 1587 five further Polish histories appeared, the *Chronica, sive Historiae Polonicae compendiosa* by Jan Herburt (after 1524–77), jurist, historian and holder of important political offices,[31] the survey published by Alessandro Guagnini (1534–1614), a Veronese in Polish military service,[32] the *Syn-*

Helth. Reformator, Humanist und Verleger zweier Völker', *Siebenbürgisch-sächsischer Hauskalender*, 23 (1978), 91–105; J.- Fr. Gilmont, 'Gáspár Heltai', *DHGE*, 23 (1990), col. 966f.

[28]   *De origine, moribvs, et rebus gestis Scotorum Libri decem* Avthore Ioanne Leslæo, Scoto, Episcopo Rossensi (Rome, 1578) – for this see Thomas Finlayson Henderson, 'John Leslie or Lesley', *DNB*, 11 (1892–93), 972–8; John Dowden, *The Bishops of Scotland. Being the Notes of the Lives of All the Bishops, Under Each of the Sees, Prior to the Reformation*, J. Maitland Thomson (ed.), (Glasgow, 1912), pp. 229–31; Forbes-Leith, *Pre-Reformation Scholars*, pp. 6, 9, 14, 65–9; Fueter, *Geschichte*, p. 172; Ross, 'Historians', 9; MacQueen, 'Latin prose literature', p. 237f.

[29]   *Rervm Scoticarvm Historia*, avctore Georgio Bvchanano Scoto, (Edinburgh, 1582); I used the edition (Edinburgh 1583) – for this see Aeneas James George MacKay, 'George Buchanan', *DNB*, 3 (1886–87), 186–93; Fueter, *Geschichte*, pp. 172–4; *Kirchenlexikon*, 1 (1975), pp. 785f.; Ian Dalrymple McFarlane, *Buchanan* (London, 1981), here esp. pp. 416–40; *idem*, 'George Buchanan and European Humanism', *Yearbook of English Studies*, 15 (1985), pp. 33–47; MacQueen, 'Latin prose literature', (1988), pp. 237f.; Arthur H. Williamson, *Scottish National Consciousness in the Age of James VI. The Apocalypse, the Union and the Shaping of Scotland's Public Culture* (Edinburgh, 1979), pp. 107–16; Roger A. Mason, '*Rex Stoicus*: George Buchanan, James VI and the Scottish Polity', in John Dwyer, Roger A. Mason et al. (eds), *New Perspectives on the Politics and Culture of Early Modern Europe* (Edinburgh, [1982]), pp. 9–33.

[30]   For this see D. Caccamo, 'Bruto, Gian Michele', *DBI*, 14 (1972), 730–4; Antal Pirnát, 'Gattungen der humanistischen Geschichtsschreibung. Historia et commentarii', in August Buck, Tibor Klaniczay et al. (eds), *Geschichtsbewußtsein und Geschichtsschreibung in der Renaissance* (Leiden, New York and Budapest, 1989), pp. 57–64, here pp. 62f.

[31]   *Chronica, sive Historiae Polonicae compendiosa* Authore macnifico viro Ioanne Herburto de Fulstin, Regni Polonici Senatore, (Basle, 1571) – for this see Roman Żelewski, 'Herburt, Jan', *PSB*, 9 (1960–61), 440–2; *Nowy Korbut*, 2, 257–9.

[32]   The *Sarmatiae Europeae descriptio* (Cracow, 1578) was reprinted by Johannes Pistorius as: *Compendium chronicorum Poloniae secundum seriem et successiones omnium principum, regumque gentis, á Lecho primo duce, Authoremque Polonorum, usque ad Regem Henricum Valesium ordine seruato* in *Polonicae historiae corpus*, (Basle, 1582), 2, pp. 341–70 – it seems to be plagiarism of a work by Maciej Stryjkowski; for this see Wlodzimierz Budka, 'Gwagnin Aleksander', *PSB*, 9 (1960–61), 202–4; *Nowy Korbut*, 2 (1964), 246–8.

opsis brevissima annalium polonicorum [33] and the *Annales, sive de origine et rebus gestis Polonorum et Lituanorum libri octo* by Stanisław Sarnicki (1532–97)[34] as well as the Polish-Lithuanian chronicle by Maciej Stryjkowski (1547–82).[35] In this context the first great text edition of Polish history by the physician and theologian Johannes Pistorius (1546–1608) should be mentioned.[36] At the end of this survey two important outlines of national history in the vernacular must not be ignored, these are the *Danmarckis Rigis Krønnicke* by the Danish chancellor Arild Huitfeldt (1546–1609)[37] and the *Kronika polska* of 1597 begun by Martin Bielski (1495–1575) and revised and continued by his son Joachim (*c.*1540–99), who had converted to the Catholic faith in 1595.[38] Finally in the 1590s two other, less important texts were edited, the *Regum Poloniae Icones* by Tomasz Treter (1547–1610)[39] and the *Chronicon regum Poloniae* by Erazm Gliczner (1535?–1603)[40] from which only the part dealing with the earliest, legendary times was published.

---

[33] *Synopsis brevissima annalium polonicorum* (Cracow, 1582).

[34] Stanislai Sarnicii, *Annales, sive de origine et rebus gestis Polonorum et Lituanorum libri octo* (Cracow 1587) – for this see *Nowy Korbut*, 3 (1965), 216–19; Barycz, *Szlakami*, pp. 56–60; Halina Kowalska/Janusz Sikorski, 'Stanisław Sarnicki', *PSB*, 35 (1994), 217–23.

[35] *Kronika polska, litewska, żmudźka i wszystkiej Rusi Macieja Stryjkowskiego.* Reprint of the edition Königsberg 1582, ed. Mikołaj Malinowski (2 vols, Warsaw, 1846 [Repr., 1985]) – for this see *Nowy Korbut*, 3 (1965), 296–9; Povilas Reklaitis, 'Maciej Stryjkowski – ein polnischer Dichter und Historiker Litauens', *Zeitschrift für Ostforschung*, 35 (1986), 406–13; Zbysław Wojtkowiak, *Maciej Stryjkowski – dziejopis Wielkiego Księstwa Litewskiego. Kalendarum życia i działnośc* (Poznań, 1990) (Uniwersytet im. Adama Mickiewicza w Poznaniu. Seria Historia 159).

[36] *Polonicae historiae corpus, hoc est Polonicarum rerum latini recentiores & ueteres scriptores, quotquot extant, uno volumine compraehensi omnes, & in aliquot distributi tomos* (3 parts, Basle, 1582) – for this see W. Gass, 'Johann Pistorius', *ADB*, 26 (1888), 199–201.

[37] *Danmarckis Rigis Krønnicke* (9 vols, Copenhagen, 1596–1603 [repr. 1976–78]) – for this see H. Ehrencron-Müller, *Forfatterlexikon omfattende Danmark, Norge og Island indtil 1814* (12 vols, Copenhagen 1924–35), IV (1927), pp. 169–72; Jørgensen, *Historieforskning*, pp. 106–16; Harold Ilsøe, 'Arild Huitfeldt', *DBL*, 6 (1980), 598–604.

[38] *Kronika polska Marcina Bielskiego*, Józef Turowski (ed.) (3 vols, Sanok, 1856) – for this see *Nowy Korbut*, 2 (1964), 24–31; Henryk Barycz, 'Bielski Joachim', *PSB*, 2 (1936), 61–4; Jerzy Topolski, 'Marcin Bielski', in Lucien Boia (ed.), *Great Historians*, pp. 303f.

[39] Tomasz Treter, *Regum Poloniae Icones* (Rome, 1591) – for this see *Nowy Korbut*, 3 (1965), 345–7; Tadeusz Chrzanowski, *Działalność artystyczna Tomasza Tretera* (Warsaw, 1984), esp. pp. 19, 157–71; Teresa Jakimowicz, *Temat historyczny w stuce epoki ostatnich Jagiellonów* (Warsaw and Poznań, 1984), pp. 85–7.

[40] *Chronicon regum Poloniae ... descriptum per Erasmum Glicznerum ...* (Torun, 1597). For this see Henryk Barycz, 'Gliczner Erazm', *PSB*, 8 (1959–60), 50–2; *Nowy Korbut*, 2 (1964), 193–5.

In the search for structural comparisons in the circumstances of composition of these national histories, one must first examine the characteristics of the 30 historians who are considered to be the authors of these works.[41]

Taking into consideration the growing declericalization of educational privileges in the early modern period, the growing majority of non-clerical authors as compared with clerics in the course of the sixteenth century is an unsurprising development. In order to understand fully the allegiance of the authors of these national histories to a Reformation perspective, one should ask which of these can be addressed as a 'man of the church' and who finally besides his historiographical activity has emerged as someone taking sides in the social controversies in the time of the Reformation.

Most of the historians listed here were distinguished men in their own right[42] and, with only a few notable exceptions, most were theologians or representatives of the supreme level of the clerical hierarchy in their respective countries.

---

[41]   It seems to be justifiable in the scope of this article, to leave aside the poetical works on national historiographical themes. See only the *Vitae Regum Polonorum* by Klemens Janicki (1516–1542/43), which the author composed in the years before his death, but which was not printed until 1563 (Klemens Janicki, *Carmina. Dziela wszystkie*, Jerzy Krókowski [ed.], [Wroclaw, Warsaw, Cracow, 1966], [Biblioteka pisarzów polskich B 15], pp. 210–47; see further *Nowy Korbut*, 2 [1964] 282–6); for Bohemia see the *Catalogus ducum regumque Bohemorum* (Prague, 1540), a collection of portraits of all Bohemian princes, each supplied with a distich by the humanist poet Martin Kuthen (Martin Kuthenus, *Catalogus ducum regumque Bohemiae, in quo summatim gesta singulorum singulis distichis continentur*, [Prague, 1540]; new impression as *Martini Cutheni Bohemi Ducum Regumque Bohemiae Gesta singulis distichis comprehensa* in: Johann Burchard Mencke [ed.], *Scriptores rerum Germanicarum praecipue Saxonicarum*, [Leipzig, 1738], 1, col. 1957–9 – for this see Josef Hejnic, Jan Martínek [eds], *Rukovět' humanistického básnictví v Čechách a na Moravě*, [Prague, 1969], 3, pp. 116–18), the *Disticha* from 1563 by David Crinitus (1531–86) (for this see *Rukovět'*, 1 [1966], pp. 472f.; Zdeněk Tichá, 'David Crinitus z Hlaváčova', *Lexikon české literatury*, 1 [1985] pp. 369f.) and the *Duces et Reges Bohemiae* by Kaspar Kropáč (*c*.1530–80) (first impression 1581, new impression as: *Caspari Cropacii Pelsinensis Bohemi Duces et Reges Bohemiae*, in Marquard Freher [ed.], *Cosmae Pragensis Chronicae Bohemorum libri III*, [Hanau, 1607] and in Mencke [ed.], *Scriptores*, col. 1960–8; for this see *Rukovět'*, 1 [1966], pp. 497–506; Heribert Sturm [ed.], *Biographisches Lexikon zur Geschichte der böhmischen Länder*, [vols 1–(3, 7), Munich and Vienna, 1979–(1993)], I, p. 214); for Hungary see the *Genealogia historica regum Hungariae. Az az magyar királyoknac eredetekről és nemzetségekről valo szép historia* (Colosvarat, 1576) by András Valkai (1540–87).

[42]   An exception in this regard may be Václav Hájek of Libočan and the authors of the minor Hungarian chronicles (Hans Hauge zum Freystein, Abráham Bakschay, Michael Siegler).

John Major and Hector Boece were professors of theology in Glasgow, St Andrews and Paris, where their Scottish histories were published in 1521 and 1527 respectively. John Leslie was a Catholic priest, last Abbot of Lindores, leader of the Scottish Catholics in the 1560s, Bishop of Ross since 1566 and living in exile in Rome since 1574, where his Scottish history was published in 1578. Poul Helgesen, author of the *Compendiosa regum Daniae historia* from 1523 was provincial of the Carmelites' Danish province and one of the outstanding representatives of the Catholic resistance against religious innovations. Olaus Petri, author of the first Swedish history in the vernacular dating from the 1530s was the leading representative of the Lutheran Reformation, while on the other side John Magnus was consecrated last Archbishop of Uppsala in 1533, but never resided in his official residence. Martin Kromer, author of possibly the most influential Polish history of the sixteenth century, was the most important representative of the Polish Counter-Reformation after Stanisław Hozjusz (Hosius) and his successor as Bishop of Warmia (1579). Tomasz Treter, temporarily working together with Hosius, stayed in Rome for many years and resided in Frombork from 1593 onwards as a canon and Chancellor of the Warmian chapter. He is also to be mentioned in this intellectual context. On the other side, from 1555 to 1570 Stanisław Sarnicki was one of the most important representatives of Polish Calvinism while Erazm Gliczner was a central figure of the Great Polish Lutherans. Václav Hájek of Libočan, author of the *Kronika česká* from the second half of the 1530s was a Catholic priest and a popular preacher in different places. Jan Skála z Doubravky (Dubravius), author of the important *Historia regni Bohemiae* had been bishop of Olomouc since 1541. Finally, Miklós Oláh, who was to become Bishop of Agram (Zagreb) and Erlau (Eger) and later Archbishop of Gran (Esztergom) was influential in the early Counter-Reformation in Hungary. Gáspár Heltai, author of the first Hungarian history written in the vernacular was one of the important Reformers in Transylvania.

Furthermore, a considerable number of these authors had become known as supporters of Reformation ideas and were involved in the Reformation controversies going on in their respective national contexts. This applies to John Leslie and George Buchanan, to Poul Helgesen, Olaus Petri and John Magnus, to Martin Kromer, Stanisław Sarnicki and Erazm Gliczner, to Václav Hájek of Libočan and Jan Dubravius as well as to Gáspár Heltai. There seems to be a clear connection between historiography, or more precisely the work on a comprehensive national view of the past, and the ideological path followed by the early modern nations in the context of the Reformation.

In order to put these reflections in concrete terms it is interesting to note when these general surveys were written. Two groups of texts may be distinguished. On the one hand there are countries where the different national historiographic outlines came into existence at the time of the controversies about the Reformation within society: Poland and Bohemia should be mentioned in this context. In Bohemia the national survey of a distinguished Catholic point of view by Hájek of Libočan and Dubravius and the Czech history of the Protestant Martin Kuthen came into existence in times of sharp conflicts between the different Reformation groups and the representatives of Catholicism.[43] In Poland the three texts by Kromer, Sarnicki and Gliczner published in the context of the Reformation were written from the Catholic, Calvinist and Lutheran position at a time when the final decision for Catholicism had not yet been made.[44] On the other hand, there are countries in which national historiographic outlines came into being at times when the country had become Protestant, as in the case of the Northern countries and Transylvania. In Scotland the Reformation had been confirmed by the parliamentary decisions of 1560 and 1567 and by the abdication of Mary Stuart;[45] only after this did the Scottish histories of the Reformation period appear: the continuation of Boece's *Scotorum Historiae* by Giovanni Ferrerio from 1574, John Leslie's book of 1578 and George Buchanan's *Rerum Scoticarum Historia* of 1582. In Denmark disregarding the work of Poul Helgesen which had remained unknown in the period, but after the Reformation had been officially accepted by 1536,[46]

---

[43]   For the background, see the surveys by Jerzy Kloczwski, 'Ostmitteleuropa: Böhmen, Ungarn und Polen', in Marc Venard (ed.) *Die Geschichte des Christentums. Religion–Politik–Kultur, vol. 8: Die Zeit der Konfessionen (1530–1620/30)*, (Freiburg, Basle and Vienna, 1992), pp. 618–61, here pp. 624–9, and Winfried Eberhard, 'Reformation and Counter-reformation in East Central Europe', in Thomas A. Brady, Jr, et al. (eds), *Handbook of European History 1400–1600. Late Middle Ages, Renaissance and Reformation* (2 vols, Leiden, New York and Cologne, 1994–95), II pp. 551–84, here pp. 556–8.

[44]   Euan Cameron, *The European Reformation* (Oxford, 1991), pp. 277f.; Kloczwski, 'Ostmitteleuropa', pp. 641–52; Eberhard, 'Reformation and Counter-reformation', (1995), pp. 574–6.

[45]   Gordon Donaldson, *Scotland. James V to James VII* (Edinburgh and London, 1965) (The Edinburgh History of Scotland 3), pp. 132–53; Jenny Wormald, *Court, Kirk, and Community. Scotland 1470–1625* (London, 1981) (The New History of Scotland 4), pp. 109–39; Cameron, *Reformation*, pp. 289–91, 385–8.

[46]   T. K. Derry, *A History of Scandinavia. Norway, Sweden, Denmark, Finland and Iceland* (London, 1979), pp. 87–9; Mikael Venge in A. E. Christensen et al., *Danmarks Historie*, 2, 1, pp. 297–301; Kai Hørby, 'Reformation. Denmark', in Byron J. Wordstrom (ed.) *Dictionary of Scandinavian History*, pp. 500–3; N. K. Andersen, 'The Reformation in Scandinavia and the Baltic', in G. R. Elton (ed.), *The New Cambridge Modern History, vol. 2: The Reformation*, (Cambridge, 1990), pp. 144–71, here pp. 144–52; Cameron, *Reformation*, pp. 272–4.

several official historiographers[47] dedicated themselves to the project of a comprehensive Danish history, which had only been realized by Arild Huitfeldt. For Sweden the first Swedish history in the vernacular by Olaus Petri and at the same time the Swedish history published only in 1554 by John Magnus during his Italian exile, were written after the Reformation had been finally pushed through in *circa* 1539/40.[48] It is striking that most of the historiographical endeavours for Hungary, which was being split into Habsburg, Osmanian and Transylvanian spheres of influence at the time, came from Upper Hungary or Transylvania. While for Habsburg Hungary only the works from the early 1530s by Hauge zum Freystein and Miklós Oláh can be mentioned, the Hungarian tradition seems to have had much stronger support in Transylvania. After the acceptance of the Reformation in Transylvania in the Lutheran or Calvinist form in the 1550s, Thomas Bomel published his short outline in 1556, in 1562–63 Michael Siegler wrote his *Chronologiae*, in 1567 Abraham Bakschay's *Chronologia* was published, while in 1565 the first edition of Bonfini's *Decades* within Hungary was edited by Gáspár Heltai.[49] In 1575, Heltai's Hungarian *Chronica* appeared in Kolozsvar, where Andras Valkai's Hungarian *Genealogia* was also printed in 1576, and by the early 1580s Gian Michele Bruto had finished his continuation of Bonfini.

The differentiation of national histories in the context of Reformation, between texts belonging to the period of active Reformation controversy and texts coming into existence after the decisive events, suggests a connection between the type of Reformation and the background for the emerging need for a comprehensive outline of history. In countries where, relatively rapidly after the arrival of Reformation influences, a decision about the Reformation was made on the supreme political level, new historiographical outlines of national his-

---

[47] After Hans Svaning (*c*.1500–84), the royal historiographer since 1553, Anders Sørensen Vedel (1542–1616) was of special importance; he had published in 1575 a free translation of Saxo Grammaticus and in 1578–81 wrote a programmatical exposé for the planned Danish history; Niels Krag (1550–1602) professor of history at Copenhagen University since 1594 and royal historiographer was busy on this project; for this see the respective entries in Ehrencron-Müller, *Forfatterlexikon*, 8 (1930), pp. 115–17, 431–8; 4 (1927) 479–82 as well as in *DBL* and Torben Damsholt in A. E. Christensen et al., 10, pp. 55–61.

[48] Michael Roberts, *The Early Vasas. A History of Sweden, 1523–1611* (Cambridge, 1968), pp. 75–91, 114–20; Andersen, 'The Reformation', pp. 156–64; Cameron, *Reformation*, pp. 274–6.

[49] For this edition see Antonius de Bonfini's, *Rerum Ungaricarum decades quatuor cum dimidia*, I. Fógel, B. Iványi, L. Juhász (eds), (Leipzig, 1936) (Bibliotheca scriptorum medii recentisque aevorum. Saec. XV. [22] 1), 1, pp. XXII–XXIV, XXXIVf.

tory developed much later. So the Scottish histories by John Leslie and George Buchanan were written approximately 15 years after the Reformation had been established. A comparable historiographical activity in Scandinavia began even more slowly: the first post-Reformation survey was published in Denmark in the last years of the sixteenth century (Arild Huitfeldt), whereas a comparable development in Sweden did not begin in that period, bearing in mind that the *Swenska Cröneka* by Olaus Petri was not printed[50] and that John Magnus wrote in Italian exile.

A further form of production of national histories is discernible in those countries where in the first generation of the Reformation no social consensus could be reached or where the central political power was not able or willing to come to a decision. This was the case in Bohemia and Poland, where in the middle or the second half of the sixteenth century complete surveys developed in a strikingly similar fashion. But especially when looking at Poland it must be stressed that, in fact, not all texts can be situated within a Reformation context, both in terms of the work's origins and reception. In sixteenth-century Switzerland, another confessionally diverse country, a comparable expansion in the number of complete surveys of the Confederation is apparent.[51] Hungary was a different case, where beyond the Reformation dynamic, historiography was stimulated by problems in the politically divided nation.

Here, it is useful to analyse more precisely the confessional background of the authors of these national histories and the character of the presentation. Of the 24 historians,[52] nine are known to have favoured the Reformation, namely Olaus Petri and Martin Kuthen before the middle of the century, and in the last quarter of the century, Thomas Bomel, Abrahám Bakschay, Gáspár Heltai, George Buchanan, Stanisław Sarnicki, Erazm Gliczner and Arild Huitfeldt. This list shows that each of the six countries compared had found a Protestant historiographer. However, not all of these were works of the first rank. While the two texts of Martin Kuthen rarely show the confessional attitude of the

---

50   Roberts, *The Early Vasas*, p. 115; Franklin D. Scott, *Sweden. The Nation's History* (Carbondale and Edwardsville, 1988), pp. 129f.; Christina Söderhjelm McKnight, 'Olavus Petri', in Virpi Zuck (ed.), *Dictionary*, pp. 454f.

51   Cf. Thomas Maissen, 'Ein "helvetisch Alpenvolck". Die Formulierung eines gesamteidgenössischen Selbstverständnisses in der Schweizer Historiographie des 16. Jahrhunderts', *Zeszyty Naukowe Uniwersytetu Jagiellonskiego*, nr. 1145, Prace historyczne 113 (Cracow, 1994), pp. 69–86.

52   As John Major and Hector Boece as well as Matthias of Miechów, Jost Ludwig Decjus and Bernard Wapowski were all pre-Reformation historiographers, they are not to be included in this number.

author and Olaus Petri's Swedish history developed its impact only to a small degree because of the prevention of printing, something similar can be said for Gliczner's *Chronicon*. Heltai, Sarnicki, Buchanan and Huitfeldt mark historiographically important positions: Heltai as initiator of historiography in the vernacular; Sarnicki, who in contrast to Kromer and Herburt, led his national history up to the present time (1586); and Buchanan and Huitfeldt as authors of the most national historiographical reference texts for a long time.

Important surveys on national history from a specifically Catholic point of view exist for Scotland, Sweden, Poland and Bohemia. While Leslie's Scottish history was overshadowed by Buchanan's text in terms of its reception, in Sweden, Poland and Bohemia 'Catholic' surveys remained most important for a long time: John Magnus's great Gothic history found its successors only in the middle of the seventeenth century, and his work was even published in a Swedish version in Stockholm in 1620.[53] It was highly important for the positive reception of his text that John Magnus decided against the writing of contemporary history for fundamental reasons: 'Cuius [Gostavi regis] gesta, cum sint varia, & multiplicia, in aliud opportunis tempus seruabuntur. Solent enim historiarum scriptores ab enarranda viuentium Principum historia prudentius abstinere.'[54] Kromer's synthesis of Polish history, which only reached as far as 1506, was not replaced until Adam Naruszewicz in the 1780s, an important fact which provides a useful comparison to Hájek of Libočan and Dubravius for Bohemia.

Finally, a further aspect of national historiography in the Reformation must be brought to light. This was the period which saw a fundamental breakthrough in vernacular historiography.[55] For Scotland, where Andrew of Wyntoun's rhyme chronicle already existed from the beginning of the fifteenth century, a translation in prose and one in verse of Hector Boece's *Scotorum historiae*[56] had been made in the 1530s as well as a Scottish version of Leslie's history in the Regensburg Scottish

---

[53] *Swea och Götha Crönika: hvarutinnan beskrifves icke allenast the inrikis konungars lefverne och namnkunniga bedrifter uthan och the utländske göthers liflighe regimente och stora mandom, som the särdeles uthi Hispanine bedrifvit hafva* (Stockholm, 1620).

[54] 'Historia Ioannis Magni', p. 781f.

[55] See for general observations Denis Hay, 'Intellectual Tendencies', in G. R. Elton (ed.), *The New Cambridge Modern History*, pp. 401–22, here pp. 419–21.

[56] *The Chronicles of Scotland*. Compiled by Hector Boece. Translated into Scots by John Bellenden (1531), R. W. Chambers and Edith C. Batho (eds) (2 vols, Edinburgh and London, 1938, 1941) (Scottish Text Society III, 10. 15). *The Buik of the Croniclis of Scotland or A Metrical Version of the History of Hector Boece*, William Stewart and William B. Turnbull (eds), (3 vols, London, 1858) (Rerum Britannicarum medii aevi Scriptores 6. 1–3).

cloister at the end of the century.[57] In Scandinavia Arild Huitfeldt[58] and Olaus Petri founded the tradition of national historiography in the vernacular; in Poland in this regard Maciej Stryjkowski and Martin and Joachim Bielski stood at the beginning of this development. Kuthen and Hájek used the Czech language which however had already been historiographically introduced,[59] apart from in Hungary where Heltai's *Chronica* can be regarded as a pioneering work. In short, one can say that everywhere, and that means in all European countries where a tradition in national historiography had been built by this time, it had also been built in the vernacular.

Conclusions based on the information provided above can now be drawn regarding the links between Reformation controversies, tendencies towards confessionalization and the rise of historiography. This is done in three stages: from the perspective of the Reformation itself, from that of nation-building, and from the historiographical perspective.

The link between national historiography and the appearance of specific characteristics of confessional identity is not easily established. Few of the national surveys were consciously intended to be confessionally militant. Perhaps the confessionally pointed, polemic function of national historiography is most clearly visible in the works of John Leslie, for whom the stress of the Catholic, anti-heretical tradition of Scottish history seems to be a function in the Counter-Reformation agitation. Perhaps the polemic was so strong, and the writing of history so focused because the political decision against the old church seems to have been so definite. Thus he is different from his episcopal colleagues

---

57   *The Historie of Scotland. Wrytten First in Latin by the Most Reuerend and Worthy Ihone Leslie, Bishop of Rosse And Translated in Scotish by Father James Dalrymple Religious in the Scottis Cloister of Regensburg the Yeare of God*, 1596, E. G. Cody (ed.) (2 vols, Edinburgh and London, 1888, 1890) (Scottish Text Society 5, 14, 19, 34) – for this see Ludwig Hammermeyer, 'Deutsche Schottenklöster, schottische Reformation, katholische Reform und Gegenreformation in West- und Mitteleuropa (1560–1580)', *Zeitschrift für bayerische Landesgeschichte*, 26 (1963), 131–255, here pp. 187f., 195–207.

58   In Denmark, the 'Danish rhyme chronicle' (Den danske Rimkrønike) was already in existence from the 1470s, having been published in 1495 in Copenhagen as the first printed book in Denmark: *Den danske Rimkrønike*, Helge Toldberg (ed.) (3 vols, Copenhagen, 1958–61).

59   In Bohemia in the beginning of the fourteenth century, the second Czech history had been written down, the anonymous old-Czech rhyme chronicle, the so-called 'Dalimil': *Staročeská kronika tak řečeného Dalimila. Vydání textu a veškerého textového materiálu*, Jiří Daňhelka, Karel Hádek, et al. (eds), (2 vols, Prague, 1988).

in Sweden, Poland, Bohemia, and Hungary. John Magnus, writing from an exile perspective, similar to Miklós Oláh and John Leslie, provided a much more integrative view. In order to avoid too pointed a polemic against the current developments in his mother country, he left out contemporary history and his hope that 'Principes, qui iam videntur pessimi, nonnunquam ad optimos, et clarissimos mores ante vltima fata conuertantur'[60] is obviously directed at Gustav Vasa. Such a hope for a return to the old faith has evidently become weaker with his brother Olaus ten years later; editing the history of Sweden he adds in a supplement a collection of exempla from medieval history on different cases of conflicts between kings or emperors with the Church and he threatens the 'heretical princes' of his time with mortal punishment:

> Ergo o Principes, qui vsque in hunc diem hæreticorum insanis consiliis seducti, Ecclesiam Dei durissimis legibus afflictis, ad cor reuersi, restitue, quæ tenetis, ne proniciamini in tenebras exteriores, vbi fletus, et stridor dentium manebit impios, quemadmodum iustis, piis, et bonis veram religionem amantibus, apud superos præparata est gloria, laus requies, amor, et concordia dulcis.[61]

In Poland, Kromer, bringing his history to a close in 1506, (the election of Sigismund I), and Herburt, closing with the death of Sigismund in 1548, and in Bohemia, Hájek of Libočan and Dubravius, both ending their report with the year 1526, the beginning of the domination of the Habsburgs, leave out contemporary history, thus offering syntheses which from the very beginning may have hoped for broader acceptance beyond current affairs.[62] Although one must not regard national historiography as a field in which confessional differences were openly shown, they worked in the background in the context of the move towards state-building which the Reformation supported especially in the countries of Northern and East-Central Europe; this was a push that promoted the productivity of national historiographic surveys. At this stage, it is more accurate to speak of the Reformation's acceptance of the past as handed down through the generations, as was the case for Buchanan, the John Magnus reception in Sweden, for Sarnicki or Heltai, than of the Reformation's pointed new approach to national historiography. With regard to the different forms of early modern confessionalization the importance of national historiography can be

---

[60] 'Historia Ioannis Magni', p. 782.

[61] Ibid., p. 787.

[62] This did not necessarily follow, as can be seen from Gustav Vasa's opposition to Olaus Petri's Swedish history, though he too did not write on contemporary history, cf. above with note 48.

stated in the following way. If one of the important differences in the impact of the Reformation in the Northern European countries is that it had a polarizing effect, although several confessions coexisted in East-Central Europe and Switzerland, this meant that in the confessionally unified countries of Northern Europe, work on a socially acceptable reference text of national history was both harder and more controversial. The works also took longer to produce, as in the case of Denmark and Sweden. In the multi-confessional countries of East-Central Europe, work on the national consciousness of history was carried out by several forces coming from different confessions. In this instance, the shaping of an early modern view of the past also had a socially integrating function.[63]

The processes of nation-building, the forming and intensifying of a national identity in the Reformation period were condensed by the culture of national historiography. Furthermore, the evidence of national history's primeval state, namely the links built between individual national histories and the mythical past, between the origins of culture from the standpoint of the Old Testament or classical antiquity and the proof of the unbroken continuity of national history, offers the historical basis for a generalized national consciousness. Indeed, many of these elements had stemmed from late medieval historical thinking. Thus the processes of the formation of a national consciousness in the shape of the national historic surveys were freed from the temporary processes and contingencies of the present. At the same time these historical foundations of national consciousness experienced a previously unknown development in three ways: first, the loosening of the clerical monopoly on literacy led to an enormous increase of national historical knowledge and views, since the authors as well as the recipients were no longer restricted to exclusive circles of the supreme clerical and courtly hierarchy. Second, this development was supported by printing, which showed a striking early interest in the publication of national histories.[64] Finally, the tendencies towards nationalization of historical thinking belong in the context of moves towards a more international perspective. As for the political system, Heinz Schilling has drawn attention to the beginning of the formation of an international system in these decades.[65]

---

63   Cf. Maissen, 'Alpenvolck', p. 86.

64   On this topic, see Anna-Dorothee von den Brincken, 'Die Rezeption mittelalterlicher Historiographie durch den Inkunabeldruck', in Hans Patze (ed.), *Geschichtsschreibung und Geschichtsbewußtsein im späten Mittelalter* (Sigmaringen, 1987) (Vorträge und Forschungen 31), pp. 215–36, here 234.

65   Heinz Schilling, 'Formung und Gestalt des internationalen Systems in der werdenden Neuzeit – Phasen und bewegende Kräfte', in Peter Krüger (ed.), *Kontinuität und Wandel*

In ideological terms the above-mentioned works of national historiography provided evidence of growing international links in three new developments. National histories were increasingly put to print in 'foreign' places of printing, not only as in the case of John Magnus or John Leslie because of external circumstances, but also with regard to an international public: one should mention in this context the Parisian printings of Major and Boece, the Frankfurt printing of Buchanan, publication of John Magnus in Basle, Cologne and Wittenberg, Kromer's publications in Basle, Frankfurt, Tübingen and Cologne, Dubravius's works published in Basle, Hanau and Frankfurt as well as the Basle, Frankfurt and Cologne editions of Bonfini. National historiographical surveys were increasingly spreading in translations in the vernacular, on the one hand in the language of an individual country, as in the case of Scotland,[66] Sweden,[67] Poland,[68] Bohemia[69] and Hungary,[70] and, on the other hand, in other European languages: Kromer's Polish history was published in 1562 in German,[71] Jan Herburt's Polish history was published twice in connection with the election of Henri Valois to the Polish throne in French,[72]

---

in der Staatenordnung der Neuzeit. Beiträge zur Geschichte des internationalen Systems (Marburg, 1991) (Marburger Studien zur Neueren Geschichte 1), p. 19–46; *idem*, 'Konfessionalisierung und Formierung eines internationalen Systems während der frühen Neuzeit', in Hans R. Guggisberg and Gottfried G. Krodel (eds), *Die Reformation in Deutschland und Europa. Interpretation und Debatten* (Gütersloh, 1993) (Archiv für Reformationsgeschichte. Sonderband), pp. 591–613.

[66] Compare with note 56f.

[67] Compare with note 53.

[68] Kromer's Polish history was published in a translation by M. Blazewski as *O sprawach, dziejach i wszystkich inszych potocznosciach koronnych polskich ksiąg XXX* (Cracow, 1611). Janicki's poem was published in a Polish version by Sebastian Fabian Klonowicz as *Królów i książąt polskich ... zawarcie i opis* (Cracow, 1576) and by Jan Gluchowski as *Ikones, Książąt Y Krolow Polskich* (Cracow, 1605).

[69] The *Historia Bohemica* by Enea Sylvio Piccolomini from 1458 had been translated in the fifteenth century into German and Czech, but these versions were not printed; the text was published twice in the sixteenth century, by Nikolaus Konač in 1510 and by Daniel Adam Veleslavín in 1585 in Czech, for this see Hans Rothe, 'Enea Silvio de' Piccolomini über Böhmen', in Hans-Bernd Harder and Hans Rothe (eds), *Studien zum Humanismus*, pp. 141–56, here p. 144 note 9.

[70] See the Bonfini-based chronicle of Heltai and Valkai's *Genealogia*, cf. above with note 27 and note 41.

[71] *Mitnächtischer Völckeren Historien ... Erstlich durch ... Martinum Chromer ... zu Latein ... beschriben. Jetzumalen aber durch Heinrich Pantaleon ... verteütschet.* (Basle, 1562).

[72] François Baudoin (tr.), *Histoire des roys et princes de Poloigne*, (Paris, 1573); Blaise de Vigenere (tr.), *Les chroniqves et Annales de Poloigne* (Paris, 1573) – for this see Stanisław Grzybowski, *Henryk Walezy* (Wroclaw, 1980), p. 112.

Dubravius was published in German in 1582,[73] as well as Hájek of Libočan in 1596[74] and Bonfini, twice, in 1545 and 1581.[75] Finally, the first national histories of the period by 'foreign' authors, written from a 'foreign' perspective, were written down; for the northern or eastern countries[76] the *Dania* by Albert Krantz[77] and the Hungarian histories by Pietro Ransano (written *circa* 1489–90 but printed only in 1558),[78] Levin Hulsius[79] and Wilhelm Dillich[80] are the earliest examples. The culture of national histories in the sixteenth century can be regarded also as an expression of the processes of growing nationalization and internationalization in the area of ideology.

Finally, from the point of view of historiography, the historical building of identity, one must stress once again that confessionalization and nationalization did not lead to new developments in the area of historiography. Furthermore, the impulses of the Reformation did not effect a rebuilding of the national view of the past or a critique of the mythological manifestations of early history which had arisen in the Middle Ages. But it cannot be denied that the progress in nationalization in which the Reformation took part, initiated an immense increase

---

73   Martin Boregk, *Behemische Chronica* (2 vols, Wittenberg, 1582). See also Heribert Sturm (ed.), *Biographircher Lexikon zur Geschichte der böhmischen Länder*, p. 325.

74   *Böhmische Chronica Wenceslai Hagecii ... Jetzt aus Böhmischer in die ... Deutsche Sprache ... tranßferiret Durch Johannem Sandel Zluticensem ...* (Prague, 1596). For this see Walter Schamschula, 'Hájek von Libočans "Kronika česká" und ihre deutsche Übersetzung', in Hans-Bernd Harder and Hans Rothe (eds), *Studien zum Humanismus*, pp. 177–93, here pp. 177–88.

75   *Des Aller Mechtigsten Künigreichs inn Ungarn warhafftige Chronick Durch Anthonium Bonfinium imm Latein beschryben und yetzt durch Hieronimum Boner ... inn diß volgende Tütsch gebracht ...* (Basle, 1545); *Ungerische Chronica ... Erstlich durch Antonium Bonfinium ... in Latein beschrieben. Jetzt aber ... in gut gemein Hochteutsch gebracht ... Durch P[aul] F[riese]*, (Frankfurt am Main, 1581).

76   Examples of early national histories from a foreign perspective in Western Europe are the *Historia Anglicana* by the Italian Polidoro Vergil (*c.*1470–1555) [Anglicæ historiæ libri XXVI., (Basle, 1534) and further editions ibid. 1546, 1555, 1556/57, 1570], the *History of Italy* from 1549 by the Englishman William Thomas (*c.*1507–54) [William Thomas, *The History of Italy (1549)*, George B. Parks (ed.) (New York, 1963 (partial edn)] or the *Two Bokes of the Histories of Ireland* (1570–71) by Edmund Campion (1540–81) [repr. of the 1st edn by James Ware: Edmund Campion, *A Historie of Ireland (1571). With an Introduction by Rudolf B. Gottfried* (New York, 1940, repr. 1977)].

77   *Chronica Regnorum Aquilorium, Daniæ, Suetiæ, Norvagiæ*, (Strasbourg, 1546).

78   Petrus Ransanus, *Epithoma rerum Hungaricarum. Id est Annalium omnium temporum liber primus et sexagesimus*, Péter Kulcsár (ed.) (Budapest, 1977) (Bibliotheca scriptorum medii recentisque aevorum. Series Nova 2).

79   *Chronologia Pannoniæ. Ein Kurtze beschreibung./ deß Königreichs Vngern / fürnembster Theil / Was sich allda seyt hero Anno Christi / 909. Biß auff dises 1595. Jars gedenckwürdig verlauffen*, (Nuremberg, 1595, 2nd edn 1596).

80   Wilhelm Dillich, *Ungarische Chronica* (Kassel, 1600, 2nd edn, 1606).

in the writing of history. The increase in productivity in this domain seems to have been fuelled at least in part by the intellectual climate shaped by Reformation controversies, and new possibilities then arose for the development of historiography in general and national historiography in particular. These developments led to ways in which historiography could progress independently, unlike in previous centuries when it had strong links with individual royal and ducal powers. In post-Reformation times this relative independence disappeared when historiography was strongly influenced by state interests. But the sixteenth century offered a rich and multiform national historiographic culture whose most eminent representatives, such as Scottish, Polish, Bohemian or Hungarian historians were never reduced to the role of commissioned court historian.[81]

This relatively free historiographical activity led to great syntheses of national historiography which at times preserved their influence and attraction until the beginning of methodical historiography in the eighteenth century.

---

[81] The commissioned writers include only Bernard Wapowski and Gian Michele Bruto, royal historiographers to Sigismund I. and Stephan Báthori respectively.

CHAPTER FIVE

Calvinism and estate liberation movements in Bohemia and Hungary (1570–1620)

Joachim Bahlcke

A correspondence between the humanist intellectual Caspar Dornau and his friend Caspar Waser in Zurich, begun in December 1604, informed the latter about the rapidly evolving events in Hungary, where a few weeks earlier the conflicts between the crown and estate opposition had escalated into an armed uprising under the leadership of the Transylvanian noble István Bocskai. In Dornau's view those responsible for the bloodshed in Hungary were undoubtedly Catholic rabble-rousers at the Vienna Court and their political and confessional spearhead, the Jesuits. In his view, the nobility, claiming its 'ancestral freedom rights' had merely been looking for shelter 'in the bosom of the Reformed Church'.[1] In later letters and essays Dornau, an enigmatic and multi-faceted personality with pronounced Calvinist sympathies, appeared likewise to be a defender of Estate rights and freedom of religion in Bohemia and Hungary. This was illustrated both by his political treatise *Menenius Agrippa* published in 1615 by Wechel in Frankfurt,[2] and by the essay commemorating the rebels executed on 21 June 1621 in Prague, which was published under the pseudonym of Adrianus Vaposcus and castigated Ferdinand II as 'tyrant', 'butcher' and 'Antichrist'.[3]

Dornau's last letter to Waser, dated 14 April 1606, surveyed events in Hungary and described the provisions of the Treaty of Vienna, which

---

[1] Robert Seidel, *Späthumanismus in Schlesien. Caspar Dornau (1577–1631). Leben und Werk* (Tübingen, 1994), pp. 110–11.

[2] The Wechel press was a Huguenot exile printing–house which in the last decades of the sixteenth century developed into one of the most important interfaces within the communication network of international Calvinism. Robert J. W. Evans, *The Wechel Presses: Humanism and Calvinism in Central Europe 1572–1627* (Oxford, 1975), p. 71.

[3] Seidel, *Späthumanismus*, pp. 129–41, 386–93; for the political and intellectual history of Bohemia and Hungary between 1570 and 1620 see the classic study of Robert J. W. Evans, *The Making of the Habsburg Monarchy 1550–1700* (Oxford, 1979) and his *Rudolf II and his World: A Study in Intellectual History, 1576–1612* (2nd edn, Oxford, 1984).

brought together the Estate representatives of the Hungarian and Bohemian lands.[4] Dornau recognized the need to develop a programme for theological and political action, in order to establish a balance against the spreading Counter-Reformation.[5] His appeal for solidarity was at the same time a call for Christianity to maintain unity. His warning against a strictly confessional foreign policy without consideration for common interests was reinforced in a revision of Georg Fabricius's historical work *De incrementis dominatus Turcici* in 1615, which he had continued to work on until the Treaty of Zsitva-Torok.

During his travels through Switzerland, France and the Netherlands, Dornau had established extensive contacts with the centres of West European Calvinism and maintained close relations with East and Central European nobles. His considerable correspondence illustrates the new lines of communication among the eastern and western Protestant brothers in faith which had begun to strengthen in the last third of the sixteenth century.[6] Unlike the Hungarian and Bohemian lands, where the growing force of Catholic renewal and a shift in favour of centralist-absolutist royal rulership was becoming apparent as late as 1600, post-Tridentine Catholicism in Western Europe and in the Empire had taken the offensive earlier. As a reaction to the 'Counter Reformation internationalism' led by the Spanish Habsburgs, a Protestant internationalism led by Calvinist powers, the Netherlands and the Palatinate, emerged. Between 1570 and 1620 this double-track European power system was consolidated in particular in the north-west of the continent, in an area of Europe most fervently contested between the two confessional systems.[7]

The St Bartholomew's Day Massacre of 1572 had led to increased politicization and greater solidarity within west European Calvinism. A

---

[4]   Josef Borovička, 'Čeští poslové do Uher roku 1606 (České přípravy k ratifikaci Vídeňského míru)' in *K dějinám československým v období humanismu. Sborník prací věnovaných Janu Bedřichu Novákovi k šedesátým narozeninám* (Prague, 1932), pp. 407–18.

[5]   'Dies XXIII Aprilis Posonii dictus est solennibus Ungarorum comitiis: in quibus de tota pace, inter Potzskaiam et Turcarum Principem ferienda, agatur, atque utinam transigatur. Delecti sunt, qui ex Silesia, Moravia, Bohemia eo abeant Barones nonnulli, Nobiles ac Doctores: uti in caussa communi consilia sua interponant: quae ut spiritu bono gubernentur, atque in Ecclessiae et Reipub. pacem redundent, Deum pacis invocemus.' Seidel, *Späthumanismus*, p. 114f. fn. 23.

[6]   Joachim Bahlcke, *Regionalismus und Staatsintegration im Widerstreit. Die Länder der Böhmischen Krone im ersten Jahrhundert der Habsburgerherrschaft (1526–1619)* (Munich, 1994), pp. 282–300.

[7]   Heinz Schilling, 'Konfessionalisierung und Formierung eines internationalen Systems während der frühen Neuzeit', in Hans R. Guggisberg and Gottfried G. Krodel (eds), *Die Reformation in Deutschland und Europa: Interpretationen und Debatten* (Gütersloh, 1993), pp. 591–613.

prophetic-eschatological interpretation of the state system, exemplified in the pamphlet propaganda of the time, had strengthened the consciousness of the international community with a common destiny to an extraordinary degree.[8] In East-Central Europe, a corresponding transnational solidarity of the confessions did not surface before the beginning of the seventeenth century. It coincided closely with the Bocskai rising, which for the first time instigated the call for interregional resistance – a fact which raises the question of a fundamental connection and interaction between Calvinism and the Estate liberation movement. In other words, in view of the longer-term intellectual and social connections and the concrete formation phases of the Estates in Bohemia and Hungary, one needs to establish whether and how far these lands were part of a 'general staff of political Calvinism'.[9] Despite scepticism concerning the degree of real political unity between the Calvinist powers, the existence of a political Calvinism, revolving around the organizing power of the Palatinate, is very much apparent in western and eastern Central Europe.[10]

The spread of Calvinist teachings evolved rather differently in Hungarian and Bohemian lands.[11] While the Reformed Church in divided

---

[8]   Heinz Schilling, 'Formung und Gestalt des internationalen Systems in der werdenden Neuzeit – Phasen und bewegende Kräfte', in Peter Krüger (ed.), *Kontinuität und Wandel in der Staatenordnung der Neuzeit. Beiträge zur Geschichte des internationalen Systems* (Marburg, 1991), pp. 19–46; Nicola Sutherland, *The Massacre of St Bartholomew and the European Conflict 1559–1572* (London, 1973); Ilja Mieck, 'Die Bartholomäusnacht als Forschungsproblem', *Historische Zeitschrift*, 216 (1973), 73–110; for Bohemia Josef Dostál, 'Ohlas Bartolomějské noci na dvoře Maxmiliána II.', *Český časopis historický*, 37 (1931), 335–49.

[9]   A. A. van Schelven, *Het Calvinisme gedurende zijn bloeitijd. Zijn uitbreiding en cultuurhistorische betekenis*, Vol. 3: *Polen – Bohemen – Hongarije en Zevenburgen* (Amsterdam, 1965); and his 'Der Generalstab des politischen Calvinismus in Zentraleuropa zu Beginn des Dreißigjährigen Krieges', *ARG*, 36 (1939), 117–41.

[10]   Claus-Peter Clasen, *The Palatinate in European History 1559–1660* (Oxford, 1963); for a case study see Joachim Bahlcke, 'Falcko-české království (Motivy a působení zahraničněpolitické orientace Falce od české královské volby po ulmskou smlouvu 1619–1620)', *Časopis Matice moravské*, 111 (1992), 227–51; Christine van Eickels, *Schlesien im böhmischen Ständestaat. Voraussetzungen und Verlauf der böhmischen Revolution von 1618 in Schlesien* (Cologne, Weimar and Vienna, 1994), pp. 228–400.

[11]   For the literature concerning the history of the Reformation in Bohemia and Hungary see especially Winfried Eberhard, 'Reformation and Counterreformation in East Central Europe', in Thomas A. Brady and Heiko A. Oberman (eds), *Handbook of European History 1400–1600. Late Middle Ages, Renaissance and Reformation* (2 vols, Leiden, 1994–95), II, pp. 551–84; Jerzy Kłoczowski, 'Ostmitteleuropa: Böhmen, Ungarn und Polen' in Marc Venard (ed.), *Die Geschichte des Christentums. Religion-Politik-Kultur, vol. 8: Die Zeit der Konfessionen (1530–1620/30)* (Freiburg, Basle and Vienna, 1992), pp. 618–61, esp. 628–9; Robert J. W. Evans, 'Calvinism in East Central Europe: Hungary and Her Neighbours, 1540–1700', in Menna Prestwich (ed.), *International Calvinism, 1541–1715* (Oxford, 1985), pp. 167–96.

Hungary had developed into a kind of Magyar National Church since the middle of the sixteenth century, its influence in Bohemia and Moravia was limited entirely to the Unity of Brethren (*Jednota bratrská, Unitas fratrum*), a small confessional union which had emerged from the Hussite movement and had a strict, sovereign church constitution as well as independent control and judicial organs. More radical than Utraquism, this Unity had opposed Rome and did not fall under the protection of the *Landrecht*.[12] The increasing calvinization of the Brethren nobility in particular, which had occurred following the victory of the Gnesio-Lutherans in the internal Protestant conflicts since the beginning of the 1570s, led to several renewals of former mandates against the Brethren. Reformed circles considered the Unity as belonging to them anyway: they had integrated the Latin confession of the Brethren, without the knowledge of the Unity, into their own collection of credal books. Since 1558 the Unity of Brethren in Ivančice owned a highly esteemed school primarily for the training of priests, whose first rector was Esrom Rüdinger, a Greek scholar from Wittenberg.[13] In the printing–press of the Unity, which was transferred to Kralice in 1578, the six-volume Kralice Bible was printed in Czech, making extensive use of Calvinist literature.[14] A reciprocal influence on Reformed ideas on the part of the Unity is demonstrated by the translation of the New Testament by the elder Jan Blahoslav.[15] But at the same time the elders Jan Kalef for Bohemia and Ondřej Stefan for Moravia, who had been newly elected shortly before Blahoslav's death, proved that there was strong internal resistance against calvinization and politicization of the Unity.

The *Confessio Bohemica* of 1575, developed in collaboration with the Brethren, considerably increased the political importance of the Unity in Bohemia. However, the initially unsuccessful attempt to unite

---

[12] Amadeo Molnár, 'Die Böhmische Brüderunität. Abriß ihrer Geschichte', in Maria P. van Buijtenen and Cornelis Dekker et al. (eds), *Unitas Fratrum* (Utrecht, 1975), pp. 15–34; Franz Machilek, 'Böhmische Brüder', *Theologische Realenzyklopädie*, 7 (1981), 1–8; Otakar Odložilík, 'Bohemian Protestants and the Calvinist Churches', *Church History*, 8 (1939), 342–55; František Hrubý, 'České svědectví o Jednotě bratrské do Svýcár z roku 1570', in *K dějinám československým*, pp. 290–8.

[13] Josef Cvrček, 'Bratrská škola v Ivančicich (Doplněk k dějinám školským na Moravě)', *Časopis Matice moravské*, 31 (1907), 193–203, 313–25; Otakar Odložilík, 'Die Wittenberger Philippisten und die Brüderunität', in W. Steinitz (ed.), *Ost und West in der Geschichte des Denkens und der kulturellen Beziehungen. Festschrift für Eduard Winter zum 70.Geburtstag* (Berlin-Ost, 1966), pp. 106–18.

[14] See Mirjam Daňková, *Bratrské tisky ivančické a kralické (1564–1619)* (Prague, 1951).

[15] Ferdinand Hrejsa, 'Náboženské stanovisko B. Jana Blahoslava', in Václav Novotný and Rudolf Urbánek (eds), *Sborník Blahoslavův (1523–1923)* (Přerov, 1923), pp. 50–120, esp. 59–63, 89–99.

the anti-Roman confessions led to a sharper internal rift within the Unity. In Bohemia the Brethren turned more towards Lutheran-orientated Utraquism in order to achieve religious freedom, which was then granted by the Letter of Majesty in 1609. In Moravia, however, where the Brethren enjoyed confessional freedom, even if it was not legally guaranteed, they remained faithful to their stronger Helvetic orientation.[16] Numerous priests and deacons bore public witness to Calvinism at the synods of Lipník (1591, 1592), Přerov (1594) and Žeravice (1595). The elder Jan Němčanský, who was elected in 1594 in Přerov, clearly supported an opening of the Unity to the Helvetic church. A decade later, at the synod of Žeravice, the question of Communion was interpreted entirely according to Calvinist ideas.[17] In Bohemia, particularly after 1609, the Reformed wing within the Unity was increasingly supported by immigrant Calvinists from the neighbouring Palatinate, who often proved to be rabble-rousers of the Estate liberation movement. The anti-Brethren sentiment, which had been predominant in the land of the Holy Wenzel's crown for some time, was exacerbated after the southern Bohemian magnate Peter Wok of Rosenberg joined the Unity in 1582. But in 1609, even such a powerful noble as Rosenberg did not dare to endorse a polemical work of the Heidelberg theologian Pitiscus, which had been translated into Czech at his own commission, and which called for unity of all Protestant confessions and solidarity with Calvinism.[18]

A special case within the Bohemian lands was territorially fragmented Silesia, which was for the most part Lutheran.[19] Here a small Calvinist community, consisting mostly of doctors and theologians, had formed and was in close contact with Polish brothers in the faith. Due to the confessional tensions with Silesian Lutheranism, their leaders decided to emigrate. Almost all of them ended up in the civil service or in the church of the Palatinate, where they took on leading positions as court

---

[16] See here the debate inspired by František Hrubý, 'Luterství a kalvinismus na Moravě před Bílou horou', *Český časopis historický*, 40 (1934), 265–309; 41 (1935), 1–40, 237–68; Ferdinand Hrejsa, 'Luterství, kalvinismus a podbojí na Moravě před Bílou horou', *Český časopis historický*, 44 (1938), 296–326, 474–85.

[17] František Kameníček, *Zemské sněmy a sjezdy moravské. Jejich složení, obor působnosti a význam. Od nastoupení na trůn krále Ferdinanda I. až po vydání obnoveného zřízení zemského (1526–1628)* (3 vols, Brno, 1900–50), III, pp. 437–48.

[18] Jaroslav Pánek, *Poslední Rožmberkové. Velmoži české renesance* (Prague, 1992), pp. 214–15, 325; František M. Bartoš, 'Výzva falcké církve k náboženskému míru v Čechách z r. 1609', *Český bratr*, 20 (1944), 28–30; Luděk Rejchrt, 'Bratrští studenti na reformovaných akademiích před Bílou horou', *Acta Universitatis Carolinae – Historia Universitatis Carolinae Pragensis*, 13 (1973), 43–82, esp. 53.

[19] Joachim Bahlcke, 'Das Herzogtum Schlesien im politischen System der Böhmischen Krone', *Zeitschrift für Ostmitteleuropa-Forschung*, 44 (1995), 27–55.

priests, members of the church authority or university teachers. From these positions they took an active part in the formation of an anti-Habsburg and anti-Catholic bloc in East-Central Europe between 1570 and 1620.[20] The extent to which this Silesian–Palatine group promoted political Calvinism in the Bohemian lands is illustrated by the success of the *Schönaichianum* in Beuthen-on-the-Oder, an academy where high-ranking Reformed scholars taught. Similar to the Goldberg School and the Altdorf Academy, it gained widespread esteem and acceptance, attracting followers of the Unity from Bohemia and Moravia.[21]

While Calvinist influence in the Bohemian lands was almost completely limited to the small minority of the Unity until 1600, accounting for about 1 to 3 per cent of the population, in Hungary around the turn of the century more than half of the Protestant population (some 85 or 90 per cent of the total) adhered to the Helvetic belief.[22] Whereas east of the Tisza up to Transylvania and in those parts of central and southern Hungary that were under Turkish occupation the Reformed Church had established itself soon after 1550, its establishment in royal western Hungary met with strong resistance on the part of a few powerful noble families maintaining Lutheranism, as well as the Court and the Roman Catholic Church. Initially, on the basis of the community organization designed by Péter Meliusz Juhász,[23] the strip of land east of the Tisza and Transylvania had been subject to a uniform clerical organization, which was largely completed by the formation of the two Reformed Church districts: Transdanubia and Samorín in West and Upper Hungary in 1591–92.[24] The fact that the formation of the indi-

---

[20] Werner Bellardi, 'Schlesien und die Kurpfalz. Der Beitrag vertriebener schlesischer Theologen zur "reformierten" Theologie und Bekenntnisbildung (1561–1576)', *Jahrbuch für schlesische Kirchengeschichte*, NS 51 (1972), 48–66; Gustav Hecht, 'Schlesisch-kurpfälzische Beziehungen im 16. und 17. Jahrhundert', *Zeitschrift für die Geschichte des Oberrheins*, NS 42 (1929), 176–222.

[21] Siegfried Wollgast, 'Zum Schönaichianum in Beuthen an der Oder', *Jahrbuch der Schlesischen Friedrich-Wilhelms-Universität zu Breslau*, 35 (1995), 63–103; Gustav Bauch, *Valentin Trozendorf und die Goldberger Schule* (Berlin, 1921), pp. 247–336; Heinrich Kunstmann, *Die Nürnberger Universität Altdorf und Böhmen. Beiträge zur Erforschung der Ostbeziehungen deutscher Universitäten* (Cologne and Graz, 1963), pp. 1–139.

[22] Evans, 'Calvinism in East Central Europe', p. 174; Mihály Bucsay, *Der Protestantismus in Ungarn 1521–1978. Ungarns Reformationskirchen in Geschichte und Gegenwart*, vol. 1: *Im Zeitalter der Reformation, Gegenreformation und katholischen Reform* (Vienna, Cologne and Graz, 1977), pp. 99–100, 104–31.

[23] Alexander Sándor Unghváry, 'Péter Somogyi Juhász (Melius), His Importance in the History of the Hungarian Reformed Church 1536–1572', in his *The Hungarian Protestant Reformation in the Sixteenth Century under the Ottoman Impact. Essays and Profiles* (Lewiston, Lampeter and Queenston, 1989), pp. 275–313, esp. 283–90.

[24] Imre Révész, *Magyar református egyháztörténet* (Debrecen, 1938), I, pp. 142–6.

vidual confessions closely followed national and language boundaries favoured the later solidarity and politicization of Hungarian Calvinism. It was mainly the Magyar nobility and the inhabitants of the approximately 800 small towns and market towns which embraced the Reformed Church, while the Germans in western Hungary, the upper Hungarian mountain villages and in the German colonies of Zips and Transylvania generally remained faithful to Lutheran orthodoxy.[25]

Crucial to the formation of estate opposition in Hungary after 1600 was the political and confessional situation of the Duchy of Transylvania, which had been independent and internally largely autonomous since 1541. Here all four religious communities, the Catholic, Lutheran, Reformed and Unitarian churches, benefited from equal rights and enjoyed legal recognition.[26] Theologically the decisive advance of the Calvinists had stemmed from Debrecen, the 'Hungarian Geneva', where after the death of Márton Sánta Kálmáncsehi in 1557, Melius and Gergely Szegedi had strongly influenced the development of the Church in Transylvania. Following the synod of Nagyenyed, which attempted to bring about a decision on the question of Communion, the *Landtag* of Torda in 1564 recognized the existence of the Reformed Church. The following *Landtage* of Nagyszeben in 1566 and Torda in 1568 confirmed this legal situation.[27] When the Jesuit diplomat Antonio Possevino visited Hungary as a representative of the Pope in 1584, he found approximately 500 Protestant preachers in Transylvania alone, 200 of whom were Calvinist, 200 Lutheran and 100 Unitarian.[28] This intellectual freedom and tolerance was unique in Europe, and was also a consequence of the differentiation and autonomy of the Estate society, which later became the backbone of the noble opposition in royal Hungary.[29]

---

[25]   David P. Daniel, 'Calvinism in Hungary: the theological and ecclesiastical transition to the Reformed faith', in Andrew Pettegree, Alastair Duke and Gillian Lewis (eds), *Calvinism in Europe, 1540–1620* (Oxford, 1993), pp. 205–30; Branislav Varsik, 'Vznik a vývin slovenských Kalvínov na východnom Slovensku', *Historický časopis*, 39 (1991), 129–48.

[26]   On this episode see particularly Erich Roth, *Die Reformation in Siebenbürgen. Ihr Verhältnis zu Wittenberg und der Schweiz* (2 vols, Cologne and Graz, 1962–64); Ludwig Binder, 'Johannes Honterus und die Reformation im Süden Siebenbürgens mit besonderer Berücksichtigung der Schweizer und Wittenberger Einflüsse', *Zwingliana*, 13 (1973), 645–87.

[27]   Ludwig Binder, *Grundlagen und Formen der Toleranz in Siebenbürgen bis zur Mitte des 17. Jahrhunderts* (Cologne and Vienna, 1976), pp. 66–88.

[28]   Gabriel Adriányi, 'Die Ausbreitung der Reformation in Ungarn', *Ungarn-Jahrbuch*, 5 (1973), 66–75, esp. 70.

[29]   Maja Depner, *Das Fürstentum Siebenbürgen im Kampf gegen Habsburg. Untersuchungen über die Politik Siebenbürgens während des Dreißigjährigen Krieges* (Stuttgart, 1938), esp. pp. 27–94.

Naturally, the superiority and the intellectual weight of the Protestant churches in Hungary was also reflected in cultural and intellectual areas.[30] After the humanist Tamás Nádasdy had founded the first printworks exclusively in the service of the Reformation in Újsziget in 1536, new printworks sprang up everywhere. *Circa* 1600, 29 of the 30 printshops served Protestant interests. Of the more than 500 books published in Hungarian in the sixteenth century, approximately 90 per cent were written by Protestants. In 1565 the most important Hungarian legal work, the *Tripartitum opus juris consuetudinarii inclyti regni Hungariae*, written by the legal scholar and politician István Werböczy, was published in a Magyar translation by Balázs Weres in Debrecen. Contemporary sources claim that as early as 1568 the works of Calvin were widely respected and read.[31] This certainly applies to Calvin's main work, the *Institutes of the Christian Religion*, even though it was not translated into Hungarian until after 1620 (in contrast to Bohemia where it was translated between 1612 and 1617). Calvin's Genevan Catechism had already been translated by Melius in 1562.[32] The production of books, which had been embracing secular topics to an increasing degree since 1570 at the expense of theological writings, increased significantly over the following decades. Only in 1577 did the Catholic Church found its first own printing-house in Trnava. According to the Papal nuncio, in 1588 there were no places in Hungary where it was possible to study theology. Of the 168 Latin schools, which had considerable authority as there was no university in the country, 134 were in Protestant hands. Among these schools the Reformed colleges in Pápa, Sárospatak and in particular in Debrecen, where the first Calvinist printworks had been founded in 1560, had high educational standards even before 1600.[33]

In both lands, intellectual contacts helped to strengthen ties between Protestants and their foreign brethren in Central and Western Europe, and this was not without consequences for the political and ideological

---

[30] László Révész, 'Die helvetische Reformation in Ungarn', *Ungarn-Jahrbuch*, 4 (1972), 72–100, esp. 87–9; Katalin Péter, 'Die Reformation in Ungarn' in Ferenc Glatz (ed.), *European Intellectual Trends and Hungary* (Budapest, 1990), pp. 39–51, esp. 47–50; Monika Glettler, 'Probleme und Aspekte der Reformation in Ungarn', *Ungarn-Jahrbuch*, 10 (1979), 225–39.

[31] Károly Erdős, *A kálvini reformáció hatása hazánkra* (Debrecen, 1909), pp. 10–24; for an introduction to the history of the Tripartitum see Janos M. Bak, *Königtum und Stände in Ungarn im 14.–16. Jahrhundert* (Wiesbaden, 1973), pp. 74–9, 121–3.

[32] Révész, *Magyar református egyháztörténet*, I, p. 125.

[33] Alexander Sándor Unghváry, 'The Reformed College of Debrecen, developed by Melius' in his *The Hungarian Protestant Reformation*, pp. 315–22; Bucsay, *Protestantismus*, pp. 161–3, 216–22.

spheres. From the victorious Ferdinand II's point of view it was definitely understandable that in a letter which he wrote from Sopron in
1622 to the Bishop of Olomouc he made the 'alluring Calvinist schools',
at which 'the youth had imbibed the poison of rebellion and resistance
against the rulers at an early age' partly responsible for the estate
risings.[34] In total more than 5 200 students from Bohemia and Moravia
were registered at foreign universities between 1503 and 1622. Even
though the aspect of confession only had a limited influence on the
choice of university, the orientation of the Unity of Brethren towards
Calvinism is nevertheless reflected in the choice of foreign universities.[35]

A detailed analysis of the enrolment registers of the Reformed academies in Basle, Geneva and Heidelberg confirms that the percentage of
Bohemian and Moravian students rose continuously after 1570 and
came to a peak in the first decade of the seventeenth century during the
great successes of the Estate liberation movement. An indication of the
strong Calvinist orientation of the Moravian Unity of Brethren is that
most of its students – apart from in Prague, which forms a special case –
were from Opava, Přerov and Uherský Brod. Between 1570 and 1620,
the share of Brethren students (15 per cent) was particularly high in
relation to the overall numbers of this religious community.[36] In individual cases the correlation between education, confession and political
thinking can be documented in detail. Jaroslav Smiřický's dissertation
'De Consiliariis Florilegium Politicum' written in 1605 in Basle, contains several references to the works of Beza, Hotman and Duplessis-
Mornay, the classic Calvinist authors, and shows the extent to which
young noble Brethren were interested in questions of legitimate resistance and rulership.[37] Smiřický defended his dissertation in the presence
of Amandus Polanus of Polansdorf, a theologian from the Silesian-

[34]   František Hrubý, *Etudiants tchèques aux écoles protestantes de l'Europe occidentale
à la fin du 16e et au début du 17e siècle. Documents*, Libuše Urbánková-Hrubá (ed.)
(Brno, 1970), pp. 309–10.

[35]   Alfred Kohler, 'Bildung und Konfession. Zum Studium der Studenten aus den
habsburgischen Ländern an Hochschulen im Reich (1560–1620)', in Grete Klingenstein
and Heinrich Lutz et al. (eds), *Bildung, Politik und Gesellschaft. Studien zur Geschichte
des europäischen Bildungswesens vom 16. bis zum 20. Jahrhundert* (Vienna, 1978), pp.
64–123.

[36]   Rejchrt, 'Bratrští studenti', pp. 43–82; Jiří Pešek and David Šaman, 'Les étudiants
de Bohême dans les universités et les académies d'Europe centrale et occidentale entre
1596 et 1620', in Dominique Julia and Jacques Revel et al. (eds), *Les Universités
européennes du XVIe au XVIIIe siècle. Histoire sociale des populations étudiantes, vol.
1: Bohême, Espagne, Etats italiens, Pays germaniques, Pologne, Provinces-Unies* (Paris,
1986), pp. 89–111.

[37]   Otakar Odložilík, 'Poslední Smiřičtí', in *Od pravěku k dnešku. Sborník prací z
dějin československých k šedesátým Josefa Pekaře* (Prague, 1930), II, pp. 70–87.

Moravian border area, who became the most important mediator between the centres of Western European Calvinism and the Bohemian lands after the death of the intellectual Johann Crato of Krafftheim from Breslau in 1585.[38]

Wittenberg, where 480 students from Hungary were enrolled between 1526 and 1597, had been the intellectual centre and university city for the Protestant élite of Hungary. With growing dogmatic tensions within Protestantism and the increasing observation of crypto-Calvinist currents by the ducal university inspectors since the 1570s, there was a sharp decline in enrolments, both of students from Hungary and from the Bohemian lands.[39] The Hungarian student organization of Wittenberg, the so-called *Coetus Hungaricus*, modelled on the Cracovian *Bursa Hungarorum*, was forced to close in 1592 on account of its Calvinist teaching. After a short resurrection it was finally dissolved in 1613.[40] Wittenberg's dwindling importance favoured the University of Heidelberg, which had been Reformed since the middle of the 1560s. It soon developed into a centre of Hungarian Calvinism. One hundred and seventy-five Hungarian and Transylvanian students were enrolled here between 1595 and 1621.[41] They were attracted in particular by the theologian David Pareus, the third leading Calvinist from Silesia next to the court preachers Bartholomäus Pitiscus and Abraham Scultetus in Heidelberg, who maintained various contacts with Hungary. Pareus intensified these contacts with the aim of playing down the differences between Lutheran and Reformed thinkers in order to strengthen the political links between the Protestant territories. This is illustrated in particular by the correspondence with the Duke of Transylvania, Gábor Bethlen after 1616, and the co-operation between Silesia and the Palatinate from 1619 onwards.[42] After Bethlen ascended the throne in 1613,

---

[38] See here Bahlcke, *Regionalismus*, pp. 274–308.

[39] András Szabó, 'Magyarok Wittenbergben, 1555–1592', in Imre Békési and József Jankovics et al. (eds), *Régi és új peregrináció: Magyarok külföldön, külföldiek Magyarországon* (3 vols, Budapest and Szeged, 1993), II, pp. 626–38; Miklós Asztalos, 'A wittenbergi egyetem és a magyarországi kálvinizmus', *A Bécsi Magyar Történeti Intézet Évkönyve*, (1932), pp. 81–94; and his 'A wittenbergi egyetem magyar hallgatóinak nyelvismerete a XVI. században', *Egyetemes Philológiai Közlöny*, (1934), 1–11.

[40] Géza Szabó, 'Geschichte des ungarischen Coetus an der Universität Wittenberg 1555–1613', theology dissertation, Halle/Saale, 1941.

[41] János Heltai, 'A heidelbergi egyetemjárás 1595–1621', in Békési and Jankovics, *Régi és új peregrináció*, II, pp. 540–48; and his 'Adattár a heidelbergi egyetemen 1595–1621 között tanult magyarországi diákokról és pártfogóikról', *Az Országos Széchenyi Könyvtár Évkönyve 1980*, (Budapest, 1982), pp. 243–347.

[42] János Heltai, 'David Pareus magyar kapcsolatai', in János Herner (ed.), *Tudóslevelek művelődésünk külföldi kapcsolataihoz 1577–1797* (Szeged, 1989), pp. 13–76; Günter Brinkmann, *Die Irenik des David Pareus. Frieden und Einheit in ihrer Relevanz zur*

Heidelberg registered a sudden increase in the number of Calvinists studying there. This was especially encouraged by János Keserűi Dajka, Bethlen's preacher and a former student of Heidelberg, who persuaded Bethlen to grant them considerable financial support.[43]

In contrast to Western Europe and likewise to the neighbouring Polish–Lithuanian noble republic, political publications and literature relating to state-theory in Bohemia and Hungary were comparatively backward.[44] The fact that, *circa* 1600, leaflets and treatises in both countries warned hysterically of the dangers of 'Calvino-Turcism', a co-operation of Calvinist powers with the Ottomans, gives an indication of the causes of this backwardness. In view of the permanent threat posed by the Turks, which made a functioning kingdom an absolute necessity, the motivation for resistance on the part of the Estates aimed at curtailing royal power was relatively limited throughout the sixteenth century.[45] The student generation of 1600, however, which had been confronted with works on theory of contract, rights of resistance and the sovereignty of the people in western academies, learned to overcome the provinciality of their homeland. They were almost forced to assume their own position within the confessional and political camps, which emerged more and more clearly after 1570. The detour via a *peregrinatio academica* helped to promote contacts between Hungarian and Bohemian Calvinists especially at a time when both lands were also coming closer to each other politically.[46]

Wahrheitsfrage (Hildesheim, 1972); Gustav Adolf Benrath, 'David Pareus' in Helmut Neubach and Ludwig Petry (eds), *Schlesier des 15. bis 20. Jahrhunderts* (Würzburg, 1968), pp. 13–23; Piroska Uray, 'Az irénizmus Magyarországon a 16.–17. század fordulóján', in Béla Varjas (ed.), *Irodalom és ideológia a 16.–17. században* (Budapest, 1987), pp. 187–207.

43   János Heltai, *Alvinczi Péter és a heidelbergi peregrinusok* (Budapest, 1994), pp. 42–9, 74–94, 155–6.

44   Jiří Hrubeš, 'Z dějin protestantského politického myšlení a jeho ohlasu v Čechách', *Strahovská knihovna*, 5–6 (1970–71), 237–53; Jaroslav Pánek, 'Republikánské tendence ve stavovských programech doby předbělohorské', *Folia Historica Bohemica*, 8 (1985), 43–62; Otakar Odložilík, 'Political thought in Bohemia in the early 17th century' in *VIIᵉ Congrès International des Sciences Historiques. Zürich 1938, Communications ...* (Paris 1938), II, pp. 635–7; Charles d'Eszlary, 'Jean Calvin, Théodore de Bèze et leurs amis hongrois', *Bulletin de la Société de l'Histoire du Protestantisme français*, 110 (1964), 74–99.

45   Jiří Hrubeš, *Politické a náboženské rozpory v Evropě v dobové publicistice 1590–1617* (Prague, 1974), p. 103; M. E. H. Nicolette Mout, 'Calvinoturcisme in de zeventiende eeuw. Comenius, Leidse oriëntalisten en de Turkse bijbel', *Tijdschrift voor Geschiedenis*, 91 (1978), 576–607, esp. 582–89.

46   Richard Pražák, 'Cesty uherských humanistů reformovaného vyznání do českých zemi v předvečer třicetileté války', *Sborník prací filosofické fakulty brněnské univerzity*,

The copious correspondence between leading intellectuals and Estate politicians in Bohemia and Hungary and the political and theological leaders of Western European Calvinism gives an insight into that world of late Humanism and into the various connections which are not always easy to trace.[47] Only for a few intellectuals such as Johann Jacob Grynaeus, the Basle theologian and father-in-law of Polanus, who had worked at the Heidelberger *Sapienzkollegium* since 1584 and who had particularly intensive relations with eastern Central Europe,[48] do we have editions for Bohemia and Hungary which allow a direct comparison.[49] Apart from being interesting in terms of learned disputes, this correspondence provides evidence of a true travelling diplomacy which is characteristic of the private network of people and institutions in international Calvinism. Examples of this type of travelling diplomat in eastern Central Europe are the Silesian Polanus,[50] the Moravian Jan Opsimathes, who accompanied the sons of Urich of Kaunitz in the first two decades of the seventeenth century to Western European universi-

---

C 29 (1982), 131–42 and his 'Szenci Molnár Albert Prágában', *A Ráday Gyűjtemény Évkönyve 1981*, (Budapest, 1982), pp. 182–7; Otakar Odložilík, 'Jan Filiczki z Filic a jeho čeští přátelé' in *K dějinám československým*, pp. 431–42; Kálmán Benda, 'Filiczki János levele 1605-böl', *Acta Historiae Litterarum Hungaricarum*, 13 (1973), 83–90; Imre Révész, 'Jegyzetek Méliusz Péter és a cseh-morva atyafiak levélváltásához', *Theológiai Szemle*, 14 (1939), 35–40.

[47] Johann Franz Albert Gillet, *Crato von Crafftheim und seine Freunde. Ein Beitag zur Kirchengeschichte* (2 vols, Frankfurt am Main, 1860); Hrubý, *Etudiants tchèques*; Josef Müldner, *Jan Myllner z Milhauzu, vol. 2: Dopisy a činnost úřední* (Prague, 1934).

[48] Kaspar v. Greyerz, 'Basels kirchliche und konfessionelle Beziehungen zum Oberrhein im späten 16. und frühen 17. Jahrhundert', in Martin Bircher (ed.), *Schweizerisch-deutsche Beziehungen im konfessionellen Zeitalter. Beiträge zur Kulturgeschichte 1580–1650* (Wiesbaden, 1984), pp. 227–52; Hans R. Guggisberg, 'Reformierter Stadtstaat und Zentrum der Spätrenaissance. Basel in der zweiten Hälfte des 16. Jahrhunderts', in August Buck (ed.), *Renaissance-Reformation. Gegensätze und Gemeinsamkeiten* (Wiesbaden, 1984), pp. 197–216; Fritz Weiß, 'Johann Jacob Grynaeus', *Basler Biographien* (Basle, 1900), 1, pp. 159–99.

[49] András Szabó (ed.), *Johann Jacob Grynaeus magyar kapcsolatai* (Szeged, 1989); Hrubý, *Etudiants tchèques*; Julius Glücklich (ed.), *Václava Budovce z Budova korrespondence z let 1579–1619* (Prague, 1908) and his *Nová korrespondence Václava Budovce z Budova z let 1580–1616* (Prague, 1912); Vincenc Brandl (ed.), *Spisy Karla staršího z Žerotína. Listové psaní jazykem českym* (3 vols, Brno, 1870–72); Noemi Rejchrtová (ed.), *Karel starší ze Žerotína. Z korrespondence* (Prague, 1982).

[50] Ernst Staehelin, *Amandus Polanus von Polansdorf* (Basle, 1955) and his 'Die Lehr- und Wanderjahre des Amandus Polanus von Polansdorf', *Basler Zeitschrift für Geschichte und Altertumskunde*, 44 (1945), 37–77; Karel Sita, 'Amandus Polanus z Polansdorfu' (PhD dissertation, Prague, 1951); František Hrubý, 'Kalvínský theolog a bouře opavská r. 1603', *Český časopis historický*, 37 (1931), 593–601; Josef Zukal, 'Polanové z Polansdorfu. Památná rodina opavská 16. věku', *Časopis Matice moravské*, 51 (1927), 99–123.

ties,[51] and the Hungarian Albert Szenci Molnár, a lexicographer, poet and translator of Calvinist literature, who worked in Heidelberg, Basle and Geneva and, finally, in the Reformed cities of Herborn and Altdorf.[52] The numerous points of contact in the widespread network of international Calvinism can only in some instances give an indication of how ideas gathered on study trips or through correspondence actually went beyond the domain of theory and had an impact on political reality. Charles Liffort's fund-raising trip to eastern Central Europe in 1592–93 shows clearly that these relations also benefited the West.[53] The trip organized on Beza's orders was meant to generate aid for the city of Geneva, which was at war with the Duke of Savoy. It took Liffort via Bohemia, Moravia and Silesia to Hungary and Transylvania. The people he contacted, at least those we know of through his visits, letters of recommendations and donations he collected, had almost exclusively studied in Western Europe and had in the meantime assumed leading political offices or intellectual functions in the Hungarian and Bohemian lands. This again underlines the key position of Silesian Calvinists for the communication between east and west and the attempt to create a political front. During the book fair in Frankfurt, the Breslavian doctor and humanist Jacob Monau (Monavius), who had close contacts with Upper Hungarian and Transylvanian Reformed circles,[54] finally gave Liffort the support monies from the eastern Central European lands which he had looked after in the meantime.

As in Western Europe, the fight for religious self-determination in Bohemia and Hungary in the sixteenth century was closely linked to internal political debates and a conflict of power between king and

---

[51]   Jar. G. Hrubant, 'Památník Jana Opsimata z let 1598–1620', Časopis Matice moravské, 40 (1916), 123–30; Otakar Odložilík, 'Cesty z Čech a Moravy do Velké Británie v letech 1563–1620', Časopis Matice moravské, 59 (1935), 241–320.

[52]   Judit Vásárhelyi, Eszmei áramlatok és politika Szenci Molnár Albert életművében (Budapest, 1985); Sándor Csanda and Bálint Keserű (eds), Szenci Molnár Albert és a magyar későreneszánsz (Szeged, 1972); Lajos Dézsi (ed.), Szenczi Molnár Albert naplója, levelezése és irományai (Budapest, 1898).

[53]   Mihály Bucsay, 'Eine Hilfsaktion für Genf in Ost- und Südosteuropa im 16. Jahrhundert. Die Kollektenreise von Charles Liffort 1592–1593', Kirche im Osten. Studien zur osteuropäischen Kirchengeschichte und Kirchenkunde, 17 (1974), 163–79.

[54]   Szabó, Grynaeus, pp. 26–9, 133–6; Hrubý, Etudiants tchèques; Gillet, Crato von Crafftheim.

[55]   László Makkai, 'A Habsburgok és a magyar rendiség a Bocskai-felkelés előestéjén', Történelmi Szemle, 17 (1974), 155–82; Jaroslav Pánek, 'Politický systém předbělohorského českého státu', Folia Historica Bohemica, 11 (1987), 41–101; Otakar Odložilík, 'Education, religion, and politics in Bohemia, 1526–1621', Cahiers d'Histoire Mondiale, 13/1 (1971), 172–203; Karin J. MacHardy, 'The rise of absolutism and noble rebellion in

nobility.[55] *Circa* 1600 a feeling of oppression was common among the Estates; a feeling that the confessional *status quo* was being disregarded and that a new model of rulership which opposed the Estate order was advancing. The tensions escalated at the beginning of the seventeenth century, when in the context of the long Turkish war Rudolf II started to use military power to implement rigorously the Counter-Reformation, almost simultaneously in the royal cities of Silesia and upper Hungary. In the autumn of 1604 the Hungarian Estates under the leadership of István Bocskai were the first to take up arms in order to defend their rights against the Habsburgs.[56] The initial attempts to organize international resistance failed and all calls for confessional solidarity went unheeded. In the end, however, the Bocskai rising did give birth to an Estate liberation movement which embraced all countries of the Habsburg monarchy.[57] This was aided by a crisis of rulership which had been growing since the Treaty of Vienna of 1606. In the wake of this movement the Estates of Hungary, Moravia, Bohemia and Silesia achieved full religious freedom. With the establishment of a Palatinate kingdom in Bohemia in 1619–20 the Estate liberation movement reached both its climax and its end. It was a daring but ultimately unsuccessful attempt to shake off Habsburg rule and to shift the weight towards political Calvinism in eastern Central Europe.[58]

The co-operative forms of the Estate liberation movement became apparent in several confederations among the individual lands, most of which had a positive legal right of resistance. The striking analogy to the Union concept of the Calvinist theoreticians and their secular contract thinking raises the question whether and to what extent a renewal of Estate resistance rights in Bohemia and Hungary originated from Calvinist motivation. Such a connection is much more obvious in neighbouring Upper Austria, where Georg Erasmus Tschernembl had published a typical resistance treatise entitled *De resistentia subditorum*

---

early modern Habsburg Austria, 1570 to 1620', *Comparative Studies in Society and History*, 34 (1992), 407–39.

[56] David P. Daniel, 'The Fifteen Years' War and the Protestant response to Habsburg absolutism in Hungary', *East Central Europe*, 8 (1981), 38–51.

[57] Gottfried Schramm, 'Armed conflict in East-Central Europe: Protestant noble opposition and Catholic royalist factions, 1604–20', in Robert J. W. Evans and Trevor V. Thomas (eds), *Crown, Church and Estates. Central European Politics in the Sixteenth and Seventeenth Centuries* (London, 1991), pp. 176–95.

[58] Joachim Bahlcke, 'Die Böhmische Krone zwischen staats-rechtlicher Integrität, monarchischer Union und ständischem Föderalismus. Politische Entwicklungslinien im böhmischen Länderverband vom 15. bis zum 17. Jahrhundert', in Thomas Fröschl (ed.), *Föderationsmodelle und Unionsstrukturen. Über Staatenverbindungen in der frühen Neuzeit vom 15. zum 18. Jahrhundert* (Vienna and Munich, 1994), pp. 83–103.

adversus Principem legitima, which bore resemblance to the teachings of the monarchomachs. In Tschernembl's state theory, which was known in Bohemia and Hungary and formed an important element in the intellectual formation of Calvinism in eastern Central Europe, unions and confederations were depicted as the most effective instrument against state and Papal tyranny.[59]

Likewise in Bohemia and Hungary, the Estates asserted a right of resistance which saw its obstruction not as a cause but as a consequence and thus placed it into a broader context of legitimization. Hungarian and Moravian Estate philosophy is illustrative of the intention to let questions of the land and *Landesfreiheiten* take priority over confessional issues in order to safeguard interconfessional unity. The Moravian Estates had, together with the estates of Upper and Lower Austria and Archduke Matthias, formed the first interregional confederation in Bratislava in February 1608. The religious ambition of the Estate first became apparent in the 'condition', an alliance which the confederates formed in 1608 in the field camp of Šterbohol not only without Matthias, but against him. According to this 'condition' he was only to be recognized as king if he was willing to permit unlimited religious freedom – as the words 'qualemcunque ob causam justem et legitimam' were interpreted. Otherwise homage was to be refused entirely. A year later the Bohemian and Silesian Estates entered a classic resistance alliance, whose severity and theoretical foundation is also reflected by the conversion of the three leading Silesian dukes to Calvinism after 1610. Ultimately, both countries were prepared to fight until the bitter end against anybody who attacked or suppressed their religion. Only the Bohemian king, who was the highest authority chosen by God, was excluded from this alliance.[60]

After the Defenestration of Prague this first wave of Estate confederations was followed by a second wave with the most prominent alliance being that of the *Confoederatio Bohemica* of July 1619. This served as a role model for the formation of alliances with Lower and Upper

---

[59]   Hans Sturmberger, *Georg Erasmus Tschernembl. Religion, Libertät und Widerstand. Ein Beitrag zur Geschichte der Gegenreformation und des Landes ob der Enns* (Linz, Graz and Cologne, 1953), pp. 90–107, 194–5, 336–65.

[60]   Joachim Bahlcke, 'Durch "starke Konföderation wohl stabiliert". Ständische Defension und politisches Denken in der habsburgischen Ländergruppe am Anfang des 17. Jahrhunderts', in Thomas Winkelbauer (ed.), *Kontakte und Konflikte. Böhmen, Mähren und Österreich: Aspekte eines Jahrtausends gemeinsamer Geschichte* (Horn and Waidhofen an der Thaya, 1993), pp. 173–86 and his 'Konföderation und Widerstand. Die politischen Beziehungen der böhmischen und mährischen Ständegemeinde vom Bruderzwist bis zum Aufstand gegen Habsburg (1608–1619)', *Folia Historica Bohemica*, 13 (1990), 235–88.

Austria in the middle of August 1619, and with the Hungarian Estates and the Duke of Transylvania in the course of 1620.[61] The political importance of humanist intellectuals for this process is exemplified in the person of Caspar Dornau, who was a member of two deputations to the Hungarian *Reichstag* in Banská Bystrica in 1620, sent by the Silesian dukes and Estates to stabilize the eastern Central European confederation system.[62]

Possibly the most attentive observer of the Bohemian and Hungarian Estate policy in the Catholic wing was Cardinal Melchior Klesl. At an early stage he had warned of the consequences of Estate emancipation and a confederation of a 'Consilium formatum' of the lands.[63] In his opinion the Estates had three major aims: to guarantee a say in foreign policy, to obtain power over the armed forces and to legalize platforms of Estate resistance. The differing opinions and arguments on the chances and dangers of such an interregional programme directed against the king were rather hard to determine in the Protestant camp. The Moravian Karel of Žerotín, for example, who was very much at home in West European resistance thought and political theories, left the Estate movement in 1618, when confrontation finally gained the upper hand over compromise. He saw that an Estate alliance like the Union of Utrecht of 1572 or an alliance such as the Protestant Union of 1608 in the Empire was impossible to realize in the political context of the Habsburg lands. In his opinion, the king alone formed the unifying link for the individual territories which were in conflict owing to religious conflicts and political particularism.[64] Žerotín's scepticism, however, was nursed by the fact that he was opposed to an overly close link with Palatinate politics and rejected an internationalization of conflicts in the region. For this reason he had also taken a critical view on the situation in

---

[61] On this episode see particularly Štefan Krivošík, 'Príspevok k dejinám stavovskej konfederácie českých a uhorských stavov z r. 1620', *Právnické štúdie*, 7 (1959), 147–87; Tibor Wittmann, 'A nemzeti monarchia megteremtéséért vívott harc a cseh-magyar szövetség keretében a terjeszkedő Habsburg-hatalom ellen. 1619–20' (PhD dissertation, Budapest, 1954); Kálmán Demkó, 'A magyar-cseh confoederatio és a beszterczebányai országgyűlés 1620-ban', *Századok*, 20 (1886), 105–21, 291–308.

[62] Josef Hejnic, 'Kašpar Dornavius a české povstání', *Zprávy Jednoty klasických filologů*, 6 (1964), 167–73; Anton Chroust, *Abraham von Dohna. Sein Leben und sein Gedicht auf den Reichstag von 1613* (Munich, 1896), 145–50; Seidel, *Späthumanismus*, 369–75; Josef Hemmerle, 'Die calvinische Reformation in Böhmen', *Stifter-Jahrbuch*, 8 (1964), 243–76.

[63] Joseph Hammer-Purgstall, *Khlesl's, des Cardinals, Directors des geheimen Cabinetes Kaisers Mathias, Leben* (4 vols, Vienna, 1847–51), II, pp. 201–2.

[64] On Žerotín see Otakar Odložilík, *Karel starší ze Žerotína 1564–1636* (Prague, 1936); František Hrubý, 'Filip du Plessis-Mornay a Karel Žerotín v letech 1611–1614 (Morava v zrcadle hugenotského zpravodaje)', in *Od pravěku k dnešku*, IV, pp. 39–69.

Transylvania since 1613: Gábor Bethlen was the first duke to be appointed by the Porte and owed his position solely to them.[65]

There are manifold impulses which the confessional resistance of the Estates in Bohemia and Hungary derived from Calvinism in that period. Before the Bocskai rising, the Hungarian Calvinist and humanist István Csulyak Miskolci, who since his stay in Görlitz in 1601 had been, together with Miklós Thököly of Késmárk, in close contact with the leaders of the Bohemian Unity of Brethren, used to praise the revolutionary traditions of Hussite Bohemia in his diary.[66] The politically and intellectually tense atmosphere of the Estate liberation movement induced the much travelled Moravian, Jan Opsimathes, to publish Calvin's *Institutes* between 1612 and 1617, a work which had been translated into Czech by Jiří Strejc in 1595.[67] The political thought of the Reformed theologian Péter Alvinczi came in useful for the Hungarian opposition. Alvinczi had studied in Heidelberg between 1600 and 1601 and had considerable influence on Bocskai after he became his court preacher in 1604. A co-author of Bocskai's *Apologia* addressed to the European powers in 1605, he published a number of radical and anti-Catholic pamphlets between 1619 and 1620, of which the *Quereles Hungariae* had the strongest effect.[68]

In 1608, in the immediate context of the foundation of the Protestant Union, Albert Szenci Molnár published a German translation of the *Apologia*, which generated widespread interest for Hungarian Protestantism in the Empire. In 1619–20 he translated numerous sermons of the Palatine Court preacher, Scultetus, into Hungarian, referring to the events in Prague after the Bohemian Estate rising.[69] In the *Confoederatio Bohemica* the king was perceived only as an instrument of divine intention ('minister dei'). Resistance, therefore, was legitimate in those cases

---

65   Katalin Péter, 'Two aspects of war and society in the age of Prince Gábor Bethlen of Transylvania', in János M. Bak and Béla K. Király (eds), *From Hunyadi to Rákóczi. War and Society in Late Medieval and Early Modern Hungary* (Brooklyn, NY, 1982), pp. 297–313; for an introduction to the literature on Gábor Bethlen see Monika Glettler, 'Überlegungen zur historiographischen Neubewertung Bethlen Gábors', *Ungarn-Jahrbuch*, 9 (1978), 237–55.

66   Pražák, 'Cesty uherských humanistů', pp. 135–8.

67   Emma Urbánková, 'Několik poznámek k českému vydání Kalvínovy Instituce', *Literární archiv*, 1 (1966), 237–46; Antonín Truhlář and Karel Hrdina et al. (eds), *Rukověť humanistického básnictví v Čechách a na Moravě* (5 vols, Prague, 1966–73), IV, pp. 67–8; V, pp. 479–80.

68   Heltai, *Alvinczi Péter*, pp. 90, 126–54; Kálmán Benda, 'Alvinczi Péter, kassai magyar prédikátor történeti följegyzései 1598–1622', *A Ráday Gyűjtemény Évkönyve 1955*, (Budapest, 1956), pp. 5–26; Kálmán Révész, 'Bocskai István apológiája', *Protestáns Szemle*, 18 (1906), 305–12.

69   Vásárhelyi, *Eszmei áramlatok és politika*, pp. 26–54, 58–62, 95–102.

in which he violated divine commandments ('defensio legitima'). The defenders of the Estates mentioned there, who were supposed to have a central control function on the regional and central level, correspond to the 'ephori speciales' and 'ephori generales', described by Johannes Althusius in his *Politica Methodice Digesta* published in 1603 in Herborn.[70]

Despite these manifold references one must bear in mind that Calvinism was only one of the currents favouring the formation of the Estate freedom movement in Bohemia and Hungary. Indeed, the idea of justified resistance against tyrannical dukes provided another impetus. In fact, the strongest influence for change came from the ancient legal consciousness of the Middle Ages and the codified law of the Estates which was easier to grasp and more substantial than political theories, and more effective than legal teachings transmitted solely by means of literature.[71] The question of the legitimization of resistance has been analysed in particular with reference to the Bocskai rising.[72] Ferenc Eckhart had established that no Calvinist notes can be found in the publications and documents of Bocskai and his followers.[73] Indeed it is noteworthy that passages on the right of resistance are missing in some translations of Calvinist confessional writings.[74] A more differentiated view was expressed by Kálmán Benda, who interprets Bocskai as someone who saw himself as a liberator sent by God, as a 'Hungarian Moses', who defended true faith against a tyrant who did not respect divine commandments. Benda thus portrays him as a typical parallel to the Calvinist royal ideal.[75]

---

[70] Bahlcke, *Regionalismus*, pp. 430–45.

[71] Ellinor von Puttkamer, 'Grundlinien des Widerstandsrechts in der Verfassungsgeschichte Osteuropas', in Konrad Repgen and Stephan Skalweit (eds), *Spiegel der Geschichte. Festgabe für Max Braubach zum 10. April 1964* (Münster Westphalia, 1964), pp. 198–219.

[72] Kálmán Benda, 'Le calvinisme et le droit de résistance des ordres hongrois au commencement du XVIIᵉ siècle', in *Études européennes. Mélanges offerts à Victor-Lucien Tapié* (Paris, 1973), pp. 235–43 and his 'A Kálvini tanok Latása a magyar rendi ellenállár ideológiájára', *Helikon*, 17 (1971), 322–30; László Makkai, 'Etat des Ordres et théocratie calviniste au XVIᵉ siècle dans l'Europe Centro-Orientale', *Etudes historiques hongroises*, 1 (1975), 329–46.

[73] Ferenc Eckhart, 'Bocskay és híveinek közjogi felfogása', in *Emlékkönyv Károlyi Arpád születése nyolcvanadik fordulójának ünnepére 1933 október 7* (Budapest, 1933), pp. 133–41.

[74] Imre Révész, 'Szempontok a magyar kálvinizmus eredetének vizsgálatához', *Századok*, 68 (1934), 257–75, esp. 272–4.

[75] Kálmán Benda, 'Absolutismus und ständischer Widerstand in Ungarn am Anfang des 17. Jahrhunderts', *Südost-Forschungen*, 33 (1974), 85–124, esp. 115–21; see also his classic study *Bocskai István* (Budapest, 1993) and 'La Réforme en Hongrie', *Bulletin de la Société de l'Histoire du Protestantisme français*, 122 (1976), 30–53.

The reasons for the strikingly traditional foundations of the Hungarian resistance under Bocskai, namely the right for political and religious freedom, are rooted in his own personality. Bocskai, who was a revolutionary against his will, was a military person, who had grown up in the traditions of the struggle against the Ottomans and had no relations with Central European humanist circles. Even in the political publications of the Bohemian lands Bocskai was sometimes greeted as an important ally against the 'poisonous Papal mob',[76] but at the same time feared as a 'tyrannus', in particular in view of possible solidarity with the Turks.[77]

In the light of these findings, the goals and motives of the interregional confederation movement and its integration into the Protestant internationalism of Europe should be considered rationally. In the Bohemian lands the confederation movement had first and foremost an emancipatory effect within the lands. With the new constitution model of 1619 the Bohemian Crown land solved a number of administrative, political and religious questions which had been contentious for decades. The *Confoederatio Bohemica* was not only designed to prevent further advances and attacks by Catholicism and royal power, it was also intended to create flexible constitutional structures for the future. The college of *defensores* which had developed since the beginning of the rising from a political and clerical instrument of the Protestant Estates into a state organ, became the most important constitutional organ. At the same time this college provided an institutional guarantee of comprehensive resistance rights on all levels. The *Confoederatio Bohemica* took on the character of a rulership contract, by means of which the Estates, the true sovereign within the State, merely bestowed government rights on the king.[78]

---

76   Josef Polišenský-Jiří Hrubeš, 'Bocskaiovy vpády na Moravu r. 1605 a jejich ohlas ve veřejném mínění', *Historické studie*, 7 (1961), 133–59, esp. 142–4 and their 'Turecké války, uherská povstání a veřejné mínění předbělohorských Čech', *Historický časopis*, 7 (1959), 74–103.

77   Josef Volf, 'Příspěvek ku vpádu Bočkajovců na Moravu r. 1605', *Časopis Musea království Českého*, 81 (1907), 466–70, esp. 470; on this episode see particularly František Kameníček (ed.), *Prameny ke vpádům Bočkajovců na Moravu a k ratifikaci míru vídeňského od zemí koruny české roku 1605–1606* (Prague, 1894); on the role of the Turks see László Nagy, 'A XVII. századi habsburg-ellenes függetlenségi harcok értékeléséhez (A török szövetség problematikája a Bocskai, Bethlen és I. Rákóczi György vezette küzdelmekben)', *Hadtörténelmi Közlemények*, 10/2 (1963), 185–241.

78   Bahlcke, 'Böhmische Krone', pp. 97–102; Josef Válka, 'Morava ve stavovské konfederaci roku 1619 (Pokus o vytvoření paralelních církevních a politických struktur v Čechách a na Moravě)', *Folia Historica Bohemica*, 10 (1986), 333–49; Winfried Becker, 'Ständestaat und Konfessionsbildung am Beispiel der böhmischen Konföderationsakte von 1619', in Dieter Albrecht and Hans Günter Hockerts et al. (eds), *Politik und Konfession. Festschrift für Konrad Repgen zum 60. Geburtstag* (Berlin, 1983), pp. 77–99.

An episode in the summer of 1620 shows that confessional solidarity had its limits and that confession was not the only determining factor for foreign policy. In that summer a meeting with Gábor Bethlen in Hungarian Bánska Bystrica failed owing to arguments over precedence among the confederate Estate representatives. It was clearly stressed that the individual alliances were definitely 'actus contrarios'.[79] But taking an overall view, the development in Bohemia and Hungary between 1570 and 1620 shows that Calvinism and the network of people and institutions emanating from Reformed Calvinist soil were decisive catalysts for the formation of the Estate liberation movement. Only after the Calvinist prophetic-eschatological interpretation of international power constellations started to spread did an interregional cooperation of the non-Catholic estates in Bohemia and Hungary develop to unite Protestantism politically against the Habsburg Counter-Reformation.

---

[79] Bahlcke, *Regionalismus*, p. 444.

CHAPTER SIX

Mural paintings, ethnicity and religious identity in Transylvania: the context for Reformation*

Christine Peters

The Protestant emphasis on the religion of the word has naturally suggested to historians the importance of linguistic and ethnic boundaries for the spread of the Reformation. It has been easy to see the adoption of the Lutheran faith by the Saxon nation of Transylvania as an expression of linguistic solidarity, and of the commercial and cultural links with German areas.[1] In the same vein, the later adoption of Calvinism by the Magyars in Transylvania has been attributed to ethnic antagonism as they sought to distance themselves from Lutheranism, which was seen as quintessentially German.[2] However, despite the fact that the Calvinist and Lutheran confessions of Cluj and Sibiu can be described as Hungarian and German respectively, the importance of ethnic antagonism and ethnic identity in determining confessional alle-

* I am indebted to the financial support of the Leverhulme Trust which enabled me to carry out research in Romania during 1993. Versions of this chapter have been given at St Andrews, Oxford and Cluj. I am grateful for comments offered on these occasions and for the assistance of John Blair and Sarah Blair in the preparation of this chapter and its illustrations. This chapter has also been published in M. Crăciun and O. Ghitta (eds), *Ethnicity and Religion in Central and Eastern Europe* (Cluj, 1995), pp. 44–63.

[1] C. Alzati, *Terra Romena tra Oriente e Occidente: Chiese ed etnie nel tardo '500* (Milan, 1982), p. 39. 'Gli ideali di Lutero trovarono in questo popolo, fiero della propria nazionalità germanica e desideroso di affermarla nel contesto transilvano, un ambiente quanto mai propizio alla loro ricezione.'

[2] C. Alzati, *Terra Romena*, p. 45. 'i nobili magiari non potevano non avvertire il carattere squisitamente tedesco della Riforma luterana e guardare con apprensione alla sua dipendenza dal mondo germanico; tanto più in Transilvania dove l'Universitas Saxonum, che aveva aderito senza riserve ai principi di Lutero, sulla base dei suoi saldi rapporti con i dottore di Wittenberg tendeva ad egemonizzare l'intera vita protestante del paese.' A slightly different view is offered by Unghváry who places greater emphasis on Luther's idea of himself as 'the German prophet', his attitude to the Turks and his theory of resistance in determining the Hungarian move from Lutheranism to Calvinism rather than on ethnic tensions within Transylvania. A. S. Unghváry, *The Hungarian Protestant Reformation in the Sixteenth Century Under the Ottoman Impact: Essays and Profiles* (Lewiston and Lampeter, 1989), ch. 16.

giance in Transylvania is not as clear as these arguments suggest.[3] In this chapter I explore the connection between ethnic identity and religious adherence in the Reformation in Transylvania. In doing so, I suggest that the different religious cultures of ethnic groups before the Reformation may provide a more satisfactory explanation of their subsequent religious histories than ideas of ethnic tension.

The division of the inhabitants into ethnic groups was fundamental to writers of descriptions of Transylvania, even if they were unable to agree on the number of 'nations' to be included. Possevino, writing in 1583, settled on three groups: the Hungarians, the Vlachs or Romanians, and the Saxons. Others saw the need to divide the Hungarians into two groups, recognizing the distinctiveness of the Szekler communities. More unusually, Gromo described the Cingara or gypsies as the fifth nation of Transylvania.[4]

Recognition of ethnic identities in such accounts does not, however, necessarily entail the presence of ethnic antagonisms. Our writers are primarily concerned to delineate the variety of rights, customs and privileges rather than to analyse the importance of ethnic identity and the relations between different groups. There is no evidence to suggest that relations between the Saxon and Hungarian communities had deteriorated to the extent of those between Germans and Czechs in Bohemia. On the political level the Unio Trium Nationum, developed in response to the 1437–38 Bobîlna peasant uprising, asserted the solidarity of the Magyar (and Magyarized), Saxon and Szekler nobilities. The consolidation and sharing of this political power in the Diets meant that the three nations need not be in competition with each other. This peaceable coexistence was further facilitated by the discrete areas of settlement and interest of the three groups. This is clearest for the Szeklers who, according to Gromo, 'habitano una parte astratta e separata da tutta la Transilvania, confinant con la Moldavia et vicini a Polonia'. The Siebenbürgen of the Saxons was similarly a well defined geographical entity. The spatial distribution of the Magyars is less clear, but, despite Gromo's assertion that they were 'sparsi per tutte le parte di quel regno', the prominence of Magyars in the Szekler lands and

---

[3] For example, the records of the diets of Sighişoara and Turda in 1564 show that the ethnic and geographical descriptions were seen as interchangeable. E.g. 'assertiones inter superintendentes et pastores ecclesiarum Coloswarensis, natione videlicet Hungara, et Cibiniensis gentis Saxonicalis.'

[4] A. Possevino, *Transilvania*, A. Veress (ed.), *Fontes Rerum Transylvanicarum* (Cluj and Budapest, 1913), p. 43; G. Gromo, *Compendio di tutto il regno posseduto dal Re Giovanni Transilvano e di tutte le cose notabili di esso regno*, A. Decei (ed.), *Apulum, Buletinul Muzeului Regional din Alba Iulia*, 1 (1945), 31; C. Alzati, *Terra Romena tra Oriente e Occidente: Chiese ed etnie nel tardo '500* (Milan, 1982), pp. 18, 34.

Siebenbürgen is questionable.[5] In the religious sphere Saxon and Hungarian relations were also characterized by separation and coexistence. In contrast to Bohemia, where German domination of church offices contributed to tension, medieval Transylvania saw a steady separation of the Saxon Church from outside influence as the privileges of the Adreanische (or Goldene) Freibrief (1224), including the right of communal election of priests, were extended from the area around Sibiu to all the main areas of German settlement.[6]

This trend towards ethnic separation was not absolute, but the existence of some fluidity probably suggests coexistence rather than antagonism. At village level some communities could clearly be ethnically mixed. A rare insight into the co-existence of Magyars and Saxons in one village is provided by the evidence of Săcalu de Pădure, which was divided by inheritance into Magarzakaal and Zaazsakal and had a separate church for each community.[7] Such arrangements appear to have been unusual. To the sixteenth-century traveller, Pierre Lescalopier, it seemed worthy of note when he came across a group of villages inhabited by people speaking Hungarian, German and Romanian.[8] In urban areas Saxon separation could be more extreme: Hungarians were not permitted to live in the cities of the Siebenbürgen and even Saxons who married Hungarians were forced to leave. However, alongside this rigour, Lescalopier also reports a recent change of policy in one of the seven cities, Cluj, which had decided to stop controlling its gates in exchange for freedom to mix with Hungarians in the

---

5   C. Alzati, *Terra Romena*, p. 205.

6   The Adreanische Freibrief was granted by Andreas II in 1224 and later extended to other areas of German settlement, for example to the Zwei Stuhle in 1318. The last stage in this process was the extension of these privileges to the Burzenland in 1422. E. Wagner, *Quellen zur Geschichte der Siebenbürger Sachsen, 1191–1975*, (Cologne and Vienna, 1976). See also O. Wittstock, 'Die Genossenschaftskirche der Siebenbürger Sachsen vor der Reformation', *Kirche im Osten*, 17 (1974), 156–62.

7   The presence of two churches is indicated by the reference in the papal taxation lists to Săcalu de Pădure as 'Duabus ecclesiis'. Wagner presumes that the village was under the supervision of a shared priest, but this seems unlikely. It is more probable that the Saxon Church was exempt from the obligation of taxation in common with the Saxon churches in the Burzenland not included in the list. E. Wagner, 'Register des Zehnten und das Schaffünfzigsten als Hilfsquellen zur historischen Demographie Siebenbürgens', in K. Benda (ed.) *Forschungen über Siebenbürgen und seine Nachbarn: Festschrift für A. T. Szabó & Z. Jakó* (Munich, 1988), pp. 207, 217.

8   The inhabitants of the villages of Fofeldea and Caşolţ may have been linguistically rather than ethnically mixed: 'le dernier iour nous disnasmes a Flalda village habité d'Hongres & d'Allemans et de Walacques, c'est a dire qui retienn<en>t le parler d'allemand et de walacque. Nous couchasmes a Casteihaulse village habité de mesmes.' P. I. Cernovodeanu (ed.), 'Călătoria lui Pierre Lescalopier in Ţara Romînească şi Transilvania la 1574', *Studii şi Materiale de Istorie Medie*, 4 (1960), 447.

countryside.[9] Such coexistence, although relatively recent in the case of Cluj, may have been a feature of some smaller towns in Transylvania.[10]

This pattern of political co-operation, broadly discrete areas of settlement and the possibility of areas of mixed occupation suggests that ethnic antagonism was a relatively unimportant feature of Saxon and Hungarian relations in Transylvania. The potential for antagonism between ethnic groups was greater in the case of relations with the Vlachs (Romanians), but here religious and social differentiation was also involved. The Vlachs lacked equal political rights and were not part of the Union of Three Nations. As Orthodox, they were viewed by Catholics as schismatics and had been subjected to periodic persecution and attempts at conversion.[11] In this context Centorio's comment in 1566 that the Saxons of Transylvania do not permit the Vlachs to build houses of stone or to live close to them need not indicate specifically ethnic tension.[12] Even if the place-name evidence for daughter settlements of Vallachian communities shows that such separation could be a physical reality,[13] the fact that the Saxons used the Vlachs to cultivate

---

[9] Lescalopier commented, 'ilz n'ont encore admis aucun Hongre resident parmi eux (in the seven cities) et si aucun y prend femme il est constraint de l'emmener demeurer ailleurs. Quant a p<rese>nt Colosvar est hors de ce nombre, pourceque depuis 8 ou 9 ans ilz avoient laissé de garder leurs porte & avoient mieux aymé la liberté du pays et se mesler en tout parmi les Hongrois', and he described Cluj as a 'belle et forte ville toutte peinte par les rües meslee d'Allemands et d'Hongrois qui peu d'annees auparauuant estoit habitee seulement par les Allemands'. Alba Iulia, the principal political centre of Transylvania, was thought to be exclusively Hungarian; 'Il n'y demeure Allemande ni Walacque mais touts parlent hongrois.' P. I. Cernovodeanu (ed.), 'Călătoria lui Pierre Lescalopier', pp. 456–7, 448.

[10] Aiud is described as a 'bourg habité d'Hongres & d'Allemands'. P. I. Cernovodeanu (ed.), 'Călătoria lui Pierre Lescalopier', p. 445.

[11] Persecution of the Orthodox was most evident in the reign of Louis of Hungary (1348–82) who ordered the expulsion of all Orthodox priests from his kingdom in 1366, and declared that only Catholics could be considered as nobles. The arrival of Johannes Capistrano in 1453 inspired a further wave of persecution in which the nobility, landowners and ecclesiastics were ordered to burn down Romanian churches and to expel all priests who refused Catholic baptism. The extent and effectiveness of these anti-Orthodox campaigns is unclear. L. Binder, *Grundlagen und Formen der Toleranz in Siebenbürgen bis zur Mitte des 17. Jahrhunderts* (Cologne and Vienna, 1976), pp. 100–2.

[12] Ascania Centorio de gli Hortensi, *Commentarii della guerra di Transilvania* (1566), L. Gáldi (ed.) (Budapest, 1940), pp. 71–2, 'a quai (Vlachs) questi Sassoni, per essere le maggiore, e principale potenza di quel Regno, non lasciano mai edificare casa di pietra, ne fermarsi troppo appresso di essi, e cosi vivono in case fatte di paglia o d'altre sorti d'herbe palustri, o fluuiatili, che loro stesso si fanno'. Cited in C. Alzati, *Terra Romena*, p. 21.

[13] E. Wagner, 'Register des Zehnten', pp. 212–15. The process of expanding settlement created Romanian daughter settlements. This is clearly documented for the villages of Rod in Reußmarkt and Wlachisch Tekes in Reps Stuhl. Wagner identifies a further 14

their lands may diminish the importance of the ethnic interpretation.[14] It may be the position of the Vlachs as a dependent peasantry, rather than as a different ethnic group, which explains the restriction of their claims to social status by the Saxon community.[15] Although the acceptance of disabilities linked to social status does not rule out animosities, legal and social restrictions do not necessarily lead to ethnic antagonism. Instead, they may be manifested in separate ethnic coexistence.

Whatever the strength of secular ethnic antagonisms, it is at least clear that ethnic and linguistic identity had no automatic connection with religious adherence. The two Hungarian peoples in Transylvania, the Magyars and the Szeklers, had dramatically different religious histories; the Magyars moving to Lutheranism and then to Calvinism, while the Szeklers remained Catholic with some later movement to Unitarianism. Perhaps the most decisive evidence for the lack of confessional ethnic identity is shown by the initial ability of Lutheranism to gain adherents among both the Magyars and the Saxons. In the early stages of the Reformation in Transylvania there was clearly no problem in Magyar acceptance of a German reform movement, whether mediated through the Saxons in Transylvania or Hungarians in other regions of Hungary.[16]

This dual German and Hungarian diffusion of Lutheran ideas suggests that attribution of the Magyar Calvinist reaction to fears of German cultural colonization is ill-founded. Even within Transylvania, Lu-

---

pairs of settlements in northern Siebenbürgen existing by 1600, of which 10 are identified by the description 'Oláh'. Romanian villages were also formed as a result of resettlement of places deserted by Catholics. The extent of settlement expansion and Romanian colonization in the fifteenth and sixteenth centuries is unclear. The main argument in favour of large-scale expansion is the extension of the obligation to pay tithe to all 'schismaticis seu valachichis' living on 'terris christianorum' by the decrees of Mathias Corvinus (1468) and Ladislau II (1500). However, settlement expansion may not be the only cause of a drive to increase ecclesiastical revenues.

14   G. Gromo, *Compendio di tutto il regno posseduto del Re Giovanni Transilvano*, 'Questa tal fattione è tutta politica, ne infra loro si ritrova alcuno povero, ma sono tutti mercanti et artefici ingegnosi si dilettano assai dell'agricoltura, ma fanno i loro terreni coltivare a i Valacchi.' Gromo also states that the Szeklers often use the Cingari (gypsies) to cultivate their fields. Cited in C. Alzati, *Terra Romena*, pp. 33, 35.

15   This is not to say that the Saxons were not conscious of Romanian ethnic identity, but that the imposition of restrictions was probably not seen primarily as a process of ethnic discrimination. The Saxons of Braşov were able to see through the superficial Magyarization of Romanian communities in the adoption of Hungarian names and described the Săcelele villages as 'villae valachales'. D. Prodan, *Iobăgia in Transilvania în secolul al xvi–lea* (Bucharest, 1968), 2, pp. 621–5.

16   An outline of the development of the Reformation in Hungary is given in D. P. Daniel, 'Hungary', in A. Pettegree (ed.) *The Early Reformation in Europe*, (Cambridge, 1992), pp. 49–69.

theranism was not dominated by a single powerful Saxon Church. Individuals such as Dávid and Heltai, who played an important part in the development of Lutheranism among the Magyars in Transylvania, may have been of Saxon origin, but organizationally their work was separate from the Saxon Lutheran Church of Brașov and Sibiu. For the latter church the focus of evangelical concern was not the Magyar or Szekler communities, but the Orthodox Romanians who lived in their midst. In 1544 a Lutheran catechism in Slavonic characters was printed in Sibiu, which met with a mixed reception from Orthodox priests. The movement towards compulsion came later, with the imposition of a Romanian Lutheran catechism on the Romanian churches of the district of Brașov in 1559.[17] This evangelization of the Romanian people would not have raised fears among the Hungarian population. Reformation of a subordinate people, living in the suburbs of the Saxon cities or cultivating Saxon lands, did not go beyond the appropriate sphere of Saxon interest, even in Magyar eyes.[18]

Rejection of the fear of German cultural hegemony as an explanation for the Magyar adoption of Calvinist ideas means that we still need to explain this development. Why do the Magyars go on to adopt Calvinist/Swiss ideas while the Saxons remain with their version of Lutheranism, and the Szeklers with Catholicism? One possible reason for the Saxons remaining Lutheran can easily be dismissed at this point. The unitary structure of the Saxon community was, of course, a significant source of strength to the Saxon Lutheran Church, but it did not guarantee resistance to Calvinist ideas. The original imposition of Lutheran ideas was primarily the work of the leaders of the Saxon community. It would, therefore, have been feasible for these same leaders to move the Church in a more Calvinist direction, whether in response to their own theological development or to pressures from a section of the community. The removal of images in Brașov in 1544, inspired by the advice of Bullinger, shows that groups holding more radical opinions could effect significant change.[19] In this context, the general continuity of Saxon

---

[17] M. Seșan, 'Die siebenbürgische Reformation und die rumänische Orthodoxie', *Kirche im Osten*, 18 (1975), 73–80. L. Binder, *Grundlagen und Formen der Toleranz in Siebenbürgen bis zur Mitte des 17. Jahrhunderts* (Cologne and Vienna, 1976), pp. 110–14. E. C. Suttner, 'Die rumänische Orthodoxie des 16. und 17. Jahrhunderts in Auseinandersetzung mit der Reformation', *Kirche im Osten*, 25 (1982), 64–5.

[18] Evangelization of the Romanian population by the Saxons may even have been carried out with Hungarian assistance. István Juhász argues that the Lutheran catechism was translated into Romanian not from German, but from Hungarian. A. Ritook Szalay, 'Il ruolo mediatore dell'Ungheria nella missione protestante orientale', in R. Sauzet (ed.) *Les frontières religieuses en Europe du xve au xviie siècle*, (Paris, 1992), pp. 292–3.

[19] Ostermayer's account clearly states that the destruction of images was officially

Lutheranism and its resistance to Calvinism cannot simply be attributed to the force of institutional inertia.

A more satisfactory answer would seem to lie in the fact that all communities were interested in adapting their existing religious ideas rather than simply adopting new ones. In Transylvania, owing to a certain degree of spatial and cultural separation, the assimilation and rejection of new ideas naturally produced unique solutions corresponding in general terms with ethnic communities. However, these associations were the result not of particular ethnic spiritual affinities, but of a long history of cultural interaction and adaptation. This can be seen most clearly in the assimilation of elements of Orthodox belief and practice into Catholicism. Thus, the Szekler community, while remaining strongly Catholic, accepted the marriage of priests under the influence of their Orthodox neighbours.[20] The Saxons, despite their somewhat disparaging view of the Romanians, also borrowed elements from the Orthodox church. At Hărman, the wall-painting of the Last Prayer of the Virgin (see Figure 6.1) is familiar in Orthodox rather than Catholic iconography and the portrayal of the Garden of Paradise has striking similarities with Orthodox representations.[21] This interaction suggests that to explain the process of the Reformation in Transylvania we need

---

sanctioned and not the result of spontaneous iconoclasm, 'Item sein mit Willen der Obrigkeit die Bilder aus den Kirchen, auch der große Altar in der Pfarrkirch abgebrochen worden'. The role of Honterus in these events is disputed by historians. Reinerth sees the leader of the Saxon Reformation rejecting Bullinger's instruction that images should be removed, and a more radical group forming around Martin Hentius, which resulted in the iconoclasm of February 1544. Roth argues for Honterus's acceptance of Bullinger's views and comments that Honterus's election as Stadtpfarrer on 22 April 1544 is incomprehensible if he had opposed the February image destruction. The subsequent destruction of silver ornaments of the church of Braşov (including monstrances, chalices and an image of the Virgin Mary) on 10 November 1544 also suggests his acquiescence, at least, in the policy. Less plausible is Roth's suggestion that all the image destruction of 1544 should be placed in November of that year. Not only does this require disregarding Ostermayer's chronology, but the events described for February and November are of a different character – the first involves the destruction of images and the high altar, the second is limited to the destruction of silver articles. K. Reinerth, 'Die Reformation der siebenbürgische-sächsischen Kirche', *Schriften des Vereins für Reformationsgeschichte*, 173 (1956), 43–7. E. Roth, *Die Reformation in Siebenbürgen: Ihr Verhältnis zu Wittenberg und der Schweiz* (Cologne and Graz, 1962), pp. 127–55.

[20]   C. Alzati, *Terra Romena*, pp. 62–3. Based on Possevino's account of the clergy in the territory of Csik and the archdeaconry of Orbai. The fact that some of these clerics married before and some after taking holy orders suggests the combined influences of Orthodox and Protestant practice by the date of Possevino's account. Cf. Possevino's account of the marriage of Catholic clergy in Moldavia.

[21]   R. Balaci, 'Noi aspecte iconografice in pictură murală gotică din Transilvania Hărman şi Sînpetru', *Studii şi Cercetări de Istoria Artei (Artă Plastică)* 36 (1989), 16.

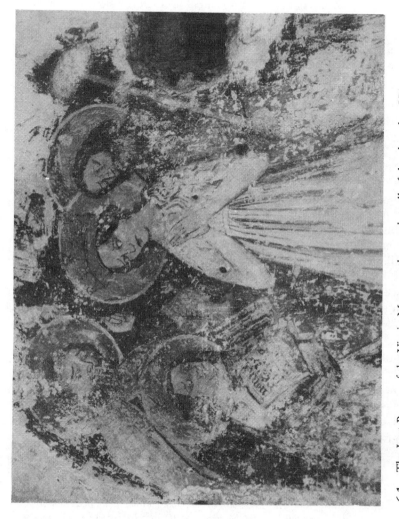

6.1 The Last Prayer of the Virgin Mary on the north wall of the chapel at Hărman

to understand the nature and diversity of the experience of Catholicism before the Reformation.

Of historians of the Reformation in Transylvania, only Ludwig Binder has attempted to explore the Transylvanian experience in terms of the continuity between late medieval piety and the Reformation.[22] The focus of Binder's concern is the search for a cultural explanation for toleration in Transylvania, but his observations also have some relevance for our attempt to explain the different religious histories of groups in Transylvania. For Binder the connection between late medieval religion and Reformation toleration is twofold. The first important factor is that the Reformation itself was not a sudden break, but one for which the way had been prepared by developments in late medieval piety. In particular, Binder suggested that the deep immersion in the Bible characteristic of pre-Reformation piety in Transylvania facilitated the transition to Reformation and the retention of Catholic ritual practices which reduced its visible impact. A second strand leading to toleration was the emergence of the Reformation in Transylvania out of the humanist tradition. The humanist faith in a conciliar solution as a means of resolving the religious fragmentation of Europe led naturally to toleration.

Binder's analysis applies only to the experience of the Saxons in Transylvania and probably tells us more about the attitudes of the intellectual leaders of the community than about the reactions of their fellow parishioners. Despite the evidence for the fairly extensive libraries of Saxon clergymen, continuity between medieval Catholicism and Reformation is more likely to be due to the presence of wider patterns of devotion favourable to the Reformation.[23] In the remainder of this chapter, therefore, I consider the evidence for the patterns of religious culture in Transylvania. The main sources for this are wall-paintings, which were of fundamental importance in a predominantly visual religion. As a source they have the additional advantage that paintings survive from churches of all ethnic groups, although patterns of survival and of concealment by whitewash mean that the evidence is more fragmentary in the Magyar areas of Transylvania.[24] The following dis-

---

22   L. Binder, *Grundlagen und Formen der Toleranz in Siebenbürgen bis zur Mitte des 17. Jahrhunderts* (Cologne and Vienna, 1976), ch. 3.

23   U. M. Schwob, *Kulturelle Beziehungen zwischen Nürnberg und den Deutschen im Südösten im 14. bis 16. Jahrhundert* (Munich, 1969), pp. 92–3, discusses the library of the sixteenth-century minister of Biertan, Franz Salicäus (d. 1567), now in the Bruckenthal Museum. G. Seiwert, 'Das älteste Hermannstädter Kirchenbuch und zwei Rechnungsfragmente', *Archiv des Vereines für Siebenbürgische Landeskunde*, 11 (1873), 323–441, includes the list of the extensive collection of books owned by the church in Sibiu in 1442.

24   Comments on wall-paintings are based on fieldwork undertaken in 1993 and

cussion therefore concentrates on a comparison of the Saxon and Szekler communities and tries to explain why the former became Lutheran while the latter remained Catholic.

Perhaps the most striking feature of the religious culture of the Saxons of Transylvania was the heightened devotion to the Virgin Mary. This can be seen in a particularly extreme form in the sermons delivered in Sibiu by Johannes Zekel in 1502, in which the status of Mary is held to eclipse even that of Christ. In his sermon on the Nativity of the Virgin Mary, Zekel makes the remarkable claim that Mary's Assumption outdoes Christ's Ascension since Christ is met only by angels, whereas Mary is met by angels, all the righteous and even the Trinity and led to her throne.[25]

This same emphasis on devotion to Mary appears in surviving wall paintings. At Biertan, early sixteenth-century paintings of the Annunciation and the Adoration of the Magi adorn the south wall of the chapel. At Mălîncrav, a probably unique representation of the Dormition of the Virgin in three scenes creatively emphasizes the sanctity of Mary and her ascension, body and soul. The Mălîncrav Dormition dates from the fourteenth century, but the lavish paintings in the choir and the elaborate Marian altarpiece suggest the continuity of Marian devotion at Mălîncrav into the fifteenth and early sixteenth centuries.[26]

The elaboration of Marian devotion and its relationship to the role of Christ in Saxon devotion can be seen especially clearly in the late fifteenth-century wall-paintings in the chapel at Hărman, near Braşov (see Figure 6.2).[27] On the south wall an elaborate image focuses on the

---

1995. The principal catalogue sources for wall paintings in Transylvania are, V. Drăguţ, 'Iconografia picturilor murale gotice din Transilvania', *Pagini de Veche Artă Românească* (Bucharest, 1972), II, pp. 9–83; D. Radocsay, *A középkori Magyarország falképei* (Budapest, 1954; German edn Budapest, 1977); M. Prokopp, *Italian Trecento Influence on Murals in East Central Europe Particularly Hungary* (Budapest, 1983).

[25] K. Reinerth, *Die Gründung der Evangelischen Kirchen in Siebenbürgen* (Cologne and Vienna, 1979), pp. 2–5. Zekel's sermon notes are in the Bruckenthal Museum, Sibiu. BBS Ms. 657, sermon on Nativity of Virgin Mary, fols 3r–5r.

[26] V. Drăguţ, 'Les peintures murales de l'église évangélique de Mălîncrav', *Revue Roumaine de l'Histoire de l'Art*, 5 (1968), 61–71. The three scenes are the Dormition with the ascension of Mary's soul, the episode with the Jew attempting to overturn the funeral bier, and the Dormition with the ascension of Mary's body.

[27] In common with many of the churches in the Burzenland, Hărman was fortified with an impressive enclosing wall during the fifteenth century. Storerooms and dwellings for temporary refuge for the villagers during Turkish raids were erected inside this wall. The 'chapel' containing the wall-paintings is on the second floor and located to the east of the church enclosure on the line of the perimeter wall and beneath one of the towers. In the literature it is usually described as a funerary chapel, although the evidence for this is not clear. In the Burzenland, there is only one other parallel. At Sînpetru, only a

purity of Mary. Drawing inspiration from versions of the *Biblia Pauperum* and *Speculum Humanae Salvationis*, the painting shows a central image of the Nativity with Mary adoring the Christ Child surrounded by four symbolic images of the Virgin taming the unicorn, the pelican tearing its breast to feed its chicks, the lion whose young awake on the third day and the phoenix. In the outer triangles four Old Testament prefigurations are illustrated: Moses with the burning bush, Aaron's flowering rod, the closed door of Jerusalem and Gideon's fleece.

A close parallel for this composition is the altarpiece from Cologne, dated *c.*1420 and now in Bonn Museum, which includes the same typological scenes and similar explanatory inscriptions and is clearly conceived as a demonstration of the Immaculate Conception.[28] However, both depictions, despite their clear focus on the purity of Mary, also emphasize the life of Christ. The illustrations of the inner set of triangles refer primarily to Christ's Passion and Resurrection. Most evidently, the pelican feeding its young with its own blood symbolizes

---

couple of miles away from Hărman, a chapel, this time on the ground floor, can be found in the angle of the north-east corner of the perimeter wall. Comparison with fortified churches in other parts of Europe, and especially in Alsace, shows that such chapels functioned as ossuary chapels and were invariably dedicated to St Michael. The lack of reference to St Michael in the Hărman iconography therefore suggests that it was not an ossuary chapel. B. Metz, 'Cellaria in cimiterio: le cimetière refuge', in M. Fixot and E. Zadora-Rio (eds), *L'église, La Campagne, Le Terroir* (Paris, 1990), pp. 21–43. The ossuary chapel dedicated to St Michael is most clearly attested at Cernay (Sennheim) (Upper Rhine) and Epfig (Lower Rhine); A. Kubinyi, 'Urbanisation in the East-Central part of Medieval Hungary', in L. Gerevich (ed.), *Towns in Medieval Hungary* (Budapest, 1990), p. 139, states that the parish church of St Stephen Miskolc has a 'grave chapel' close by. At Hărman, removal of plaster and brickwork during the summer of 1994 showed that the westernmost arch did not originally form the west wall of the chapel. Paintings of the five wise and five foolish virgins on the intrados of the arch continue on the external face and this subject is more usually associated with the decoration of the chancel arch as at Cisnădie. Parallels for churches being built into the defensive walls of fortified churches in Transylvania are found at Moşna, Şaroş, Curciu and Şoala and it is usually assumed that these churches were no longer functioning as complete buildings at this time. J. Fabritius-Dancu, *Sächsische Kirchenburgen in Siebenbürgen* (Sibiu, 1983), nos 63, 72.

28 *Das Rheinische Landesmuseum – Auswahlskatalog* (Bonn, 1977), vol. 4, pp. 53–8; C. J. Purtle, *The Marian Paintings of Jan van Eyck* (Princeton, 1982), pp. 137–8. The function of the Cologne altarpiece as a demonstration of the Immaculate Conception is emphasized by the concluding inscription: 'Hanc per figuram noscas castam parituram' (Learn through this painting – proof of the Virgin Birth).

Panel paintings similar in conception to the images at Cologne and Hărman occur at Holy Cross, Rostock, St Lorenz, Nuremberg (Friedrich Schön epitaph), and St Sebald, Nuremberg (Elsbeth Starck epitaph). Other images with elements of this composite design can be found at Neuwerk (Mönchen Gladbach), Stettin, St Sebald, Nuremberg (Margaretha Löffelholz epitaph) and Ottobeuren. A. Stange, *Die Deutschen Tafelbilder vor Dürer*, 3 vols (Munich, 1967–78), vol. 1, pp. 117, 189, 196, vol. 2, p. 181, vol. 3, pp. 29, 45, 49.

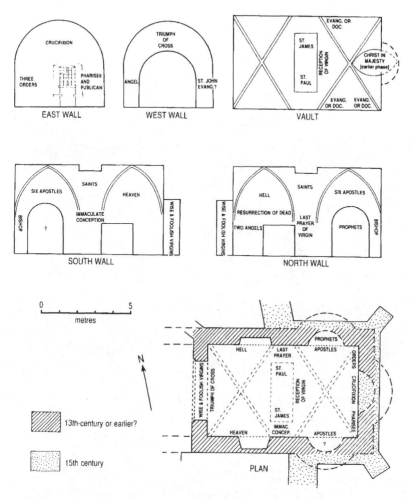

6.2   Plan and iconographical scheme of the chapel at Hărman

the Crucifixion. The belief that lion cubs awoke after three days relates this image to the Resurrection. Of the four images in this set only the unicorn refers directly to Mary, but this is clearly in the context of her role in the Incarnation of Christ. This emphasis on Mary's role in relation to Christ is developed even more strongly in the Hărman example. The central image at Hărman is the Nativity of Christ with Mary adoring the Christ Child, whereas in the Cologne altarpiece it is the Madonna and Child enthroned (see Figure 6.3).

The Immaculate Conception composition at Hărman is painted directly opposite the scene of the Last Prayer of the Virgin. As mentioned

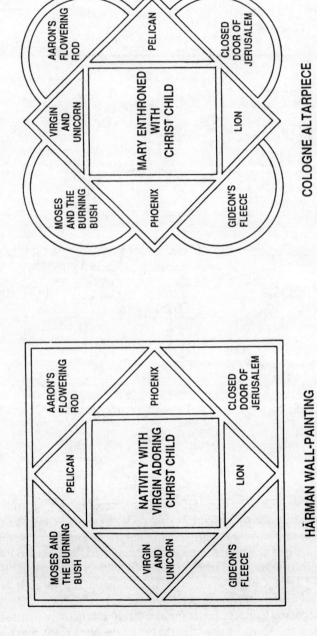

COLOGNE ALTARPIECE

AARON'S FLOWERING ROD

PELICAN

CLOSED DOOR OF JERUSALEM

VIRGIN AND UNICORN

MARY ENTHRONED WITH CHRIST CHILD

LION

MOSES AND THE BURNING BUSH

PHOENIX

GIDEON'S FLEECE

HÄRMAN WALL-PAINTING

AARON'S FLOWERING ROD

PHOENIX

CLOSED DOOR OF JERUSALEM

PELICAN

NATIVITY WITH VIRGIN ADORING CHRIST CHILD

LION

MOSES AND THE BURNING BUSH

VIRGIN AND UNICORN

GIDEON'S FLEECE

6.3   Iconographical schemes of the Immaculate Conception in the wall-painting at Härman and in the altarpiece from Cologne

earlier, this image is characteristic of Byzantine rather than Catholic iconography. It is therefore highly unlikely that it came from the same source as the image of the Immaculate Conception.[29] In choosing to pair these two images, the artist and/or his patrons were not slavishly copying a pre-existing model but creating a composite meaning of their own. Where the image of the Last Prayer of the Virgin does appear in Catholic iconography, as in the polyptych of St George, Prague, it is not as a separate image but in the context of the Dormition. The scene of the Dormition does not appear at Hărman and therefore Ruxandra Balaci has suggested that the addition of a crown in the Hărman Last Prayer was meant to conflate the ideas of the Last Prayer and the Dormition.[30] However, the presence of an image of the Reception of the Virgin in Heaven, lavish in its use of gold, spanning the ceiling space between the two images of the Last Prayer and the Immaculate Conception would seem to make this conflation redundant (see Figure 6.4). Instead, the importance of the crowned figure of the Virgin in the Last Prayer may be to suggest her exceptional status even before the moment of her Assumption. The iconography of the Reception of the Virgin also supports this interpretation. The detail and luxuriousness of the mantle of the Trinity and of the cloak held behind them by several angels, together with the insignificant scale of Mary herself and the probable absence of a crown, suggest that the focus of the scene is not the act of coronation, but the enfolding of Mary into the celestial world. The absence of the Dormition or Assumption corresponds with a lack of emphasis on transition. Mary's status is asserted by her purity, validated by Old Testament prefigurations, and manifested in the devoutness of her life on earth. As Johannes Zekel preached in Sibiu, on admission to heaven the composition of the reception committee was an important measure of prestige.

The concentration on the purity of the life of Mary on earth in the paintings of Hărman should not, however, make us conclude that Saxon devotion was overwhelmingly Marian. In the Saxon churches of Transylvania, Mary has very little role in the process of salvation. She does not appear as the Madonna of Mercy in the Last Judgement, but is seen as operating at one stage removed. At Biertan, Mary as the Madonna of Mercy appears in a separate image from the Last Judgement and intercedes for the souls beneath her mantle by tugging at the cloak of St Michael. The Crucifixion on the east wall at Hărman includes the standard figures of Mary and John, but it is the groups on either side,

---

[29] The absence of border inscriptions also suggests a different source.
[30] R. Balaci, 'Noi aspecte', p. 16.

6.4 The Reception of the Virgin in Heaven at Hãrman

the pharisee and the publican to Christ's left and the Three Orders to his right, which interpret ideas of prayer and intercession.

At Hărman the Marian iconography is clearly conceived as a part, and probably a subordinate part, of the general scheme which emphasizes the importance of the Passion of Christ in the process of salvation. The prominence of the Crucifixion on the east wall of the chapel has already been noted. On the west wall, separating the resurrecting souls from the entrance to Paradise, we do not have the usual Doom with a majestic Christ presiding over the judgement of the saved and the damned. Instead, the central image at Hărman is the cross itself garlanded with the crown of thorns and flanked by apostles. In life, as the east end imagery demonstrates, it is possible to intercede with the human suffering Christ. At the Last Judgement, it is the fact of Christ's Crucifixion which makes salvation possible. The depiction of the five wise and five foolish virgins on the intrados of the arch underlines the message that salvation depends on the use the individual makes during life of the chance offered by the Passion of Christ. However, this idea does not require fear and apprehension. The artist devotes much more space and attention to the garden of Paradise than to the torments of the damned on the opposite wall. The purpose seems to be to encourage viewers of the prospect of salvation through the sacrifice made by Christ. The possibility of reaching heaven through a virtuous and pure life on earth and also refers back to the Marian imagery in the centre of the chapel. Mary's experience may not have been that of all women, but the inscription at the base of the image of the Immaculate Conception emphasizes her kinship with ordinary humanity: 'Sicut spina rosam genuit Judea Mariam'. From sinful humanity, symbolized by the thorn and Judea, the emergence of virtuous and pure individuals is possible.

An emphasis on the Passion of Christ is also found in other Saxon churches. At Homorod two superimposed layers of painting suggest a subtle shift in emphasis from the late fourteenth to the fifteenth centuries (see Figure 6.5). The earlier image combines elements of the Pietà and the Vir Dolorum and emphasizes the human context of Christ's sufferings. Christ in the tomb shows the wound in his side and is supported by Mary. On the other side, St John the evangelist holds a scroll. The early fifteenth-century layer stresses the eucharistic significance of the Passion. The painting shows the Crucifixion with a kneeling donor collecting Christ's blood in a chalice at the foot of the cross. Devotion to the Holy Blood was more developed at Mălîncrav and in 1424 the Pope granted the right to issue indulgences to the Holy Blood chapel there.[31] In the parish church itself the image of the suffering

---

[31]   J. Fabritius-Dancu, *Sächsische Kirchenburgen*, no. 73.

6.5 Two layers of paintings at Homorod showing Christ as the Man of Sorrows, and the crucified Christ with a layman collecting his blood in a chalice at the foot of the cross

Christ was painted in perhaps the most important symbolic position, on the central axis at the east end of the chancel.

The Saxon emphasis on the Passion of Christ also had a strong eucharistic focus. The Corpus Christi brotherhood dominated the parish churches of St Mary in Brașov and Sibiu, attracting rich endowments. Other parishes could have a Corpus Christi chapel, as was the case at Ghimbav.[32] A heightened devotion to the sacrament was also evident in other parishes. In richer churches in the course of the fifteenth century, the simple aumbry or sacrament niche gave way to the towering sculptured sacrament house.[33] The elaborate sacrament houses, especially the fine examples at Sighișoara and Moșna, are testimony to the strength of eucharistic devotion, and it is unfortunate that any imagery they possessed usually does not survive.[34] However, this gap can be filled by the decoration of the humbler sacrament niche. The oldest example, dating from the end of the fourteenth century, survives at Mălîncrav and includes a small relief of a rood group framed by a canopy.[35] Later examples place more emphasis on the sufferings of Christ. A group of sacrament niches, dating from the end of the fifteenth and beginning of the sixteenth century and mainly from the area around Mediaș, show Christ as the Man of Sorrows pointing to the wound in his side (see Figure 6.6).[36] At Valea Viilor the message is reinforced by the inscription, 'Christus salvator mundi'. The same idea is expressed symbolically at Richiș, c.1500, in the image of the pelican tearing her breast to feed her young.

To sum up, in Saxon churches the sacrament of the eucharist is very prominent and there is also a strong connection between the Passion and suffering of Christ and the possibility of human salvation. At the

---

[32]   G. Seiwert, 'Die Bruderschaft des heiligen Leichnams in Hermannstadt', *Archiv des Vereines für Siebenbürgische Landeskunde*, 10 (1872), 314–60. F. Zimmermann and G. Werner, *Urkundenbuch zur Geschichte der Deutschen in Siebenbürgen* (Bucharest, 1892) 3. Some early fifteenth-century endowments given to the Corpus Christi brotherhood of St Mary's, Brașov are given in docs 1601, 1632, 1714 and the grant of an indulgence in doc. 1635. Details of an endowment of a mass in the Corpus Christi chapel of Ghimbav in 1413 by Margaret, widow of Peter Sadeler are given in doc. 1726.

[33]   V. Roth, 'Gotische Sakramentsnischen und Sakramentshäuschen in Siebenbürgen', *Beitrage zur Kunstgeschichte Siebenbürgens* (Strasbourg, 1914), pp. 102–15.

[34]   The 10m high sacrament house at Moșna includes the portrayal of three lions hunting a dragon, symbolizing the fight of good versus evil. J. Fabritius-Dancu, *Sächsische Kirchenburgen*, no. 63. Painted decoration on the walls around sacrament niches rarely survives, but the fragmentary remains at Băgaciu suggest that such schemes could have been very elaborate.

[35]   V. Drăguț, *Artă Gotică in România* (Bucharest, 1979), fig. 323.

[36]   Good examples can be found at Bazna, Ighișul Nou and Dupuș. J. Fabritius-Dancu, *Sächsische Kirchenburgen*, p. 18.

6.6   The sacrament niche at Bazna showing Christ as the Man of Sorrows

same time the figure of Mary is not unimportant. But she is venerated for her own purity and her exemplary life on earth, rather than as a vital intercessor in the process of salvation.

In the churches of the Szeklers the interpretation is rather different, although there are significant shared elements. As in the case of the Saxons, the stress is on mercy rather than judgement. Consequently, a common feature is the lack of emphasis on the sufferings of the damned. At the Szekler church of Mugeni, for example, it is the moment of the damned being hauled off to hell that is selected rather than their torments. Even the moment of resurrection need not be a cause for fear, as angels raise the slabs of the tombs and assist the resurrecting souls (see Figure 6.7). Both areas also show a striking lack of concern for scenes of moral instruction or warnings of the need to prepare for impending death. Such scenes as the warnings to sabbath breakers, the seven deadly sins and the seven works of mercy do not occur, despite their presence in other regions with strong artistic links with Transylvania.[37]

However, the common offer of mercy in the religion of Saxons and Szeklers in Transylvania was made in different ways. It is this variation which can explain their diverging religious histories in the Reformation period. In the Saxon areas, mercy was linked to the Passion of Christ. By contrast, mercy was offered in the Szekler communities by saintly figures. At Dîrjiu, instead of the usual representation of St Michael as the stern figure of justice weighing souls in his balance, we see a compassionate figure holding an interceding soul in the crook of his arm (see Figure 6.8). More commonly, and in the context of the Last Judgement, it is Mary who offers mercy. In Saxon paintings Mary as the Madonna of Mercy appears only as a separate image,[38] whereas in Szekler iconography she has a crucial role to play in the Last Judgement.[39] At Ghelința, the intercessors flanking the figure of Christ in the Last Judgement are the Madonna of Mercy and St John the Baptist. The role of Mary is portrayed even more elaborately at Mugeni where the

---

[37] V. Drăguț, 'Probleme comune al picturii murale medievale din Transilvania și Cehoslovacia, așa cum rezulta din studiile publicate in revista *Uměnî*, *Studii și Cercetări de Istoria Artei (Artă Plastică)*, 10 (1963), 263–6; F. Stele, *Slikarstvo v Sloveniji od 12. do srede 16 stoletja* (Ljubljana, 1969). For example, Christ (or St Nedelya) of the Trades occurs at Bodešée, Zanigrad v Istri, Crngrob and Pristava pri Polhovem Gradcu. V. Dvořáková, J. Krása and K. Stejksal, *Stredovká nástenná malba na Slovensku* (Prague and Bratislava, 1978). See for example, the works of mercy and the seven deadly sins at Levoča.

[38] Saxon depictions of Mary as the Madonna of Mercy occur at St Bartholomew's church, Brașov (exterior and no longer visible), Biertan and Mălîncrav.

[39] The Madonna of Mercy is integrated into the Last Judgement at Sic, Ghelința and Mugeni.

6.7   An angel assisting resurrecting souls in the Last Judgement at Mugeni

6.8   Detail from the painting of St Michael on the south wall of the nave at Dîrjiu showing the soul in the crook of his arm

figure of Mary is shown twice in the same Judgement scene. She appears first, as expected, in the role of intercessor beside the central Christ. More interesting is the depiction of Mary as the Madonna of Mercy, sheltering souls beneath her cloak. The addition of a hurrying figure seeking admittance into the folds of Mary's cloak at the last moment adds a sense of immediacy and urgency to Mary's protection, and dramatically underlines its availability to all in the ultimate hour of need (see Figure 6.9).[40]

Curiously, this emphasis on the role of Mary's protection in the churches of the Szekler communities was not matched by an interest in the life of Mary herself. It is striking that none of the images of the Coronation of the Virgin occur in Szekler churches. Mary is shown in composite images together with St Anne and the Holy Family, as at Sîntana de Mureş, but this scene hardly represents a devotion strongly focused on the life of Mary herself.

At the same time, the imagery of the Szekler churches does not focus on the suffering of Christ's Passion and its eucharistic significance. The elaborate sacrament houses and sacrament niches seem to be a feature of Saxon rather than Szekler areas. At Mugeni, the cloth of Veronica is depicted, but this is an isolated image and not part of a general emphasis on the role of the human sufferings of Christ's Passion in the process of salvation.

We must now consider how these distinct patterns of religion in Saxon and Szekler areas can explain the different reactions to the Reformation. The Saxon focus on the Passion of Christ and the sacrament of the eucharist may have eclipsed devotion to other saints and so have paved the way for their renunciation in the course of the Reformation. It may also account for the appeal of communion in both kinds. At the same time the excesses of eucharistic devotion could produce reaction and ridicule, as in the disruption of the Corpus Christi processions at Sibiu where priests were ridiculed for believing that Christ was a child who wanted to be carried around the city in the arms of old women.[41] When a crucifix fell down in the church of Viseud, the

---

[40] V. Drăguţ, 'Picturile murale ale bisericii reformate din Mugeni', *Studii şi Cercetări de Istoria Artei (Artă Plastică)*, **11/2** (1964), 307–20, is the most comprehensive discussion of the iconography at Mugeni, but does not note the presence of the figure seeking admittance into Mary's cloak. The similarity, noted by Drăguţ, with the paintings at Rakoš (Slovakia, Goemoer district) does not extend to the portrayal of the Madonna of Mercy, but does include the unusual representation of the group of righteous *leaving* the heavenly city.

[41] K. Reinerth, *Die Gründung der Evangelischen Kirchen*, p. 18. According to the letter from the dean and the preacher of Sibiu to the Archbishop of Esztergom in June 1526 detailing the activities of the Protestant heretics, the Corpus Christi processions

6.9 Scene from the Last Judgement at Mugeni showing Mary as intercessor and as the Madonna of Mercy

reaction of a bystander was to order it to stand up and prove itself.[42] This ridicule of excesses could simultaneously entail an acceptance of eucharistic devotion: the problem was foolish superstition, not the spiritual value of the eucharist. The ability to criticize in this way was a feature of a personal, active religion which could arise from a devotional emphasis on the opportunities provided by the Crucifixion for the salvation of the individual Christian who lived a good life on earth. For such people, the adoption of Lutheran ideas may have seemed a natural step.

The subsequent inability of the Saxons to move towards a more austere Swiss/Calvinist position may therefore only partly be due to the Marian emphasis of Saxon devotion. Of greater significance is the attachment to eucharistic devotion and the importance of the Passion of Christ. Under the influence of Swiss ideas, images were removed from the churches of Braşov in 1544, but significantly the large crucifix next to the font was specifically retained.[43] In Sibiu in 1545 the figures of Mary and John were painted out of the Crucifixion scene in the centre of the altarpiece and scriptural texts in humanist script were added, emphasizing the connection between salvation and the Passion of Christ.[44]

In view of this analysis of the situation in the Saxon lands, the continued loyalty of the Szeklers to Catholicism is less surprising. The absence among the Szeklers of a prominent eucharistic devotion and an emphasis on the human sufferings of Christ meant that there was no natural impulse to Reformation. At the same time the stress on the mercy offered by Mary even at the last moment offered the comfort of protection and did not foster active individual religion.

For the Saxon and Szekler communities, therefore, the nature of late medieval parish devotion can explain their religious options in the era of Reformation. In this process ethnic identities and antagonisms were

---

were disrupted by blasphemous catcalls: 'Tunc pridem [recte quidem] nonnulli Cibinienses blasphemiam magnam perpetraverunt, et cives aliqui dixerunt: Sacerdotes nostri credunt Deum factum esse coecum, ex quo tot luminaria incendunt. Alii dixerunt: Sacerdotes nostri arbitrantur Deum esse puerum, qui velit instar puerorum duci et portari in brachiis vetularum circumcirca per civitatem', in V. Bunyitai (ed.) *Monumenta ecclesiastici tempora innovatae in Hungaria religionis illustrantia* (Budapest, 1902), vol. 1, p. 261.

[42]   K. Reinerth, *Der Gründung der Evangelischen Kirchen*, p. 24. Cites the words of the peasant as given in the report of 5 September 1524 of the incident in Zied (Schenk district), 'Da affichter koblen Herrgott, bestu gefallen, zo stand wider auff.'

[43]   K. Reinerth, *Die Reformation der siebenburgische-sachsischen Kirche (Schriften des Vereins fur Reformationsgeschichte* 61, 173) (Gutersloh, 1956), pp. 43–7.

[44]   The texts are, 'Venite ad mei omnes qui laboratis et onerati estis, ego refocillabo vos et invenietis requiem ani[m]abu[s]' from Matthew 11:28–9 and 'Iustus servus meus cognicione sui justificabit multos ib ipse peccatum multorum tulit et pro iniquis rogavit,' from Isaiah 53:11–12.

less significant than the medieval development of ethnically distinct religious cultures. Linguistic and ethnic boundaries may have been important for the spread of types of Reformation, but the explanation for this lies in devotional receptivity rather than in ethnic or linguistic determinism.

CHAPTER SEVEN

The image controversy in the religious negotiations between Protestant theologians and Eastern Orthodox Churches

Sergiusz Michalski

For the Protestants of the sixteenth century, locked in a seemingly interminable combat with Rome, the Eastern Orthodox Church presented the welcome example of a Christian church whose roots went back to the apostolic times and who was not subservient to the papacy. References to the special situation of the 'Greek' churches of the East abound in the polemical writings of the sixteenth century, starting with Luther's famous statement in the Leipzig disputation of 1519. Rarely, however, did the Protestant references go beyond certain stereotypical views about the beliefs and habits of the 'Greeks' (the Russian religious situation was less known). And to put it succinctly, the encounters between these two Christian confessions were on the whole neither frequent nor far-reaching in their consequences prior to the nineteenth century.[1]

These contacts and their results have been characterized in a number of ways. One of the more popular catchphrases has been the antonymic pair of the pulpit and the icon.[2] In this view, the pulpit stood for the Protestant negation of the visual side of religion, a negation resulting ultimately in iconophobia and iconoclasm. There is no need to dwell here on the oversimplification inherent in this assumption, a simplification which overlooks the nuanced, relatively iconophilic attitude of the Lutheran Church. Nevertheless the divergences as regards the image

---

[1] In a vast secondary literature, see E. Benz, *Wittenberg und Byzanz* (Marburg, 1949); G. Hering, 'Orthodoxie und Protestantismus', *Jahrbuch der Österreichischen Byzantinistik*, 31/2 (1981), 823–74.

[2] C. S. Calian, *Icon and Pulpit: The Protestant–Orthodox Encounter* (Philadelphia, 1968). For the relations of Protestantism and Eastern Orthodox Churches as regards the image question see Sergiusz Michalski, *The Reformation and the Visual Arts. The Protestant Image Question in Western and Eastern Europe* (London and New York, 1993), ch. 4.

question constituted one of the most important points of conflict between the two churches. From the point of view of fundamental theology, more important issues divided the two confessions. But for a number of reasons – some of which we shall try to present here – the divergences as regards the 'Bilderfrage' shaped the mutual perceptions of both confessions to a large extent.

Nowhere does this appear more clearly than in the two religious negotiations undertaken by these two great Christian confessions. The first was the exchange of letters carried out in the years 1574–1581 between a group of theologians affiliated with the University of Tübingen (Jakob Heerbrand, Jakob Andreae, Martin Crusius and others) and the Patriarchate in Constantinople under Jeremiah II.[3] The second was the exchange of letters between a group of dissident Anglican bishops and theologians – known as the 'Nonjurors' – and the Patriarchates of Constantinople and Jerusalem in the years 1716–25.[4] The term 'religious negotiation' constitutes no doubt an exaggeration of some sort – the participants never met, in both cases exchanging more or less formal letters. Many negative factors weighed heavily on these exchanges: the non-representative status of both the Tübingen and the Anglican group and the manifest weaknesses in theological doctrine and scholarship which plagued the Patriarchate in Constantinople, to name but a few.

Though with hindsight these conciliatory attempts seemed to have been doomed to failure from the very outset, they raised a number of interesting problems nonetheless, and deserve our topical interest. The image question treated somewhat lightly by both sides at the beginning proved to be one of the main stumbling blocks to negotiations, as these exchanges progressed. The starting-point of the negotiations of 1574–81 between Tübingen and Constantinople on images was provided by

---

[3] An English translation of the Tübingen–Constantinople exchange is in G. Mastrantonis, *Augsburg and Constantinople. The correspondence between the Tübingen Theologians and the Patriarch Jeremiah II of Constantinople on the Augsburg Confession* (Brookline, MA, 1982). See also W. Engels, 'Tübingen und Byzanz', *Kyrios*, 5 (1940–41), 240–87; W. J. Jorgensen, *The Augustana Graeca and the Correspondence between the Tübingen Lutherans and the Patriarch Jeremiah: Scripture and Theological Methodology* (Ph.D. dissertation, Boston, 1979); D. Wendebourg, *Reformation und Orthodoxie. Der ökumenische Briefwechsel zwischen der württembergischen Kirche und Patriarch Jeremias II. von Konstantinopel in den Jahren 1574–1581* (Göttingen, 1986).

[4] The correspondence is printed in G. Williams, *The Orthodox Church of the East Being the Correspondence between the Eastern Patriarchs and the Nonjuring Bishops* (London, 1868); See also J. H. Overton, *The Nonjurors, their Lives, Principles and Writings* (London, 1902), pp. 451 and following; K. Minkner, 'Die Non-jurors und die Ostkirche', *Eine Heilige Kirche*, 21 (1939), 207–18; H. W. Longford, 'The Nonjurors and the Eastern Orthodox', *Eastern Church Review*, 2 (1966–67), 118–32.

the terse statement to be found in the Augsburg Confession, which the Tübingen theologians had sent earlier to the Patriarchate, denying that the Protestants had abolished 'all of the ceremonies' in the Church. Since the question of images as such was not explicitly mentioned in the Augsburg Confession, the first letter of the Patriarch Jeremiah II to Tübingen, a letter commenting on its tenets and arguments, referred only to the problem of the legitimacy of the cult of the saints. In their first response, when discussing the invocation of saints, the Tübingen theologians mentioned in passing the problem of images by endorsing the views of the well-known patristic opponent of religious art, Bishop Epiphanius of Cyprus (fourth cent.): 'Let those things be destroyed which have penetrated the hearts of the deceived. Let the allurement of the idol be taken from our eyes - Epiphanius has in mind here first and foremost images that are worshipped'[5] - concluded the German Lutherans. Epiphanius was a classic reference of the iconophobes.[6] In the context of this particular dialogue the reference was particularly tactless - Cyprus was a traditional Eastern Orthodox territory - and bound to infuriate the Patriarchate. The Patriarch thus felt provoked to take up in detail the question of images and this in close connection with the cult of saints. In his second letter the Patriarch, after accusing the Germans of misinterpreting Epiphanius who had not, in his opinion, expressed iconophobic sentiments, forcefully reiterated the legitimacy of the cult of images. The saints and their icons are to be venerated relatively (with schesis or douleia), not absolutely (with latreia), since worship is due to God alone. A leitmotif of the Patriarch's argument was the notion of St Basil that veneration passes to the prototype. The cult of images cannot under any circumstances be conceived as idolatrous, since the faithful adore not matter but the divinity represented in the image. Jeremiah appended to this thought of St John the Damascene long quotations from his anti-iconoclastic works. However, the Patriarch refers continually to images of saints - only once mentioning images of Christ - thus avoiding the incarnational argument.

Where Jeremiah II attempted to link Christology with the problem of reference he fell into rather dubious theological constructions that constituted fallacious reminiscences of anti-Arian polemics ('Thus he who does not honour the Son ... does not honour the Father, just as he who does not venerate images does not venerate the thing to which the image refers').[7] The Tübingen theologians had no difficulty in refuting

---

5   Mastrantonis, *Augsburg*, p. 201.

6   K. Holl, 'Die Schriften des Epiphanius gegen die Bilderverehrung', in K. Holl, *Gesammelte Aufsätze zur Kirchengeschichte*, (Tübingen, 1928), vol. 2, pp. 351–87.

7   Mastrantonis, *Augsburg*, p. 201.

this contention by pointing out that God and the Son are one essence, which cannot apply to the relation of the image with its prototype. The Patriarch also quoted at length the mystical image theory of Dionysius the Aeropagite, thus weakening the cohesiveness of his argument. Weaknesses do appear both in his Christological and in his exegetical elements. In Jeremiah's formulation the story of the brazen serpent is seen only in the light of a prefiguration of Christ; it is a very narrow interpretation which leaves aside the problem of abuse. Luther had shown in his famous polemic with Karlstadt in 1522 that this 'image' had to be destroyed only then, when intolerable iconodulic abuses had been committed. On the other hand Jeremiah's response in defence of church tradition, pointing to the pitfalls of unavoidable subjectivity when choosing – as the Lutherans did – only particular elements of the cult, was unquestionably pertinent to the needs of the dispute and soon became a standard Eastern Orthodox argument.

The Tübingen theologians now had no choice; in their second response (1580) they attacked the very concept of a relative cult and the usage of St Basil's formula (' ... even the excuse, which states that worship is not offered to the material of the icon but to the person who is depicted in it, is not able to gloss over the worship of icons').[8] The cult of images, as such, goes against the testimony of scripture. Despite the fact that they allowed the existence of images of saints in the churches ('we will allow the martyrdom of saints to be depicted as an example of perseverance in the faith'), they categorically negated any cult of their images as well as the theological basis of the cult of saints as such. Only Christ could be a mediator and the virtues of the saints – repeating Luther's classic formulation – could not be imitated. They rejected out of hand the distinctions in the grades of veneration, since they considered this to be conceptually flawed and absolutely inapplicable for the faithful in practice. All the observed practices of worship testify that the cult of images comes to stand deceitfully between man and God.

In this persistent though sometimes camouflaged reference to the main assumptions of the doctrine, especially the immediacy of the man–God relation, we can see the unquestioned force of the Lutheran argument, despite some willingness to compromise on ceremonial matters. God does not want the elements of sacrality to be transmitted to humanity through the cult of images. The Tübingen theologians also rejected the argument of the Patriarch that the homage paid to the portraits of famous people and rulers should imply the relative venera-

---

[8] Ibid., p. 279.

tion of icons. As they stated, the first was a kind of civil honour where a form of symbolic identity between image and prototype did in fact exist and should not therefore be compared with the aims of the cult of images. The refutation of this charge of Eastern iconodulism is unquestionably consistent, but this strand of the polemics is more a reflection of the dispute with Catholic than with Orthodox iconodulism.

On the other hand, the pronouncements of the Tübingen theologians on the subject of the spiritual fathers of the cult of icons did have direct reference to Eastern iconodulism. It is not surprising that St John the Damascene was the main target of strongly worded attacks nor that the decisions of the second Nicean Council were also questioned in turn. This part of Lutheran polemics limited itself to summary judgements given without wider argument. None the less, the entire early Christian theoretical heritage of iconodulism was undermined.

By their intermittent attacks on the cult of images the Lutherans from Tübingen weakened their position in the negotiations, for this naturally obscured the fact that they were against the strict aniconism of the Calvinist type. Moreover some of their arguments were derived from the radically iconophobic repertoire ('it is much better to lighten the ... needs of the living holy icons of God ... than honour painted icons which neither see, nor hear, nor feel anything').[9] That is why their assurances of toleration of images of the saints (though of a historical rather than devotional nature), a concession which went against contemporary Lutheran Church practice, could not have made much of an impression on the Patriarch.

The last exchange of letters on this matter thus produced a brief, but extremely grave pronouncement by Jeremiah II: the Lutherans were accused of continuing the tradition of Jewish hostility to religious imagery, that is in short, they were accused of 'Judaizing'. Though this was a traditional argument in the context of the image controversy, its use did signal that a point of no return had been reached in the debate itself. Though the Patriarch put a greater stress on the aspect of 'Judaizing' as a traditional constituent of various heresies[10] (the Patriarchate must have had some information about the iconoclast 'Judaizing' heresies in the Russian Church at the end of the fifteenth and the mid-sixteenth century), and less on its specific Old Testament connection with the 'ban of images', this accusation clearly put an end to all hopes of finding an agreement. A shocked denial by the Lutherans in their third and last letter refuted the charge of 'Judaizing' without mentioning the image

---

[9]   Ibid., p. 278.
[10]   L. I. Newman, *Jewish Influence on Christian Reform Movements* (New York, 1925), pp. 613–17.

controversy specifically: the theologians from Tübingen seem belatedly to have realized their mistake in opening this Pandora's box after all.

Almost a century and a half elapsed until the next Protestant–Orthodox religious negotiations. Once again the Patriarchate in Constantinople (aided by that of Jerusalem) represented the Eastern Orthodox side. Their Protestant partners, the Nonjurors, constituted a small group of Anglican bishops and clerics which had refused on grounds of conscience to take the oath of allegiance to the new monarch after 1688.

The Nonjurors displayed a wide-ranging readiness for compromise. This stance no doubt reflected their weak position not only in European Protestantism as a whole but also as against the mainstream Anglican Church. As some potential thorny issues of fundamental theology had been eliminated from the outset, in the course of the eight-year exchange of letters a growing disagreement regarding the cult of saints and the cult of images was given room to develop.

The prospects for an agreement were auspicious from the outset: the Nonjurors had decided to accept the existence and legitimacy of religious art. They considered this rightly as a tremendous concession in itself ('And for a further declaration of our settlement on this article we willingly acknowledge, that the use of images in churches is not only lawful, but may be serviceable for representing the history of the Saints, for refreshing the memory and moving the devotion of the people').[11]

The scope of this concession can be ascertained only if one takes into account the traditional terminology of the image controversy and the various confessional standpoints associated with it. The acceptance not only of biblical 'histories' but also of quasi-legendary scenes from the lives of the saints went beyond the relatively iconophilic Lutheran practice. The Tübingen theologians had accepted scenes of the saints' martyrdom, but they were reluctant to concede more. The formulation elaborated by the Nonjurors comes close on the whole to Catholic positions, especially as regards the phrase 'warming the devotion of the people'.

However, the Nonjurors could not go much further: they saw no possibility of accepting the veneration of images, a practice which in their view gave scandal to 'Jews and Mohammedans alike'. Obviously they intended a reference to the particular dialectics of the 'skandalon' as such – a concept which had been brilliantly used by Luther in his diatribes against Karlstadt in 1522 in the context of the debate over images. But by referring to the strictly aniconic Jews and Mohammedans they had clearly chosen a wrong example – as the protest of the Greek side was to show later on.

---

[11] Williams, *Orthodox Church*, p. 100.

Interestingly enough the Nonjurors tried earnestly to develop a historical basis for their arguments. Like the Tübingen theologians they felt themselves bound to repudiate the iconodulic statements of the seventh Nicean Council held in 787 and referred therefore to its critique in the resolutions of the Frankish Council at Frankfurt in 794. The mere fact that the Council at Frankfurt had taken place should – in the opinion of the Nonjurors – put an end to all pretensions to ecumenicity on the part of the Nicean Council. In itself, this argument constituted an affront to the Greeks. The Nonjurors, however, went even further: they claimed that thanks to the virulent Frankish critique of Nicean iconodulism, the growth and the spread of the cult of images in the West had been impeded for almost half a millennium. So, as they tried to demonstrate at length, the cult of images proper really began in Germany in the thirteenth century, in France and England even later. This fact should be taken into account in all discussions about the cult of images, since 'Christianity is not a gradual religion, but was active and perfect when the Evangelists and the Apostles were deceased. Thus whatever variations there are from the original state ... or practice ... ought to come under suspicion.'[12] The reference to the simplicity of the apostolic times had – in the context of the image debate – a distinct iconophobic ring. By prolonging the 'imageless epoch' until the High Middle Ages the Nonjurors amplified the polemical aspect of this topos. Needless to say this argument was unacceptable to the Greek side.

The Patriarchate defended stubbornly the cult of images and did not display any readiness for compromise at this point. While they commended the Nonjurors at the outset for their relatively iconophilic introductory statements, the Eastern Orthodox demanded much stronger affirmative action. They rejected vehemently the notion of avoiding 'giving offence' to hesitant Christian and non-Christian alike. The Greek churches reaffirmed the teachings of John of Damascus and stated that the Basilian notion 'that the honour paid to the image ascends to the prototype' still constituted the prime motivation of the cult of images as practised among the Christians of the East. The Patriarchate also elaborated at length about the different grades of worship – the latreia (adoration) due to God alone, the hyperdouleia due to the Virgin and the douleia (veneration) due to the Saints proper and their continued relevance for the practice of the cult of images.

The Nonjurors completely rejected this latter scheme: 'The distinction between latria, doulia and hyperdoulia is what we do not understand.'[13] Scriptural evidence does not lend itself to such a differentiation.

---

12   Ibid., p. 101.
13   Ibid., p. 139.

As noted above the Tübingen theologians had dealt with the matter from a more pastoral and pragmatic point of view, disregarding strictly spiritual aspects.

Despite all these reservations the Nonjurors were ready, in what amounted to a plea for a kind of ecclesiastical *laissez-faire*, to leave the problem unresolved and to accept regional variations. They asked the Eastern Orthodox side for toleration of their opposition to the cult of images and of their desire to return, in some domains, to the simplicity of Apostolic times. For if Christianity is to be compared with a long stream, 'the stream runs clearest towards the fountains head'.[14] The Eastern Orthodox did not provide any further response to this entreaty but no doubt the Patriarchates of the East must have found the attitude of the Nonjurors – who dealt with tradition in both a very doctrinal and very lax fashion – very infuriating.

In terms of the tenets of fundamental theology the Nonjurors – whose importance in the 1720s was rapidly diminishing – represented what could be called the Catholic aspect of the Anglican Church. Though they maintained quite strongly the principle of sacramental grace they had some misgivings about the Real Presence. Their doctrine of virtualism was of course unpalatable to the Eastern Orthodox Churches, though the Greeks did not seem to have realized the extent of the fissure. None the less it was the image controversy which came to the fore and dominated in the final exchange of letters. The position of the Nonjurors with their curious mixture of Lutheran and Catholic accents did not satisfy the Eastern Churches who clung to the strongly iconodulic confession of Dositheos from the year 1672 (one copy reached England and was duly translated, but did not seem to have elicited any direct response).[15] Conversely, in England, besides deriding the political ambitions of the Nonjurors and their pretensions to a role in the whole of Christendom the mainstream Anglican opinion was openly critical of their tactics as regards the image question (Blackmore): they were accused of having capitulated to the obstinate iconodulism of Eastern Orthodox Christianity.

---

[14] Ibid., p. 101.
[15] C. R. A. Georgi, *Die Confessio Dosithei (Jerusalem 1672)* (Munich, 1940), pp. 50–2.

CHAPTER EIGHT

Protestantism and Orthodoxy in sixteenth-century Moldavia

Maria Crăciun

From the fourteenth century onwards, Moldavia was a semi-independent state, ruled by a Voyvode or Grand Duke, originally a vassal of the Hungarian King. Ties with Hungary were broken, however, as successive Voyvodes began to see themselves as rulers by divine right, but from the fifteenth century onwards, any nascent independence evaporated, as Moldavia came into contact with the Turks, and began paying tribute to the Porte, the court of the Ottoman sultan.

In the sixteenth century, dependence on the Ottomans intensified. The 'ahidname' proclaimed that Moldavia was part of the House of Peace, paying tribute to the Emperor.[1] The increasing Turkish influence made itself felt in the appointment of the Moldavian rulers, who tended to be selected by the Porte. Those elected by the Boyars, or Moldavian landed nobility, still needed to have their election ratified by the Sultan, and could easily lose their throne and their lives by being called to Constantinople and executed. Other princes prudently converted to Islam, and received appointments elsewhere in the Empire as Ottoman dignitaries. Moldavia itself suffered territorial losses, as areas like Brăila, Tighina and the Bugeac passed under direct Ottoman administration. Equally, Moldavia's foreign policy was generally directed by the Ottomans, in spite of the efforts of the Capuchehaia, or Moldavian representative in Constantinople, to form anti-Ottoman alliances with other powers. Moldavia's Ottoman overlords also removed its right to mint its own coinage, leading to a reorientation of trade routes and commerce towards the Empire itself. However,

---

[1] 'Ahidnames' or 'ahdnames' were capitulations or peace and commerce treaties concluded between the Ottoman Empire and Christian states. Non-Muslims who had concluded a treaty with Ottoman Sultans were called 'ahl al'ahd' or 'muahidin' (treaty people). The term derived from 'ahd' meaning agreement, convention or oath. The Romanians had concluded several treaties or ahidnames with the Sultans; Viorel Panaite, 'Ethnicity and Religion in the Terminology of Sixteenth and Seventeenth-Century Ottoman Documents. A Case Study: Ahdnames', in Maria Crăciun and Ovidiu Ghitta (eds) *Ethnicity and Religion in Central and Eastern Europe* (Cluj, 1995).

Moldavia did preserve its internal autonomy, its traditional institutions, administrative and social structures, and religious and cultural life.

Within Moldavia itself, the Boyar élite, which often controlled vast tracts of land, followed the Polish model by challenging the authority of the prince. However, factionalism and divided support for various claimants to the throne weakened the Boyars' political influence in spite of their role in the government council. Significantly, the élite's main obligation to its overlord was that of military service.

Demographically, Moldavia was relatively densely populated, mainly with villages of about 20 houses each, but there were also 29 small towns, whose populations were an ethnic mix of Romanians, Transylvanian Saxons, Galician Germans, Hungarians and Armenians.[2]

In the context of the history of the Reformation, Moldavia presents an interesting case, because of the existence of Protestant communities in an Orthodox state. In order to understand the impact of Protestantism in Moldavia, one must examine the state of the pre-existing Moldavian Orthodox Church. The Church was led by a Metropolitan in Suceava and two bishops, one in Rădăuti and the other in Roman. The Moldavian Church had links with the other eastern Orthodox churches, as its Metropolitan was recognized by the Patriarch in Constantinople, although the tense relations with Constantinople after the Council of Florence meant that the bishops of Moldavia were often ordained in Ochrid.

One particularly crucial period in the history of Protestantism in Moldavia was the brief reign of Jacob Basilicos Heraclides, known as Despot, who held the Moldavian throne between 1561 and 1563. Described as a Greek adventurer,[3] he played a vital part in establishing the Reformation in Moldavia. Firmly ensconced in the Orthodox world, Moldavia was not at first glance the most fertile ground for Protestant ideas. Yet the evidence suggests that already by the 1530s, the Reformation was gaining ground in the previously Catholic areas of the country. As for Despot himself, the exact nature of his own Protestantism has long been a matter for debate. Indeed, it is likely that he moved through various confessional standpoints in the course of his lifetime. During his travels in Germany and Scandinavia, he adopted Lutheranism, and was well thought of by Lutheran leaders such as Melanchthon, as evidenced by the latter's letters of recommendation

---

[2] For estimates concerning Moldavian towns see: C. C. Giurescu, *Târguri sau oraşe şi cetăţi moldovene*, (Bucharest, 1967).

[3] C. Marinescu, *Jacques Basilicos 'le Despote', Prince de Moldavie (1561–1563), Ecrivain Militaire* (Cluj, 1938), pp. 1–3.

for Despot, written in June 1556.[4] By the time Despot reached Königsberg, however, his views had changed, as he expressed approval of Osiander's theology. As he travelled eastwards, to Wilno and Cracow, his confessional perspective evolved as well, probably through an intermediate Calvinist stage during his stay with Calvinist Polish nobility between 1557 and 1561 and ending up as a supporter of the Radical Reformation.[5] Evidence for his increasingly radical perspective comes, first, from the report of Commendone, the papal nuncio in Poland. Commendone noted that Despot shared the Calvinist prince Radziwill's views.[6] Despot's biographer, Antonio Graziani, confirmed that it was in Poland that Despot had become accustomed to 'impieties'.[7] Despot's growing adherence to the Radical Reformation was reflected in his choice of associates who were themselves Antitrinitarians, such as Jan Lusinski, a former priest who is thought to have ended his life as a Socinian. Another Antitrinitarian collaborator was Johann Sommer, ordained as a Lutheran minister in Wittenberg in 1548. By 1570, he had become the principal of the Unitarian school in Cluj. In a further sign of the links between Despot and the Radical Reformation, Sommer wrote a biography of Despot, and dedicated it to Jacob Palaeologus, another prominent figure in the Radical Reformation.

Despot's own religious beliefs are more difficult to define, not least because he seems to have adapted his confession to the changing circumstances around him. He refused to support Wolfgang Schreiber's project to print Reformation texts in Romanian, and instead sent him on to Constantinople, where Schreiber was cast into prison. Despot's decision to sacrifice Schreiber was due to political circumstances rather than religious affiliations,[8] but his attitude has often been interpreted as a refusal to show his preference for the Reformation, demonstrating instead his loyalty to the Turks or his Orthodox beliefs. In contrast to this episode, however, were the persistent criticisms of Despot as a Jew. Both the papal nuncio, Commendone, and the bishop, Peter Myszkowski

---

4   Hans Petri, *Relațiunile lui Jacobus Basilius Heraclides zis Despot Voda cu capii reformațiunii atît în Germania cît și în Polonia precum și propria sa activitate reformatoare în principatul Moldovei* (Bucharest, 1927), pp. 16–24.

5   On Despot's life see: Nicolae Iorga, 'Un Heraclide à Montpellier et un courtisan valaque de Henri IV', in *Analele Academiei Romane, Buletinul Secțiunii Istorice*, seria II, 17, 1930; Ernst Benz, 'Melanchton et l'Eglise orthodoxe', in *Irenikon*, 29, 2, 1956; Ernst Benz, 'Wittenberg und Byzanz', in *Kyrios*, 4, 1939; Cesare Alzati, *Terra Romena tra Oriente e Occidente, chiese ed etnie nel tardo 1500*, (Milan, 1982).

6   Nicolae Iorga, *Nouveaux materiaux pour servir à l'histoire de Jacques Basilikos l'Héraclide dit le Despot, prince de Moldavie* (Bucharest, 1900).

7   Antonio Maria Graziani, 'Vita Jacobi', in Emile Legrand (ed.) *Deux vies de Jacques Basilicos* (Paris, 1889), p. 162.

8   Dosachi Hurmuzaki, *Documente Privind istoria românilor*, II, 1, p. 418.

(1555–68), referred to Despot as a Jew.[9] Less explicit, but no less relevant, were the accusations that Despot could not be a Christian, accusations made in the papal nuncio's report concerning Despot's wish to become a priest. There were, in fact, Radical Reformation communities in Poland which had adopted Jewish practices. As both sources calling Despot a Jew were Polish, this could explain the confusion. Generally, the Christian community condemned Unitarians for denying the divinity of Christ. The epithet of Jew was a common one, as more and more Orthodox critics of Unitarians accused them of Judaizing tendencies.

In many ways, therefore, Despot appears to have supported the Radical Reformation, and his religious views had a clear impact on his policies for Moldavia. One of the most important questions is whether Despot in fact intended to introduce the Reformation in Moldavia, and whether his policies in favour of Protestantism were directed against Catholics, that is the German and Hungarian population of Moldavia, or against Orthodox communities. Before examining these matters, one must bear in mind that Despot was not the first to introduce the Reformation to Moldavia. In fact, his actions relied on the Protestant proselytizing carried out in Moldavia during the preceding decades and, tellingly, on support from his associates in Poland and Germany.

Contemporary documents show that Despot had evolved a proselytizing programme even before he occupied the Moldavian throne. He had used this programme to obtain Polish support for his political ambitions. On 2 April 1560, Albert Laski wrote to Maximilian presenting Despot as an evangelist for Moldavia.[10] On 5 October 1560, the papal nuncio in Poland, Everardo Buongiovanni, outlined Despot's actions for the conquest of the Moldavian throne with the assistance of Polish Protestants and his intention to establish the Reformation in Moldavia. On several occasions, Despot promised that he would reform the country he was about to conquer. Later, his Polish supporters were to accuse him of having failed to fulfil his promises. Significantly, the proclamation of Vaslui was issued at the beginning of his reign, announcing his religious policy. It was effectively a decree of toleration. He was practically inviting all the Protestants persecuted for their beliefs in France, Spain and Germany, to come to Moldavia.[11] Consequently, the evidence suggests that Despot fully intended to support the Reformation in Moldavia.

---

[9] Nicolae Iorga, 'Notițe', *Revista Istorică*, 20 (1934), 191.

[10] Hurmuzaki, *Documente*, II, 1, p. 385.

[11] Andrei Veress, *Documente privind istoria Transilvanei, Moldovei și Țării Românești* 1, pp. 201–2.

The urban areas of Moldavia offered Despot constant support, even until the end of his reign. This leads one to suppose that his policies met with the approval of townspeople. It is probable that upon his arrival in Moldavia, Despot had already found a population which had come into contact with the Reformation. The influence of the Catholic hierarchy was weak, and priests were mainly recruited in neighbouring Transylvania, thus leaving the path free for the development of a Moldavian Reformation.

Yet beyond this spontaneous movement, Despot developed a clear programme of Reformation for the formerly Catholic communities. Contemporary texts show an articulated and decisive programme of reform, which aimed to annihilate Catholicism in Moldavia. This programme implied the exile of Catholic priests and their replacement with Protestant pastors, and the destruction of sacred objects and images. On 9 April 1589, the Archbishop of Lemberg, I. D. Solikowsky, wrote to Cardinal Montalto, outlining the difficult situation the Catholics had experienced under Despot, and the actions taken by Despot to destroy Catholicism.[12] This is confirmed by Bottero in his 'Le relazioni universali'.[13] Yet the removal of Catholic clergy had to be accompanied by the arrival of Protestant pastors. Despot's plan to bring Jan Lusinski to Moldavia as a Protestant bishop seems to have been part of his programme. In 1562, in the same year as the official establishment of the Antitrinitarian Church in Poland during the Calvinist synod of Pinczow, Despot decided to appoint a Protestant bishop, 'episcopus nationis Saxonicae et Hungaricae'. Belsius's report to Emperor Ferdinand on 13 April 1562 made it clear that Lusinski's mission in Moldavia was not restricted to the repair of churches, but was mainly intended to strengthen the Protestants in their faith.[14] The evidence suggests that Despot continued to work to bring into Moldavia clergy trained for the Protestant Church.[15]

The second component of Despot's programme was the reform of morals. The first issue to be dealt with was that of divorce. In Moldavia, divorce was relatively simple, following the payment of a fine. The German and Hungarian communities in Moldavia had apparently begun to copy the Orthodox custom in this regard. Consequently, Lusinski's episcopal duties included jurisdiction over matrimonial litigation among the Germans and Hungarians. Marriage as an indissoluble bond be-

---

12   Hurmuzaki, *Documente*, I, p. 123.
13   N. C. Burghele, 'Despot Vodă Ereticul Domnul Moldovei (1561–1563)' *Convorbiri Literare*, 31 (1897), 718.
14   Hurmuzaki, *Documente*, II, 1, p. 407.
15   Graziani, 'Vita Jacobi', p. 170.

came a principle in Despot's legislation, and penalties were applied accordingly. Johann Sommer provided an eyewitness account of the execution of six men under the terms of the legislation.[16] The most interesting aspect of this control of morals is that Despot wanted to extend this jurisdiction to the Moldavian Orthodox population. This was probably an attempt to establish the Reformation among the Moldavian Orthodox through its moral component. An improvement in their morals was supposed to make them more receptive to other Protestant ideas.

The third component of Despot's Reformation programme was education. The success of the Reformation was dependent on knowledge of the Bible in the vernacular, and on the circulation of catechisms, hymn books and children's Bibles. One of the cornerstones of Despot's educational project was the establishment of a school at Cotnari. Whether the school was a college, a centre of higher education, or simply a grammar school has been debated at length. There is no doubt, however, that the school played a key role in the introduction of Protestantism in Moldavia. Under the direction of Johann Sommer, the school became the training ground for future Protestant clergy. It was also meant to educate a larger segment of the population in a Protestant context. Cotnari itself was home to a numerous German and Hungarian colony, whose members were already Protestant. However, Sommer's description of the school tends to suggest that it was not intended for the German and Hungarian population alone. Apparently, children were brought to the school from all over the province and were provided for by the prince. Thus, it seems that the educational programme was directed at the Moldavian Orthodox as well, and that the school was an integral part of the proselytizing action initiated by the prince.[17] At the same time, Despot had also built a Protestant church in Cotnari, intended for the local faithful. Again, this building programme is consistent with Despot's plans to consolidate the Reformation in Moldavia, and is confirmed by internal chronicles.

These preoccupations show how well Despot was able to co-ordinate the establishment of the Reformation in Moldavia through the provision of clergy, discipline and education. An educated clergy was essential for efficient proselytizing, for the success of the Reformation was not dependent on the Bible alone, but also on powerful preaching of the new confession. Despot strengthened the nascent Protestant community by bringing to Moldavia leading Reformation figures who were familiar

---

[16] Johannes Sommer, 'Vita Jacobi Despotae, Moldavorum reguli', in Emile Legrand (ed.) *Deux vies de Jacques Basilicos*, (Paris, 1889), p. 32.

[17] Sommer, 'Vita Jacobi', p. 35.

with the task of supporting an emerging church. Graziani confirms this impression when he insists on Despot's desire to bring in strangers who would introduce the new religion and the new cults in accordance with his wishes.[18] Therefore, the evidence suggests that Despot had a coherent programme to encourage Protestantism among the Hungarians and Germans living in Moldavia. However, his relations with the Moldavian Orthodox communities remain less clear.

Despot's position regarding the Orthodox church in Moldavia was a delicate one. When he accepted the throne, he became 'dominus' through God's mercy, and was installed in his office by the Metropolitan of the country. In order to have any measure of success his Reformation policies had to take the existing Orthodox Church in Moldavia into account, and thus he could only proceed with caution in his attempts to bring Protestantism and Orthodoxy together. Yet in many instances he appears to have proceeded with a total disregard for Orthodox sensibilities, as in the case of the confiscation of vessels and other sacred objects made from precious metals, which had been kept in monasteries. These confiscations are described both in internal chronicles and in the *Chronologia* of Martin Siglerius.[19] The internal chronicles reinforce the idea of Despot's sacrilege by pointing out that he had destroyed icons by removing the precious stones which served to adorn them.

Equally, Despot's attitude to Orthodox practices and doctrines was hardly conciliatory, as he adopted the Protestant theologians' polemical views on Orthodoxy, disdaining the Orthodox cult, liturgical books and clergy, especially the monks, refusing to participate in religious festivals and equating Orthodox worship practices with superstition. Graziani, Commendone, and even Sommer comment on Despot's hostility to the Orthodox church.[20]

Despot's policies aimed at introducing the Reformation to Orthodox Moldavian communities attracted the interests of other Reformers, who attempted to seize the opportunity to bring the Protestant message to the Orthodox, chiefly through books in their own language. One such advocate of the need for Protestant works in Romanian was Dimitrie, a Serbian who had become a Lutheran, and had stayed with Melanchthon in Wittenberg. Having been forced to flee Moldavia during the last years of Alexandru Lăpușneanu's reign because of the anti-Lutheran persecution ordered by the prince, Dimitrie returned to Moldavia when

---

18   Graziani, 'Vita Jacobi', pp. 182–9.

19   Martin Siglerius, *Chronologia* in Alexandru Lapedatu (ed.) *Stiri privitoare la istoria țărilor române din Cronologia lui Siglerius,* in *Annarul Institutului de Istorie națională, București,* 2, 1923.

20   Nicolae Iorga, *Nouveaux Materiaux*, p. 18; Graziani, 'Vita Jacobi', pp. 188–9.

Despot ascended the throne. On 5 November 1562, Protestant books printed in Slavonic were sent to Moldavia from Germany, intended for the Orthodox population. Dimitrie was active in this work, as he was mentioned as one of the translators into Slavonic, along with the Slovene Primus Trubar.[21]

Wolfgang Schreiber, mentioned above, was also a participant in a project aimed at providing Protestant works in Romanian for the Orthodox population of Moldavia. Schreiber had been sent to Moldavia by Hans Ungnad with a proposal for Despot. Ungnad wished to print the Romanian translation of the Gospels with cyrillic characters. Ungnad offered Despot his services, in case the prince wished to have the Romanian version of the Gospels printed in Germany. In order to convince Despot of the feasibility of the project, Ungnad sent him various versions of the Scriptures in Slav languages.[22] Schreiber's mission as Ungnad's envoy was part of the efforts made by the groups in Urach and Tübingen to translate the Scriptures into the national idioms of the lands of southeastern Europe.[23] The mission to Despot was encouraged by the Emperor Maximilian, who gave Schreiber a letter of recommendation to facilitate his task, expressing the hope that Schreiber would be able to organize the printing of the books and advance Christian faith.[24] Both Dimitrie and Schreiber came to Moldavia to help Despot introduce the Reformation to the Orthodox communities by providing translations of the Scriptures into vernacular languages. Although neither was really successful, they represent the link between Despot and the Reformers elsewhere in Europe, who were equally interested in fostering the Reformation in Orthodox settings.

These examples highlight Despot's programme regarding the Moldavian Orthodox, and help to explain the hostility which Despot triggered among the Orthodox élite, a hostility which later led to his assassination. Graziani claimed that the Orthodox clergy, who had tried to protect the sacred objects being removed from the churches, were also involved in encouraging the hostility against Despot, and made them responsible for starting the rebellion.[25] The most dramatic move

[21] Serban Papacostea, 'Diaconul sîrb Dimitrie şi penetraţia reformei în Moldova', *Romanoslavica* (1969), 213–16.

[22] Hurmuzaki, *Documente* II, 1, pp. 445–6.

[23] For the efforts made to convert the South Slavs it is worth looking at: Maria Holban, 'En marge de la croisade protestante du groupe d'Urach pour la diffusion de l'Evangile dans les langues nationales du sud-est européen. L'épisode Wolff Schreiber', *RESEE*, 2, 1964; M. Murko, *Die Bedeutung der Reformation und Gegen Reformation für das geistige Leben der Sud Slaven* (Prague and Heidelberg, 1927).

[24] Hans Petri, *Relaţiunile*, p. 50.

[25] Graziani, 'Vita Jacobi', pp. 181–90.

of the clergy to rid themselves of Despot was their attempt to kill him with a poisoned wafer on Easter Day. Although their plot failed as the prince was forewarned, the clergy's hatred of Despot's Protestant policies was clear. They especially resented his bringing a Socinian bishop (Lusinski) into the country and giving the bishop a prominent position at court, his attack on church possessions and his Protestant propaganda promoted through education.[26] This plot, and others carried out more efficiently by the boyars allow us to point to the existence of a powerful conservative reaction to Despot's policies in Moldavian society, particularly in Orthodox areas.

Indeed, this Orthodox resentment of Despot led to his downfall and that of people associated with him in any way. Lusinski, his widow, and Despot's illegitimate child were all killed by the boyars, as were a number of the German and Hungarian inhabitants of Cotnari. All of the victims were suspect because of their supposed loyalty to Despot.[27] The prince himself was besieged in Suceava by the rebels. In a note dated 11 August 1563, intended for the English authorities, it was reported that the Despot of Valachia was besieged in Suceava by his own subjects, because he had taken the gold and silver from the churches, had tried to change religion, and had intended to marry a foreigner.[28]

In spite of his brief reign and violent death, Despot was an important Protestant ruler, both because of his links with Reformers elsewhere and because of his actual policy in Moldavia. Despot's international role is particularly significant in Hans Ungnad's ill-fated attempt to interest the prince in providing Reformation works in vernacular languages for the Orthodox of Moldavia. Ungnad believed that he was dealing with a prince who was favourable to the Protestants. Indeed, Despot's intentions of encouraging the Reformation were known and supported in Protestant circles outside Moldavia.

Despot's approach was a dual one: on the one hand, he wanted to support the ethnically distinct communities in Moldavia, who were largely already Protestant, and on the other, he wanted to bring the Orthodox population of Moldavia to the Protestant fold. His supporters outside Moldavia were particularly interested in the second of these approaches, and were critical of Despot's inability to establish any confessional changes among the Orthodox over the long term.

---

[26]   Mathias Miles, *Siebenbürgisches Würgengel oder Chrönicalischer Anhang des 16 Saeculi nach Christi Geburth*, (Hermannsstadt, 1670).

[27]   Sommer, 'Vita Jacobi', pp. 47–8, Martin Siglerius, 'Chronologia', p. 370.

[28]   E. D. Tappe, *Documents Concerning Romanian History 1427–1601 Collected from British Archives* (London, 1964), p. 36. His intended bride was Christina Zborowski. The latin note is from Graziani's 'Vita Jacobi'.

Despot hoped to bring these Orthodox communities to the Reformation through his reform of morals, through the creation of a school in Cotnari, open to all and directed by a notorious Protestant, and finally by reforming worship practices by removing certain cult objects from the churches. The impact of this relatively modest and unambitious programme was very great, as evidenced by the hostile reactions of the boyars and the Orthodox clergy. As the effects of these policies survived until the end of the century, it is fair to say that Despot was the most important princely supporter of the Reformation in Moldavia. Despot's death meant the loss of a valuable agent for the Reformation in Eastern Europe, while Moldavia lost a European prince.

CHAPTER NINE

Church building and discipline in early seventeenth-century Hungary and Transylvania

Graeme Murdock

The Reformed Church in Hungary and Transylvania was the product of a late and incomplete sixteenth-century reformation. By the early seventeenth century the building blocks of a Reformed confession for the Hungarian Church were however largely in place, with consistent adherence to the Helvetic confession and Heidelberg catechism. The Bible, Psalter and other key texts were available in the vernacular, and a settled, if regionally variable, administrative structure was established with Reformed Church regions and districts under the control of superintendents, archdeacons, synods and all-clergy area presbyteries. Indeed, hierarchical controls over Reformed communities in Hungary and Transylvania were strengthened during this period, with canons and state laws aiming to defend church doctrine and order. From the accession of Gábor Bethlen in 1613 a series of Reformed Transylvanian princes offered their co-religionists protection against local confessional rivals, ennobling the clergy as a class, and supporting the development of Reformed educational centres across the region. The Reformed Church achieved the status of orthodoxy in the early seventeenth century Transylvanian state, as the public church which informed the ideology of the area from the Szekler lands in eastern Transylvania to the counties of north-eastern and eastern Hungary.[1]

During the early seventeenth century the Reformed Church of Hungary and Transylvania became increasingly involved in a web of European contacts between Calvinists and Calvinist churches. This broad engagement encouraged Hungarian Reformed ministers to compare their experience of foreign churches with domestic practices, even if disagreements emerged on the need to copy what interested outsiders considered best for Reformed religion in Hungary and Transylvania. Hungar-

---

[1] Jenő Zoványi, *A reformáczió magyarországon 1565–ig* (Budapest, 1921). Jenő Zoványi, *A magyarországi protestantizmus 1565–tol 1600–ig* (Budapest, 1977). János Pokoly, *Az erdélyi református egyház története* (5 vols, Budapest, 1904).

ian Reformed schools prospered by attracting prominent foreign teachers to the region, while large numbers of so-called academic ministers from Hungary and Transylvania were sponsored by princes, nobles and towns to travel to Western universities, before returning to work as rectors and ministers in Hungarian schools and parishes. This clerical élite became the leading protagonist in the defence of Hungarian Reformed religion in strident interconfessional disputes against local Catholics, also renewing attacks on Antitrinitarians, while some ministers offered irenic olive branches towards Lutherans in the interest of Protestant unity. University-educated ministers translated many recent foreign texts on Reformed worship and liturgy, church music, public prayer, homiletics and sacramental theology. Some reform-minded academic ministers returned to Hungary and Transylvania also determined to encourage individual religiosity and personal piety in the Hungarian Church, and were subsequently stigmatized by local traditionalists as puritans.[2]

Early modern Reformed religion was marked out across Europe from its confessional rivals, above all, by its commitment to reform church practices further, and to undertake a reformation of public and private morality through church discipline. Churches and rulers everywhere were concerned with questions of social order, however, a discernably Reformed morality pervaded the issues concentrated on by Calvinist Church discipliners, and distinctive institutions were formed through which Calvinist community discipline was exercised. In this chapter I shall examine the imposition of Reformed patterns of discipline and punishment for sin in local communities across Hungary and Transylvania as one product of the broad engagement with the rest of continental Calvinism outlined above, with the morality and procedures of Hungarian Reformed discipline entirely comparable to the disciplinary issues and practices of Reformed churches elsewhere.[3] I shall high-

---

[2]   Heinz Schilling, 'Confessionalization in the Empire: religious and societal change in Germany between 1555 and 1620' and 'The second Reformation – problems and issues', in *Religion, Political Culture and the Emergence of Early Modern Society* (Leiden, 1992), pp. 205–301. R. Po-Chia Hsia, *Social Discipline in the Reformation: Central Europe 1550–1750* (London, 1989). Andrew Pettegree, 'The Clergy and the Reformation: from "devilish priesthood" to new professional elite', in Andrew Pettegree (ed.), *The Reformation of the Parishes* (Manchester, 1993), pp. 1–22. Andrew Pettegree, Alastair Duke and Gillian Lewis (eds), *Calvinism in Europe 1540–1620* (Cambridge, 1994), pp. 231–53. Menna Prestwich (ed.), *International Calvinism, 1541–1715* (Oxford, 1985).

[3]   E. W. Monter, 'The consistory of Geneva, 1559–1569', *Bibliothèque D'Humanisme et Renaissance*, 28 (1976), 467–84. R. A. Mentzer, 'Disciplina nervus ecclesiae: the Calvinist reform of morals at Nimes', *The Sixteenth Century Journal*, 18 (1987), 89–115.

light the application of discipline by the Hungarian Reformed clergy in two areas in particular: Zemplén county in north-eastern Hungary, and the town of Kiskomárom in western Hungary. I shall argue that during the early seventeenth century there was a novel determination to impose in these areas, as elsewhere in Hungary and Transylvania, tighter standards of discipline and moral conduct which were the hallmarks of Reformed Church building. I shall then reinforce this picture of greater disciplinary zeal among the Reformed clergy, by examining the stresses which such enthusiasm caused between the agents of Reformed Church building: the Transylvanian princes, Hungarian godly nobles, and the clergy. I shall further support the case for the early seventeenth century as a period in which Hungarian Reformed Church builders attempted to impose tighter disciplinary standards, by looking at the conscious efforts of the clergy to set themselves apart as a disciplined and disciplining order, and gauge the reaction among Reformed congregations to this social separation.

Authority to uphold the law, establish good order, and punish wrongdoing in Hungary and Transylvania lay with local landowners, and their noble county assemblies. There was no great codification of crimes and customary punishments, with either monetary or physical punishment handed out for different offences. In each county a high sheriff was supported by sheriffs and county justices, and in each parish a selected justice was responsible for reporting local scandals to each local noble. The justices were supported by village councils of jurymen and a curator of village works, while in self-governing towns councils of justices and jurors dealt with all legal matters, with difficult cases referred as a last resort to the Transylvanian prince.[4]

The Reformed Church tried hard to mould the attitudes of the civil authorities and especially the Transylvanian princes towards sin. Princes were encouraged to fulfil the requirements of Reformed godly magistracy in setting high standards of morality at court, and in the country at large. In 1619 Gábor Bethlen responded favourably to a request from the Küküllő Reformed area synod of central Transylvania, and introduced stringent new laws on public behaviour. Reacting to apocalyptic fears raised by the appearance of a comet in 1618, the Küküllő synod had requested Transylvanians to embark on a national penance, to adopt more modest lifestyles, humbler dress, and to keep fasts on

---

G. Parker, 'The "Kirk By Law Established" and the origins of "The Taming of Scotland": St Andrews 1559–1600', in L. Leneman (ed.), *Perspectives in Scottish Social History: Essays in Honour of Rosalind Mitchison* (Aberdeen, 1988), pp. 1–33.

4   E. Illyés, *Egyházfegyelem a magyar református egyházban* (Debrecen, 1941). Géza Nagy, *Fejezetek a magyar református egyház 17. századi történetéből* (Budapest, 1985).

Sundays. The synod also demanded that sinners, especially Sabbath breakers and fornicators, should be punished without regard for their social status, and that the punishment of adulterers and blasphemers should be pursued according to God's law. New articles, which Bethlen supported at the Transylvanian Diet of 1619, imposed tight regulations on Sabbath activities. Swearing was made punishable for nobles by a one forint fine, and for peasants by a morning to be spent in the stocks. Local authorities were also ordered to impose the death penalty consistently in future against all thieves, murderers and adulterers.[5]

While the Hungarian Reformed Church sought to influence the ruling Transylvanian princes, it had also obtained a great deal of administrative autonomy with guaranteed rights to hold all-clergy synods at the discretion of regional superintendents, and for senior clergy to conduct regular visitations of Reformed parishes. Canons for all the Hungarian and Transylvanian Reformed Church districts indeed ordered frequent visitations to examine the behaviour of ministers and their congregations, specifying offences to be watched out for, and appropriate punishments to be meted out. Reformed canons from the late sixteenth century had stressed the role of the prince and nobles as partners in this disciplining process, yet the clergy were also instructed to rebuke the nobility when necessary, particularly for living opulently, or for failing to observe the Sabbath, to partake regularly in communion, or to carry out their duties as magistrates and administrators of justice. While the Reformed Church tried to influence and shape the policies of the civil authorities, by highlighting the importance of particular sins and suggesting appropriate punishments for them, it also had a range of spiritual weapons at its disposal to deploy in the battle against sin, with the power to excommunicate as the most potent in its arsenal. Exclusion orders and excommunications were applied by Reformed ministers against those who refused to take communion, or to come to church. After warnings from a minister, unreformed thieves, adulterers, blasphemers, false oath makers and drunkards were generally deemed worthy of excommunication. Transylvanian canons drawn up by superintendent István Geleji Katona in 1649 concluded that exclusion from the Church could follow when reprimands from a minister were clearly having no effect. Open sinners who justified their actions despite such warnings could be first temporarily excluded from the Church, and then excommunicated, but only with the agreement of the local synod. It was however stressed that 'the truly repentant are not to be left

---

5 G. Illyés, 'Az 1619. évi küküllővári zsinat felterjesztése Bethlen Gábor fejedelemhez', *Református Szemle* (1934), 501–5.

outside the church in misery for long in the land of Satan, but when they have mended their ways they shall be called back'.[6]

Sinners could be reaccepted into Reformed communities after exclusion if they showed a willingness to repent. Repentance required an admission of guilt and a renunciation of sin, which was marked publicly during church services by the penitent sitting on a stool of repentance or standing at the church door, and by wearing dark clothing, or covering his or her head. The procedure followed in the northern Danube church district detailed that local ministers should first preach against a particular sin, and then expel any repeated offenders from their congregations. Return to the Church community required kneeling penitence in mourning clothes before absolution could be granted, and the penitent was kept out of church for some more weeks before a ceremonial public confession of the sin which had been committed, and a further rebuke from the minister.[7]

The annual visitations of the Zemplén Reformed Church district in the northern Tisza region were conducted by the local archdeacon, accompanied by the senior clergy who were usually members of the Zemplén clergy presbytery. These visitations were the prime means of investigating general standards in the hilly, flood-prone Zemplén county, whose southern region was dominated by ethnic Hungarians, and its north populated largely by Slavs. The visitors travelled across Zemplén county throughout the year with letters sent by the archdeacon warning parishes that a visitation party was about to arrive. Disciplinary issues were also discussed at regular meetings of the Zemplén area synod, and Zemplén's archdeacons looked to the synod for support especially when called upon to intervene in difficult local disputes, and satisfy competing claims from ministers, their noble patrons and local communities. The synod in turn co-operated with the county noble assembly on local disciplinary matters, particularly where a case involved a noble offender.[8]

---

6   A. Kiss, *A XVI. században tartott magyar református zsinatok végzései* (Budapest, 1882), pp. 241, 584–5, and 686; and Transylvanian canons of 1649, no. 44 in A. Kiss, *Egyházi kánonok* (Kecskemét, 1875).

7   János Samarjai, *Helvetiai vallason levő ecclesiaknak ceremoniajokrol* (Lőcse, 1636).

8   These visitation records are in the Hungarian National Archive (Magyar Országos Levéltár, hereafter MOL), box 1907 and 1908: from three volumes of the 'Zempléni egyházmegye protocolluma' (hereafter ZEP) 1629–45, 1638–51, and 1653–72. The original copies are in the Tiszáninneni református egyházkerület nagykönyvtár kézirata (Sárospatak), vols 16–18. Some visitation records for the period under István Miskolczi Csulyak were published by Jenő Zoványi, 'Miskolczi Csulyak István zempléni ref. esperes (1629–1645) egyházlátogatási jegyzőkönyvei' in *Történelmi Tár* (hereafter *TT*), 54 (1906), 48–102, 266–313, and 368–407.

Instructions from the early seventeenth century for visitation parties in Zemplén laid down that the standards of maintenance of the church building, graveyard, minister's house and sacramental plate were to be thoroughly investigated. A check had also to be made on all church property, and on the income paid to each parish minister. Visitors were to gather the local congregation together and to inquire about the minister's soundness of doctrine, diligence in teaching and catechizing, conduct of the sacraments, care of church property, and personal conduct. An investigation was also to be made into the behaviour of the local schoolmaster and his students. The minister was then questioned about his congregation's attendance at services and at communion, about their general behaviour, and about the punishments handed down by the local authorities for different offences.[9]

The disciplinary reports of the clergy about their congregations, and the findings of visitations on general standards in Zemplén varied enormously during the early seventeenth century. The first visitations completed by archdeacon István Miskolczi Csulyak in 1629 revealed widespread abuses and a lack of standardized punishment, or no punishment at all, by local justices and councils of many sins emphasized as important by the Reformed clergy. Annual visitations continued under Miskolczi's leadership until his death in 1645, then under János Simándi and Pál Tarczali. By the 1650s it became more common for reports from parishes in Zemplén to contain praise both from the congregation about their minister, and from the minister about his people. This, on the evidence of outspoken reports in previous years, can hardly be attributed to reticence on the part of members of the Zemplén Reformed community to criticize one another. Visitations by Pál Tarczali in 1655 and 1656 seem to have gone particularly well, with comparatively little scandal reported, and congregations even complimented on their diligent attendance at church services.[10]

The central aim of Reformed spiritual discipline was to discourage sin and to encourage repentance, and the main deterrent used to this end was punishment by public shaming. On frequent occasions however the standards of punishment and ritual public humiliation which the Zemplén archdeacons were encouraging their ministry to apply, were baulked at by many parishioners who tried to evade making public repentance for their sins during church services. Sometimes not

---

[9] Jenő Zoványi (ed.), 'A zempléni ref. dioecesis egyházlátogatási kerdőpontjai', *Protestáns Szemle*, 17 (1906), 40–1.

[10] Reports from Szécs, Lasztócz, Velete, Radvány, Kajata and Fűzér in 1655, and from Karcsa, Kövesd, Szerdahely and Luda in 1656, ZEP/1653–72, pp. 75–81, and 126–30.

only ordinary parishioners but local law enforcers as well refused to co-operate with the Church. In 1639 at the village of Kápolna, the minister reported that the local justice and council were not punishing swearing or fornication at all, and that theft in the area only resulted in a fine of alcoholic drink donated by the offender for the rest of the village to enjoy. Individuals who resisted the Church could, however, invite more severe sanctions to be directed against them. A justice in Zétény for example had been required by his minister to repent publicly, but refused to do so, and while on visitation the archdeacon advised that if the justice died without making a public confession of his faults, then he was not to be given an honourable funeral.[11]

The majority of discipline cases reported by ministers in Zemplén to their superiors on visitation involved some failure to keep moral or behavioural standards, but there were also incidences of more purely religious offences. Individuals were commonly accused of non-attendance at church services and communion, and whole congregations were frequently rebuked for tardy attendance, particularly at weekday services. The minister at Bénye in 1635 noted that there were sometimes only three people present in his congregation, and that many did not attend church on the slightest pretext. Threats were also made against Ambrus Vajda who nevertheless absolutely refused to attend his local church, saying that even if they killed him he did not want to go. The visitors instructed the local council that the church bell should not be rung at Vajda's death and he was not to be buried in the graveyard, the classic marks of a so-called 'ass's funeral'. There were also frequent complaints by visitors about the state in which churches were kept, with some described as smelly, and others being used to store meat. Objections were also raised by ministers about the behaviour of congregations once at church. In Ricse in 1639 for example the minister protested that there was always shouting or noise near the church during prayers and services, and that he wanted his congregation to depart quietly after services and not to stand around 'contending with one another'.[12]

Throughout the course of visitations in Zemplén during the early seventeenth century a crusade conducted by the Reformed clergy against foul language, cursing and blasphemous swearing stood out as the most prominent aspect of the campaign against public immorality. Zemplén's archdeacons and clergy wanted to stiffen the punishment for swearing, oaths invoking the devil, blasphemies in 'sayings about the spirit' and 'sayings about baptism', and generally foul and sexually explicit lan-

---

11   *TT*, 54 (1906), 304, 312 and 371; ZEP/1638–51, March 1648; ZEP/1653–72, February 1656, pp. 112–13, and 115.
12   *TT*, 54 (1906), 56, 71, 85, 301, and 402.

guage. In Kisazar in 1648, the minister accused his congregation of 'devilish and abominable blasphemies', and a list of names which the son of János Horvát used at Szilvásujfalu in 1651 included 'son of the devil, son of the devil's wife, son of a devil-given whore, and son of a thieving whore'. It was also noticeable that women were commonly those reported using the spirit of God, or their own spirit and baptized status in oaths and blasphemous curses.[13]

It proved very difficult however for the Reformed ministry to gain acceptance in Zemplén for the standards of language which they wished to impose. When for example the minister at Viss tried to reprimand a girl guilty of blaspheming, he was upbraided by the girl's mother for doing so. However the archdeacons exerted pressure on local clergy to urge more rigorous punishment by civil discipliners of swearing and blaspheming. At Horvát in 1629 István Miskolczi Csulyak found that blasphemous swearing was not being punished at all by the local justice, while at Szőlőske such offenders had their hands placed in the stocks. Miskolczi thought that even this punishment was insufficient, since he reasoned that the mouth and not the hands had offended, and therefore the offender's neck needed to be put in the stocks. Miskolczi indeed suggested that one oath or blasphemous saying should be punished by the person remaining in the stocks for the duration of a sermon, for two offences the offender should stay in the stocks until the evening, and on the third occasion the culprit was to be beaten as well.[14] The minister at Toronya reported, however, that while the custom in his locality was for swearing to be punished by a place in the stocks, 'when they want to punish someone lightly, they gather together and make him pay for drink, and if there is little to drink, they demand more from him, and then drink until they are drunk'. Better news was reported to the archdeacon at Kozma in 1641, where blasphemy led to the offender's head being put in the stocks and a beating, and at Kazsu in 1639 where offenders stood in the stocks and were publicly rebuked by the minister.[15]

---

[13] Women were those seen to have been blaspheming at Gálszécs in June 1641, *TT*, 54 (1906), 387, and at Saava in 1648, ZEP/1638–51, pp. 100–1, 147 and 219. Pál Medgyesi included sayings which showed lack of honour for God's name, such as 'God preserve you', and 'God help you' as well as oaths such as 'devil spirited', 'my spirit, my spirit', and 'God overcome you' in *Igaz magyar nép negyedik jajja s-siralma* (Sárospatak, 1657), pp. 17–18.

[14] *TT*, 54 (1906), 59, 269, and 285. Blasphemy was weakly punished at Olaszi in 1629, Pelete in 1632, Zsadány in 1633, Ujlak, Jesztreb and Szőlőske in 1636, Rozvágy, Imreg and Redmecz in 1639, *TT*, 54 (1906), 51, 53–4, 277, 279, 287–8, 290, 300, 309, and 370. At Szerdahely and Kápolna in 1639, Miskolczi found that cursing was not punished at all, *TT*, 54 (1906), 305, and 371.

[15] *TT*, 54 (1906), 273, and 384.

The punishment of offences such as swearing could vary according to the social status of the transgressor. At Szilvásujfalu in 1639, ordinary people were put in the stocks and beaten for swearing, while jurymen could pay off punishment by a fine of wine to be provided for the community. In November 1638 Miskolczi commented on the punishment handed out to blasphemers at Olaszi, that although offenders were sometimes placed by their hands in the stocks, members of the local council were only punished by providing one forint's worth of drink. In 1641 the archdeacon attempted to change this customary punishment, and at Vitány and Kajata recommended that the one forint fine for theft, blasphemous swearing, and other roguery should not be drunk in wine, but instead the money should be set aside for the common use of the village.[16] This picture of mixed enforcement of punishments, and only partial acceptance by local élites of the punitive requirements of the Reformed Church continued during the visitations of the 1640s and 1650s. At Pelejte in June 1641 the minister and local nobility had come to an agreement to outlaw swearing and curses. Those who offended were to have their necks placed in the stocks, and if they made any difficulty, they would also have to pay one forint to be used by the village. However in two neighbouring villages, Izsép and Lasztócz, swearing was still not even recognized as a sin, and went completely unpunished by the local authorities.[17]

Drink and drunkenness were also viewed by the Reformed clergy to be serious problems in Zemplén's parishes, with scandals usually centred on local taverns. The Reformed clergy acted to enforce tighter standards on the availability of drink, and to reform customary behaviour at festivals. At Olaszi in 1650 the minister complained about the behaviour of Gergely Bolyko, whom he knew often went to the local pub on Sunday afternoons. The minister was particularly annoyed since he thought Bolyko, as a juryman, should have been setting an example to others. Christmas drinking was reported against the youth of Hotyka in 1629, as were the taverns set up at Whitsun in Toronya and at the castle of Gercsely. At Ujváros in 1632 a scandalous festival tavern was reported with beer-drinking, dancing, and whistling. Meanwhile at Szécs the servants of local nobles organized holiday taverns, and had prevented the local justice from punishing anyone for it, while at Nagyazar in 1635 there had been fighting at Christmas in the tavern, and a certain Jancsi Kotnyeles had demonstrated his reputed magical skills.[18]

---

16   *TT*, 54 (1906), 76, 82, 97, 99, 296, 372, and 383.
17   *TT*, 54 (1906), 388, 396, and 406.
18   ZEP/1638–51, p. 187; In Hotyka at Easter in 1629, *TT*, 54 (1906), 56, 59, 63, 73, and 275–7. The pub at Kajata was causing problems in 1648, and at Bári in 1648, those

New disciplinary rigour, if not altogether higher standards, were being slowly introduced across Zemplén county by the conscientious application of visitation rights by its archdeacons to supervise standards of public morality, and encourage punishments of public shaming for blasphemy, foul language, drinking and festival immorality. Close attention was also paid by visiting senior clergy to sexual morality, the behaviour of the unmarried, and to problems concerning marriage. A major area of concern in the protection of village morality was the winter attraction to young men provided by spinning-rooms. Zemplén's archdeacons consistently repeated encouragements to local ministers to have this practice stopped altogether, or at least to have it controlled since it was 'nothing other, than a cover for roguery'. At Szentes in 1629 István Miskolczi Csulyak intoned that 'the spinning-room is forbidden amongst Christians. It gives opportunities for wrong-doing'. However at Zétény in 1639 Miskolczi conceded that if the locals were determined to spin together, then it should at least take place in an honourable home and absolutely no men were to be admitted.[19]

The Zemplén visitation records also show a consistent drive to create a harsher climate of discipline against fornicators. Fornication was punished by the civil authorities before offenders came to church to offer public repentance, and the clergy wanted their initial punishment by justices to be severe. At Szerdahely in 1629 weak punishment for fornication was criticized, and the archdeacon demanded that the hands of sinners be beaten so that they cried out in pain. When fornicating youths in Jesztreb were unwilling to undergo public repentance, the visitation party ordered that if any of them died without repenting they would not receive a proper burial. There were still however villages in Zemplén where punishment was apparently not handed out at all to fornicators, such as Rad in 1629 where fornicators, thieves and false believers were reported not to have received any public discipline, nor at Battyán where the local noble patron was deemed to be at fault for failing to punish fornication.[20]

Apart from offering instructions on the desired punishment regime for sexual immorality, difficult cases were also reported to visiting senior clergy for advice. In Toronya suspicion of a woman whose house was frequented by local students sparked an immediate investigation,

---

who had resorted to the devil were to be excluded from the congregation until they recognized their fault, ZEP/1638–51, pp. 145, and 150–1.

[19] Imreg in 1639, *TT*, 54 (1906), 309; Also Szentes, Kajata, Szilvásujfalu, and Szécskeresztur in 1629; Pelete, Nagyrozvágy, Kozma in 1632; Ujlak in 1636, and Zétény in 1639; *TT*, 54 (1906), 66, 68, 70, 89, 96, 275, 277, 287, and 304.

[20] *TT*, 54 (1906), 87, 89, 90, and 96.

while the visitation of Sárospatak in 1641 revealed an extraordinary case of bigamy, where the wife of Tamás Magyar was found to have another husband living in Tarczal, while Tamás Magyar himself was revealed to have two other wives. Other problematic marriage cases were also reported to church visitors, and divorces and marriage annulments were usually investigated by local clergy synods with requests for divorce normally successful only on the grounds of impotence, adultery, bigamy or abandonment. Secret promises of engagement, and the secret exchange of signs of engagement between a couple were strictly forbidden, and such cases were brought before the regional synod for official annulment. For example, in 1641 the Zemplén synod held at Sárospatak heard a case from Szerdahely where György Békési asked to be freed from an engagement on the grounds that he had been bound by diabolical possession. The Church synod agreed to his request, and required that the gifts exchanged between the couple had to be returned in front of the minister, and also ordered that the parties undertake to be publicly reconciled.[21]

The archdeacons of Zemplén and their local clergy also battled to have punishments enforced in cases of theft, scandals, quarrelling and violent arguments. Visitations revealed examples where the punishment of thieves gave the archdeacons grounds for concern. Bee thieves in Viss had been fined by their local justice, but István Miskolczi Csulyak noted they had not yet made public repentance, while at Zétény in 1639, Miskolczi found that there were thieves who had made public repentance three times, yet still continued in their activities. A more satisfactory case was recorded at Zsadány in 1639 with a pig thief called György Kovács, who had been punished by the civil authorities, and had since lived such a godly life that the archdeacon released him from the necessity of public repentance and confession, and from the humiliation of a ministerial rebuke. Meanwhile local disputes ranged from petty quarrels, fights, and arguing, again especially recorded among women, to more serious cases involving violence. The unruly also came under scrutiny during visitations such as the 'violin-playing and drinking cobblers' living in a house in Szőlőske in 1635, or the 'women of bad repute' at Nagyrozvágy in 1629 who were to be punished for fear that they would bring sin into the village.[22]

In various localities across Hungary and Transylvania during the early seventeenth century increasing pressure was being placed upon traditional methods of social disciplining to produce a tighter regime in

---

21   *TT*, 54 (1906), 71, 80, 267, 273, 372, and 380.
22   *TT*, 54 (1906), 60, 63, 96, 304, and 313.

line with the demands of the Reformed Church. This resulted in some places in the organic reform of traditional local authorities, and elsewhere in the adoption of lay presbyteries. In western Hungary the Reformed Church had a comparatively decentralized administration, and Catholic repression and fear of the Turks hampered the progress of visitations. In the face of such difficulties the example of foreign Reformed churches in local administration was consciously copied by the minister at Pápa, János Kanizsai Pálfi, who in 1616 gained the support of his noble patron to follow the Heidelberg model of presbyterial church government. The presbyters subsequently appointed at Pápa were given the responsibility for the good running of church services and sacraments, as well as looking after order and discipline. In 1630 Kanizsai, as superintendent of the western Hungarian Church, also led a synod at Pápa which adopted presbyteries as the model for church government in all of western Hungary.[23]

Kanizsai moved to Kiskomárom in 1634 and began a *senatus ecclesiasticus* there, with 11 presbyters to look after moral discipline, and be vigilant to maintain order in the town. The first meeting of the presbytery was held in the Kiskomárom church in August 1634, and was attended by the local deputy commander of the town's garrison. The presbytery subsequently spent much of its time reconciling disputes and petty arguments between family members and neighbours. In December 1634, for example, an unmarried woman was reprimanded for being short-tempered, and in August 1635 János Szabó was warned to live peaceably with his wife. Punishments regularly handed down by the presbytery included demands for repentance in church, and formal public rebukes of offenders in front of the whole presbytery. Such public humiliation was not viewed as a soft option, with for example the Kiskomárom presbyters hearing a case in March 1635 against the wife of Gergely Szakos, who had been caught with a young man at night. It was noted that she had been sentenced to death for this by the civil authorities in Kiskomárom, but the presbytery instead enforced three Sundays of public penance, to be followed by a full public confession. The woman was required to stand alone at the outer door of the church, and to wear sober clothing. She was specifically warned that this repentance must be shown to be sincere taking into account the seriousness of her offence. Similarly a thief in June 1635 was sentenced to be hanged, but the presbytery imposed three weeks of public penance in church, to be followed by a public confession of his sins over a

---

[23] E. Thury, *A dunántúli református egyházkerület története* (Pápa, 1908), pp. 179–87. János Pokoly, 'Az első magyar ref. presbyterium keletkezése és szervezete', *Protestáns Szemle*, 2 (1890), 202–20.

further four weeks. The presbytery had quickly established its authority in the town, and in July 1635 the town justice consulted the presbyters on how to tighten local disciplinary policies. Kanizsai and the presbytery suggested the outlawing and harsher punishment of blasphemous swearing, and better protection of the Sabbath, with a prohibition on the passage of carts into the town on Sundays, and on religious festivals. The presbytery also wanted to prevent pubs from opening until the end of afternoon church services, and a ban on wine-selling after eight in the evening.[24]

Presbyterial discipline did not however transfer easily to the more hierarchical church structure of eastern Hungary and Transylvania. Support for presbyteries in the east came from a section of the Reformed clergy, driven not merely by the conviction that lay presbyters offered the prospect of better control over public behaviour than even the most conscientious archdeacon ever could, but also by the assertion that presbyterial government formed an inescapable part of a properly organized Reformed Church. However the national synod of all Hungarian and Transylvanian church districts meeting at Szatmár in 1646, while accepting the usefulness of presbyteries, decided that the time was not yet right for their general introduction. Presbyterial church government however remained a live issue into the 1650s, supported by noble patrons such as the dowager princess Zsuzsanna Lórántffy and her younger son, Zsigmond Rákóczi, and promoted by reform-minded ministers. Some of these ministers found themselves described as puritans, and supporters of presbyteries were frequently accused of hypocrisy with claims that their excessive disciplinary ambitions were in fact merely a cover for personal immorality. In 1654 for example an anonymous complaint was received by the Transylvanian prince, II. György Rákóczi, against the presbytery set up by Zsuzsanna Lórántffy at Sárospatak. Presbyters at Sárospatak had apparently excommunicated some nobles, and stood accused of grasping power from local civil magistrates and ruling 'on the necks of the congregation', 'prohibiting every Christian conversation, youthful pleasure, and honourable enjoyment' with 'pharisaical holiness'.[25]

Disagreements among the Reformed clergy over church government, and over how to involve the ordinary laity in church disciplining, were matched by conflicts between the increasingly assertive claims of the clergy for authority in localities as discipliners, and the demands of

---

[24]   Dunántul Református Egyház Levéltár (hereafter, DREL/Pápa), no. 131, 'A kiskomáromi ref. egyházközség legrégébbi anyakönyve 1624–1732', pp. 198–208.

[25]   S. Szilágyi (ed.), 'Levelek és okiratok II. Rákóczy György fejedelem diplomacziai összeköttetései történetéhez', in *TT*, 37 (1889), 475–9.

nobles to exercise their traditional rights in the administration of justice. In November 1641 the noble assembly of Szatmár county in eastern Hungary forwarded an 11-point complaint to their local Reformed Church, with concerns that the Church's drive for discipline was infringing upon traditional noble rights and privileges. The Szatmár nobility complained about the use of excommunication as a disciplinary tool, demanding that public repentance not be imposed on the nobility, especially not for so-called minor offences such as if a noble killed someone in self-defence. The noble assemblies in the neighbouring Szabolcs, Bereg, and Ugocsa counties supported their colleagues in Szatmár, and jointly forwarded their grievances to the 1642 general synod of the eastern Tisza church. The synod in response demanded full public repentance for sins regardless of the rank of the offender, but conceded that for minor theft public penance might not be necessary for nobles.[26] The eastern Tisza church was supported by the archdeacons of northern Hungary who asserted that the proposals of the noble assemblies were 'ill-considered', and that there were many in Hungary who disregarded the authority of the Church, or who tried to destroy it completely. The archdeacons confirmed the scriptural and historical basis of the Church's sole rights over excommunication free from the intervention of 'kings, landowners, nobles, or royal constitutions'.[27]

Hungarian nobles were not however completely unsympathetic to the ambitions of the Reformed disciplinary crusade, and in 1653 the noble assembly of Szabolcs county drew up a new punishment code. Among the measures of this code, blasphemous swearing was made punishable, in the first instance, by a period in the stocks and a beating, and, after a second offence, landowners were to place offenders in irons, have them beaten with a cane, and then the blasphemer was to be compelled to undergo public repentance. The nobility of Hungary and Transylvania were being urged not only by the clergy hierarchy but also by the prince, to tighten the punishment of immorality, and to put into effect regulations of this kind. In October 1654 II. György Rákóczi wrote to the Szatmár county nobility expressing his concern at the daily growth in swearing and immoral behaviour, and ordering them not to impede the work of the clergy or prevent the prosecution of sin and evil-doing. In response the noble assembly denied that they were in any way restricting the activities of the church, but indicated that the problems of the 1640s with the clergy of their county had still not been resolved.

---

[26] 'Debrecen egyházmegye jegyzőkönyvei' vol. 1, 1615–1655, at the MOL box, 1884, pp. 442–5.
[27] ZEP/1629–45, pp. 380, and 384–6.

> In those things which affect the direction of the church and disci-
> pline, we [the Szatmár nobility] are servants of the true church, of
> which we are members, but we are not aware by which privilege
> the clergy of whatever rank can impose things on us by themselves,
> without our knowledge and will, and set every direction of the
> church by themselves. About which we could have made our com-
> plaints; but we do not wish to burden Your Grace with an enu-
> meration of them.[28]

The tensions which arose between the increasingly assertive disciplinary force of the Reformed clergy, and a nobility accepting the need for
discipline, yet on occasions defensive in the face of clerical power, were
experienced at first hand by Zsigmond Lónyai, a high sheriff in the
eastern Tisza region. In letters to I. György Rákóczi in 1646, Lónyai
related that he had been brought under discipline by his own minister,
and was not allowed to travel freely, because of a claim that he had
failed to punish local miscreants quickly enough. Lónyai wrote that

> in so far as in other Reformed churches there is a lay presbytery to
> bridle ministers, I cannot disapprove of it, with relation to the way
> in which they [the clergy] are beginning to dominate over us, which
> has never been the case before, but only since God encouraged
> Your Grace the prince to be on their side, ... and if Your Grace
> does not take care over the lords and nobility, then some of the
> clergy will gladly dominate us, ... and I do not know what to do
> with them, if Your merciful Grace does not assist us.[29]

However the impression given by Lónyai that the nobility needed support against the clergy, was exactly contrary to that given to the new
prince II. György Rákóczi in a 1648 letter from the four archdeacons of
the northern Tisza district. The archdeacons reminded the prince of the
approach made by the eastern Hungarian nobles against the church in
1642 as a sorrowful example of how the nobility, 'want to take for
themselves a free life, and using all their ability want to pull themselves
from under every discipline of the church'. The archdeacons argued that
neither the authority of archdeacons nor superintendents could com-
pensate for this recalcitrance, and that only the prince could bring the
Hungarian nobility completely under Reformed Church discipline.[30]

The early seventeenth century witnessed the building-up of the Reformed clergy in Hungary and Transylvania as a class of discipliners,

---

[28]   The code of 1653 in 'Liber Protocolaris Venerabilis Districtus Szatmariensis ab
anno 1670 inchoatus', pp. 119–20, and 156, published by K. Kiss, *A szatmári reform.
egyházmegye története* (Kecskemét, 1878), p. 12.

[29]   A letter of 19 June 1646, in S. Szilágyi (ed.), 'Lónyay Zsigmond pere saját
papjaival', *Magyar Protestáns Egyházi és Iskolai Figyelmez*, 8 (1886), 147–9.

[30]   A letter of April 1648 in L. Hegedüs, 'A zempléni helv. hitv. egyházmegye
jegyzőkönyvéből', *Sárospataki Füzetek*, 1 (1857–58), 472–3.

bringing increased devotion and enthusiasm to the cause of curbing immoral behaviour. There was also an ever stricter regime of control over the clergy themselves during this period. There were detailed rules on behaviour in Reformed schools and from synods, governing the lives of Reformed students and ministers. Reformed ministers were becoming increasingly socially distinct as an order, with ministers often coming from the same families. Instructions from synods concerning the dress and activities appropriate for ministers and their families represented a concerted effort during this period to set the clergy apart from the rest of society. The social status of ministers was enhanced by this stricter regulation and better education, but this process also brought increased isolation from congregations and the clergy became on occasions the targets of resentful criticism from below.

The early seventeenth century saw a series of new and revised regulations adapted from German models for the expanding network of Reformed schools in Hungary and Transylvania. This raft of regulations was preoccupied with appropriate and morally proper dress for students, which also allowed Reformed students to be easily distinguishable from the rest of urban youth. In 1624 the school orders at Debrecen, for example, described a compulsory uniform for its students of a long ankle length cloak, a green toga highlighted with yellow cord, and a high fur cap with green trimming. Students were not allowed to go bare-headed like Turks, nor wear Tatar hats, nor soldier's clothing, and were to avoid wide belts, and only wear black or white gloves. If any student did not comply with any of these regulations he could be expelled from the college.[31] Hungarian and Transylvanian Reformed Church synods were also very concerned to regulate dress, and made frequent pronouncements on approved clothing for teachers, ministers, and their wives. Transylvanian canons from 1606 advised that clergy clothing be appropriate and lacking in luxury, and in 1638 a synod at Nagyenyed ordered ministers never to wear boots. In 1642 another Transylvanian synod at Nagyenyed threatened expulsion from the ministry for those who wore inappropriate clothes, particularly velvet, or coloured and decorated clothing, but an exception was made for the superintendent, court preachers and senior archdeacons.[32]

---

[31] István Juhász and Zsigmond Jakó, *Nagyenyedi diákok, 1662–1848* (Bucharest, 1979), pp. 5–46. R. Békéfi (ed.), 'A sárospataki ev. ref. főiskola 1621–iki törvényei', *Értekezések a Történelmi Tudományok Köréből*, 18 (3), (Budapest, 1899), 54–61. R. Békéfi (ed.), *A debreczeni ev. ref. főiskola xvii. és xviii. századi törvényei* (Budapest, 1899), pp. 87–97. G. Lampérth, *A pápai református főiskola története, 1531–1931* (Pápa, 1931), pp. 21–35.

[32] Sándor Payr, *A magyar protestáns papi öltöny története* (Sopron, 1935). 1567 Debrecen articles, no. 67; 1570 Szatmár synod, no. 48; the 1577 Nagyvárad articles, no.

In eastern Hungary archdeacons were empowered by a synod of 1624 at Nagyvárad, to admonish those who failed to keep up to expected standards of dress. Teachers and students were allowed to wear short-heeled boots in winter, or when it was muddy, but were not to wear fur. In 1630 a synod at Debrecen ordered ministers to wear clothes 'appropriate to their order', strictly outlawing the wearing of boots, shorter decorated fur-lined coats or golden collars. In 1632 by order of the Zemplén area synod, iron-shod boots and short fur-lined coats were forbidden for ministers, 'so that people go about in clothes appropriate to their office'. The dress of ministers' wives too was subjected to detailed scrutiny, and articles prohibited clergy wives from any luxury or immoderation in dress and hairstyles. In 1624 the synod at Nagyvárad ordered ministers' wives to avoid wearing golden shirts or rings, red or yellow boots, wide fur belts or straps, short-sheepskin coats or multi-layered skirts. In 1642, meanwhile, a Transylvanian synod at Nagyenyed ordered clergy wives to avoid golden robes and luxurious clasps, pearls or any neck decoration, and boots that diverged from normal fashions.[33]

There were therefore not only warnings against decorative, immoderate and inappropriate clothing, but also a deliberate attempt to make ministers easily visually distinguishable from other orders. The Köveskút synod in 1612 instructed ministers to be discernably different from traders, soldiers and cobblers, in particular recommending long gowns and cloaks of 'an appropriate colour for their office'. The 1649 Transylvanian canons included an order for ministers' dress to be distinguishable both from Anabaptists, and from the excessive splendour of Catholic priests. It was not however only in dress that ministers and their families, Reformed teachers and student ministers were to be distinct, but also in their language, general deportment, activities at work, and in recreation. Transylvanian canons detailed how ministers' lives were to be temperate and sober, exemplary in personal relationships, beyond reproach in conversation, and avoiding secular preoccu-

---

7 all in A. Kiss, *A XVI. században tartott magyar református zsinatok végzései* (Budapest, 1882). Results of Transylvanian synods of 1606, 1638 and 1642 in István Szilágyi, 'Az erdélyi anyaszentegyház közzsinatainak végzései kivonatban', *Magyar Protestáns Egyházi és Iskolai Figyelmező* (hereafter *MPEIF*) 3 (1872), 1–9, 77–84, and 473–9. Transylvanian canons of 1649, nos 83, 94 and 96; and conclusions of the 1646 synod, no. 28, in A. Kiss, *Egyházi kánonok* (Kecskemét, 1875).

33 János Lugossy, 'Constitutiones in generali synodo varadina anno 1624, 1 die Julii', *Protestáns Egyházi és Iskolai Lap* 6 (1847), pp. 235–6. ZEP/1629–45, pp. 147–63. Debrecen articles of 1567, no. 43 in A. Kiss, *Zsinatok végzései*, pp. 563–613. Transylvanian canons of 1649, no. 84, in A. Kiss, 'Egyházi kánonok', *MPEIF* 3 (1872), 1–9, 77–84, 473–9.

pations. Swearing and arguing, particularly with other ministers, was specifically forbidden, with good company advised, and conversations to be engaged in only to build up neighbours and friends. All usury and business trading was prohibited as ministers were not to 'sink into the problems of life'. The clergy were neither allowed to keep weapons, hawks nor hunting dogs, since instead they were to be 'fishers of men'. Ministers were also prevented by canons from taking part in singing and dancing, and articles from the late sixteenth century ordered that if a minister was invited to a party, he could freely go, but that if music and dancing began he must get up and leave the room. For those whose attitudes and actions fell short of these ideals, warnings could be given by senior clergy to disobedient ministers, to be followed ultimately by dismissal from office.[34]

Parish ministers needed to balance successfully different constituencies of support, with clergy superiors closely monitoring their performance, local noble patrons holding annual rights of reappointment over them, and parishioners who had a direct channel of complaint to ministers' superiors during visitations. The expression of serious grievances against any minister could initiate internal church disciplinary action. Cases could be referred by archdeacons to area synods for resolution, or the archdeacon could decide on disciplinary action himself during a visitation. Some congregations did praise their ministers' behaviour and application to duties during visitations, but the willingness of congregations to complain to outside visitors reflected some breakdown in local loyalties between the parish clergy and their congregations. When dissatisfaction was expressed about ministers, drunkenness was frequently cited as the cause of neglect and immorality. Accusations against ministers included being drunk during services, and while preaching. At the village of Olaszi in Zemplén in 1629, the congregation reported that they would prefer their minister not to preach while drunk, rather than have him preach scandalously. At Sára in 1641, the minister was reported to have got so drunk one Sunday lunchtime, that he was unable to conduct the evening service. Drunkenness during services was also reported about the minister at Jesztreb in 1639, and the visitors were informed that he also argued with his wife, regularly hit her, and had been neglecting his teaching duties.[35]

---

[34] E. Thury (ed.), '1550–1617 adatok a dunántúl és felsödunamellék egyházkerületekről', *Magyar Protestáns Egyháztörténeti Adattár*, 7 (1908), 127–40. A. Kiss, *Egyházi kánonok*, 1649 canons 78–82, and resolutions of 1646, nos 14–22; Nagyvárad articles of 1577, no. 15; in A. Kiss, *Zsinatok végzései*.

[35] Accusations of drunkenness were made against the minister at Nagygéres in 1629, Zétény in 1634, Olaszi in 1638, Hotyka in 1639, Sára and Ujváros in 1641, *TT*, 54 (1906), 89–90, 199, 295, 308–9, 312, 377–9, and 385.

Reformed ministers in Hungary and Transylvania formed a class of discipliners in the early seventeenth century, increasingly tightly regulated in their duties by their own hierarchy. Reformed clergy worked in this period wherever possible in co-operation with local civil officers, to tighten moral and behavioural standards particularly on issues of language, drinking, and sexual and public morality. The array of Reformed punishments centred on public shaming and denial of access to the sacraments, aiming to encourage repentance on the part of the sinner. Only in some urban centres did a sector of local lay élites become actively involved in the exercise of spiritual discipline. On occasions when the alliance of noble and clergy power broke down, both sides appealed to the prince as the ultimate authority in the Reformed Church and in society, to come to their aid in the cause of social order. The price paid by the clergy for their leading role in disciplining Reformed communities was some popular resentment against their demands. Occasionally individuals tried to avoid or challenge spiritual punishments, and congregations were more than willing to criticize the clergy, when in turn a minister's standard of behaviour fell below what was expected. Internal disciplining of the Reformed ministry was more severe than that of anyone else during this period, and increasingly the clergy formed a class apart, ennobled as an order, frequently changing parishes, comparatively well educated, inbred, and forming an increasingly assertive disciplined and disciplining élite. This separation of the Reformed Church clergy from their congregations, was, however, essential to the moderate advances made during this period in the crusade against popular immorality, and towards achieving the Reformed Church's goal of taming Hungary and Transylvania.

CHAPTER TEN

Morals courts in rural Berne during the early modern period

Heinrich Richard Schmidt

This chapter investigates the role of the morals courts in the everyday life of the ordinary Reformed Protestant believers in Berne until the end of the eighteenth century. Our main focus is on the long-term effects, and not on the causes of the Reformation, and we stress the actions of peasants and craftsmen who, as believers, formed the church together with the pastor and who sat as elders in the morals courts. Consequently, we will be offering a view of the everyday life of the Reformed Church rather than of its doctrine or its written norms. In the second place our intention is to provide an insight into the motives and influences that may have formed the evangelical movement, seen retrospectively from the point of view of confessionalization. This chapter summarizes a detailed published study,[1] in which the presbytery records of morals courts from the canton of Berne, and the city of Biel, between 1540 and 1800, were analysed against the background of leading theories about the role of the church in early modern times.[2]

The grand theories of Max Weber, Norbert Elias and Gerhard Oestreich have all explained the development of European culture in the early modern period through similar concepts.[3] They all assume a more or less linear process of 'modernization'. The thesis of Oestreich is of particular importance since research into confessionalization, which is the focus of my own study, has adopted it as an essential paradigm.

---

[1] Heinrich Richard Schmidt, *Dorf und Religion. Reformierte Sittenzucht in Berner Landgemeinden der Frühen Neuzeit* (Stuttgart, Jena, New York, 1995).

[2] I will not repeat the apparatus of footnotes taken from the book, but mention only some of the most important titles. Facts taken from the study itself, especially those depending on the examination of the Bernese archives, will not be noted. I thank Dr Wulf von Lucius for his permission to take the English summary of the book as basis for this essay. Mark Furner was very helpful with the English translation of the text.

[3] Schmidt, *Dorf*, pp. 360–75 for a detailed discussion of their concepts. For a first approach see Schmidt, 'Die Christianisierung des Sozialverhaltens als permanente Reformation. Aus der Praxis reformierter Sittengerichte in der Schweiz während der frühen Neuzeit', in Peter Blickle and Johannes Kunisch (eds), *Kommunalisierung und Christianisierung* (Zeitschrift für Historische Forschung, Supplement 9, Berlin, 1989), pp. 113–63.

Gerhard Oestreich has described the process of the diffusion of civilized standards as 'social disciplining'. Disciplining was a long-term process, which began with the employees of the absolutist states, the army and the civil servants (*Stabsdisziplinierung*),[4] but during the eighteenth century widened into a disciplining of the whole society (*Fundamentaldisziplinierung*).[5] All these disciplining processes, according to Oestreich, 'combine together into a forceful process of empowerment that fundamentally changed the basic structures of political, social and intellectual life, concentrating them towards a central authority'.[6] Oestreich's ideas are marked by a bias towards the state and by their teleological character. He accordingly attributes the crucial role in the modernization of human character (in Europe) to the state-enforced impulse towards discipline. His concept is therefore very 'etatist'.[7] The contribution of the church is seen as only marginal.[8] This is purely a consequence of the concept alone, because Oestreich defines social disciplining (*Sozialdisziplinierung*) as a reaction to confessionalization.[9]

---

[4]   Gerhard Oestreich, 'Justus Lipsius als Theoretiker des neuzeitlichen Machtstaates', in Gerhard Oestreich, *Geist und Gestalt des frühmodernen Staates. Ausgewählte Aufsätze* (Berlin, 1969), pp. 35–79, here p. 64; also Oestreich, 'Strukturprobleme des europäischen Absolutismus', in Oestreich, *Geist und Gestalt*, pp. 179–97, here p. 194 f., for the eighteenth century. See also Gerhard Oestreich, 'Policey und Prudentia civilis in der barocken Gesellschaft von Stadt und Staat', in his *Strukturprobleme der frühen Neuzeit. Ausgewählte Aufsätze* (Berlin, 1980), pp. 367–9, here pp. 377–9 (concerning Elias). Siegfried Breuer, 'Sozialdisziplinierung. Probleme und Problemverlagerungen eines Konzepts bei Max Weber, Gerhard Oestreich und Michel Foucault', in Christian Sachße and Friedrich Tennstedt (eds), *Soziale Sicherheit und soziale Disziplinierung* (Frankfurt am Main, 1986), pp. 45–69, here p. 55: 'Parallel dazu gewinnt der Neustoizismus auch für das "sitzende Heer" der Beamten an Bedeutung, deren höhere Ränge an den Universitäten zunehmend unter den Einfluß der "prudentia civilis" geraten, einer Morallehre, die Gehorsam und Disziplin sowie die "Meisterung der Affekte zur Bewältigung des individuellen Lebens wie zur widerstandslosen politischen Unterordnung lehrt" … [und] als Voraussetzung einer geordneten Herrschaft betont.'

[5]   Oestreich, 'Strukturprobleme des Absolutismus', p. 193 f.

[6]   Breuer, 'Sozialdisziplinierung', p. 55. All quotations in the text are translated by me. The original text is written in the footnotes, here 'Alle diese Disziplinierungsprozesse addieren sich nach Oestreich zu einem gewaltigen "Vermachtungsprozeß", der die Grundstrukturen des politischen, gesellschaftlichen und geistigen Lebens tiefgreifend umgestaltet, indem er sie auf eine Zentralinstanz hinordnet.'

[7]   Heinz Schilling, 'Die Kirchenzucht im frühneuzeitlichen Europa in interkonfessionell vergleichender und interdisziplinärer Perspektive – eine Zwischenbilanz', in Heinz Schilling (ed.), *Kirchenzucht und Sozialdisziplinierung im frühneuzeitlichen Europa* (Zeitschrift für Historische Forschung, Supplement 16, Berlin, 1994), pp. 11–40, here p. 12.

[8]   Paul Münch, *Zucht und Ordnung. Reformierte Kirchenverfassungen im 16. und 17. Jahrhundert (Nassau-Dillenburg, Kurpfalz, Hessen-Kassel)* (Stuttgart, 1978), p. 183, note 61.

[9]   Oestreich, 'Strukturprobleme des Absolutismus', p. 189 f. On Calvin and Puritanism see ibid., p. 192.

Nevertheless research into the early modern period, in so far as it studies the influence of confession and church on social historical development, has adopted social disciplining as a central paradigm,[10] but has changed it fundamentally by integrating religion and extending the temporal space back into the years 1530–1650.[11] Confessionalization becomes, according to Wolfgang Reinhard and Heinz Schilling, part of the process of social disciplining and the indoctrination of people with religion, Christian norms and morality, primarily through the morals courts and presbyteries, its essential means.[12] The amalgam of paradigms thus formed – the combination of confessionalization and social disciplining – is of German origin, but claims European validity.[13] Through a 'criminalization of sin' – that is the message – confessionalization becomes an agent of absolutism at the expense of communal self-regulation.[14] The individuals and the village and city communes were 'virtually overrun by the "apparatus" of the early modern state and the confessional churches. In the cities and the villages the people increasingly got the clear impression of being exposed to an inescapable influence from "above"'.[15]

Besides this form of confessionalization, there was a niche-variant: the self-made, not state-enforced, church discipline of the autonomous communal churches of the Huguenots, of the Dutch and of some North German churches such as Emden, in which 'the church congregation was not only the object, but equally the subject, of church discipline'.[16] But

---

[10]   For the reinterpretation of Oestreich's concept through research into confessionalization see Schilling, 'Die Kirchenzucht', p. 12.

[11]   Winfried Schulze, 'Gerhard Oestreichs Begriff "Sozialdisziplinierung in der frühen Neuzeit"', *Zeitschrift für Historische Forschung*, 14 (1987), 265–301.

[12]   Wolfgang Reinhard, 'Zwang zur Konfessionalisierung? Prolegomena zu einer Theorie des konfessionellen Zeitalters', *Zeitschrift für Historische Forschung*, 10 (1983), 257–77, here p. 268. Heinz Schilling, *Aufbruch und Krise. Deutschland 1517–1648* (Berlin, 1988), p. 274; see also p. 366.

[13]   Heinz Schilling, 'The Reformation and the rise of the Early Modern state', in James D. Tracy (ed.), *Luther and the Modern State in Germany* (Kirksville, 1986), pp. 21–30, here pp. 23, 24 f., 30. See Heinz Schilling, '"History of Crime" or "History of Sin"?', in E. I. Kouri and Tom Scott (eds), *Politics and Society in Reformation Europe* (London, 1987), pp. 289–310, esp. pp. 297–306.

[14]   Schilling, 'History of Sin', pp. 297, 304.

[15]   Heinz Schilling, 'Konfessionalisierung im Reich. Religiöser und gesellschaftlicher Wandel in Deutschland zwischen 1555 und 1620', *Historische Zeitschrift*, 246 (1988) 1–45, here p. 43: 'durch den neuzeitlichen "Apparat" des frühmodernen Staates und der Konfessionskirchen geradezu überfahren … In den Städten und Dörfern gewannen die Menschen immer deutlicher den Eindruck, einer unentrinnbaren Einwirkung von "oben" ausgesetzt zu sein.'

[16]   Schilling, 'History of Sin', p. 297. See also his 'Reformierte Kirchenzucht als Sozialdisziplinierung? Die Tätigkeit des Emder Presbyteriums in den Jahren 1557–1562',

these phenomena were marginal to the mainstream drift towards absolutism. Through the amalgamation of the two concepts of social disciplining and confessionalization, the latter is given an 'etatist' touch. It becomes an action enforced by the State, strongly and effectively exercised to change popular culture along the lines defined by the élites.[17] One thing, concluded Heinz Schilling, 'must be said of all three confessionalizations – they were the actions of the princes'.[18] The theory of Oestreich is very close to the acculturation thesis of French historiogaphy, which postulates a struggle of élite culture against popular culture.[19]

However, Schilling recently expressed doubts, calling for a reconsideration of the role of the communes and their autochthonous efforts towards discipline even in a state–church system.[20] This is an important anti-etatist turn,[21] through which he withdraws from the standpoint of Wolfgang Reinhard, who repeated his position of 1983[22] in 1993 unchanged.[23]

One can summarize the research on Central European confessionalization by postulating two main emphases for the work of morals courts:

---

in Heinz Schilling and Winfried Ehbrecht (eds), *Niederlande und Nordwestdeutschland. Studien zur Regional- und Stadtgeschichte Nordwestkontinentaleuropas im Mittelalter und in der Neuzeit* (Cologne, 1983), pp. 261–327, here pp. 273, 275 relating to Emden. He stresses, p. 275, that the commune supported church discipline.

17   Schilling, 'Konfessionalisierung', p. 6: 'Verzahnung mit der Herausbildung des frühmodernen Staates und mit der Formierung einer neuzeitlich disziplinierten Untertanenschaft.'

18   Ibid., pp. 11, 34: 'Das gilt von allen drei Konfessionalisierungen – sie waren Fürstenkonfessionalisierungen.'

19   Peter Burke, *Helden, Schurken und Narren. Europäische Volkskultur in der frühen Neuzeit* (Munich, 1985), pp. 221–5. English version as *Popular Culture in Early Modern Europe* (London, 1978). See Kaspar von Greyerz, 'Religion und Gesellschaft in der frühen Neuzeit (Einführung in Methoden und Ergebnisse der sozialgeschichtlichen Religionsforschung)', in *Religiosität – Frömmigkeit – Religion populaire* (Veröffentlichungen der Schweizerischen Gesellschaft für Wirtschafts- und Sozialgeschichte 3, 3, Lausanne, 1984), pp. 13–36, here p. 21. See also the survey of Günter Lottes, 'Popular culture in England (16.–19. Jahrhundert)', *Francia*, 11 (1984), 614–41. On popular culture studies see also Schmidt, 'Christianisierung', pp. 120–3.

20   Schilling, 'Die Kirchenzucht', pp. 30 f., 38–40; *idem*, 'History of Sin', pp. 296, 304. Geneva, with the membership of magistrats in the presbytery, looks like the etatist variant of discipline.

21   Schilling, 'Die Kirchenzucht', p. 30.

22   Reinhard, 'Zwang', p. 268.

23   Wolfgang Reinhard, 'Was ist Katholische Konfessionalisierung?', in Wolfgang Reinhard and Heinz Schilling (eds), *Die katholische Konfessionalisierung* (Gütersloh, 1995), pp. 419–52, esp. pp. 425–35. See also Wolfgang Reinhard, 'Gegenreformation als Modernisierung? Prolegomena zu einer Theorie des konfessionellen Zeitalters', *ARG*, 68 (1977), 226–52.

1. They were means by which the state disciplined an unwilling people.

2. They succeeded in discipling and civilizing the subjects, thereby creating new mentalities.[24]

Both assertions are of wide-ranging importance for the understanding of the whole epoch, even for our historical conscience. Must we understand ourselves as products of absolutism and its educational programme? Is history the effect of the élites? A study that focuses on morals courts, which have been called the 'apparatus' of social disciplining, will help to find answers and to re-examine the main paradigms of confessionalization.[25]

The object of the present study is the canton of Berne, and in it two villages near the capital, Vechigen and Stettlen.[26] Two clear differences are immediately apparent in this study: between the villages and between centuries. Vechigen is approximately 25 km² and Stettlen only 3.5 km² (see Figure 10.1). While Stettlen was mainly an enclosed village with few surrounding farmsteads, Vechigen was characterized by small villages with many individual farmsteads. Vechigen was approximately four times larger than Stettlen (in 1764, 1 569 inhabitants as against 415). Stettlen was not only smaller, but it was also clearly more densely populated and, as far as one can judge, a poorer settlement dominated by weavers. Those groups that were not in a position to live off the land formed a clear majority in Stettlen. The population there grew faster, and the productive capacity of the agricultural land was more quickly and clearly exceeded. Common lands in Stettlen were broken up earlier. Social distinctions between poor and rich were greater: 15 per cent of the population owned 70 per cent of the land, but in Vechigen, by comparison, this percentage was owned by 26–29 per cent of the population. In Stettlen the remaining population owned an average of 1.6 hectares, whereas in Vechigen the remainder owned nearly 2.7 hectares. Proto-industrialization was more intensive in Stettlen and achieved a higher proportion of the spectrum of occupations.

---

[24] For a new survey of Protestant church discipline all over Europe see Heinrich Richard Schmidt, 'Gemeinde und Sittenzucht im Europa der Frühen Neuzeit', in Peter Blickle and Elisabeth Müller-Luckner (eds), *Theorien kommunaler Ordnung in protestantischen Europa* (Munich, 1996), pp. 181–214.

[25] Ibid.

[26] See above, note 2: all the evidence is in Schmidt, *Dorf*. There is also a diskette accompanying the book, containing all relevant data in digital form (dBASE, Lotus-wks, SPSS) together with an English explanation. See also the English summary of the study: Schmidt, *Dorf*, pp. 377–400.

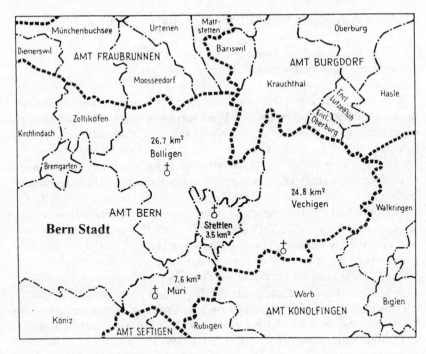

10.1 Map of the region of Berne

The difference between centuries lay in the sudden increase in the number and intensity of structural social stresses evident in both communities from the beginning of the eighteenth century. The population grew rapidly. Strangers and the poor within the community turned increasingly to proto-industrialization as a source of livelihood. Market connections became more and more prominent, whether from peasants' surplus production or from textile workers. The traditional orientation towards the village and its social controls disappeared.

In this investigation the small town of Biel, which is now part of the canton of Berne, is also included in order to take the sixteenth century into account, a period hardly touched by the rural records. Until the nineteenth century Biel belonged to the Prince-Bishopric of Basle, although it retained a largely autonomous position. Finally, data from an earlier study of the territory of Berne in Aargau is recalculated and incorporated into the discussion.[27] But the main conclusions rest on the two villages, Stettlen and Vechigen.

---

27 Willy Pfister, *Das Chorgericht des bernischen Aargaus im 17. Jahrhundert* (Aarau, 1939).

In these villages Christian discipline was exercised through the local morals courts in Berne, called *Chorgerichte*, whose aims were the enforcement of the Ten Commandments. They were implemented in the great mandates on morality, which attempted to instruct the people of God, that is the authorities and subjects of the state of Berne, how they should pay homage to the holy majesty of God.[28] God was to be honoured through the reform of morals, through obedience and piety, and through a Christian life. Those who did not honour God would suffer His severe punishment both in this world and in the next. This also affected the innocent, who did not actively resist the sins of others. The instructional appeal of the authorities to the conscience demanded repentance, conversion and improvement.

The *Chorgericht*, the local consistory, put this increased aspiration to sanctification, typical of Reformed Protestantism, into practice. It brought with it the innovation that each parish had a court staffed by parishioners. The election of elders (the *Chorrichter*) and of the *Ammann*, the *de jure* representative of the city magistrates, by the community became common after the Reformation. In sociological terms, most judges were elected from among the more wealthy farmers (represented at double the level justified by their share of the population). The judges were the local notables, the 'fat peasants' (*dicke Bauern*), who represented the whole community but could also control it (see Figure 10.2). The apparatus of the modern state, as Heinz Schilling called the morals courts, were the subjects themselves.

The prerogative of punishments held by the *Chorgericht* ranged from minor warnings to fines such as five shillings or more, prison sentences of a maximum of three days and public humiliation. Bernese *Chorgerichte* never acquired the right to excommunicate. All men and women who were brought before the local *Chorgericht*, and all their offences, that is transgressions of Christian norms, have been analysed through a detailed description and through a quantitative evaluation: a total of 12 983 male and 6 375 female offences were calculated, in all 19 358 offences. Because a person could commit more than one offence at a time, the actual number of people brought before the courts was lower: approximately 12 113 people were tried. Women formed approximately one-third of this number. In this study, the activities of the morals courts are analysed in four sections: church discipline in its narrowest

---

28   Sources with normative writings (mandates, statutes, letters) concerning state and church in Berne are published in *Sammlung Schweizerischer Rechtsquellen. Die Rechtsquellen des Kantons Bern*, part 1: Stadtrechte, vol. VI, 1 and 2: Staat und Kirche, revised by Hermann Rennefahrt (Aarau, 1960–61).

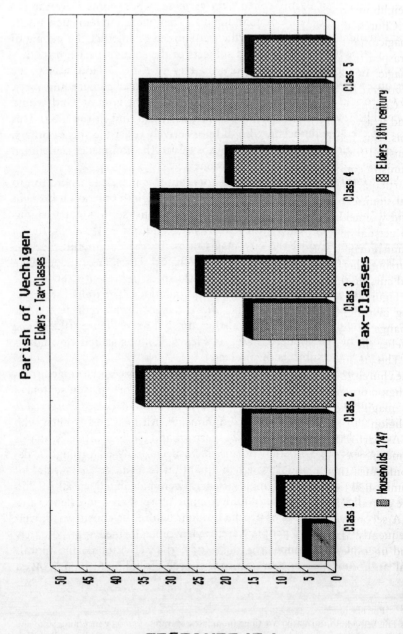

10.2 Tax classes of elders

sense, sexual discipline, matrimonial order, and the social regulation of neighbourhood relations.

Church discipline in the narrowest sense confronted paganism and magic on the outside, and battles for piety on the inside. Magical action is grasped through an analysis of cursing, which is essentially word-based magic. Witchcraft and casting magic spells were not brought before the *Chorgericht* of Biel, Stettlen or Vechigen, in contrast to cursing.

Cursing means the malediction of another in order to cause harm, and is a verbal form of harmful magic.[29] Common scolding is close to this, but has little to do with magic. Everyday oaths can be distinguished from cursing, in the period of this study, by the severity of the punishment meted out. The high female proportion of 'heavy cursing' is particularly worthy of note: in Vechigen, which is of particular statistical significance, the relation of men to women severely punished is 1:2 and women, who were less often accused, were four times more likely to get harsh punishments than men (see Figure 10.3). If the degree of punishment is a measure of the magical, blasphemous quality of the cursing, then women were clearly more imputed to be inclined to magical cursing than men.

Figure 10.4 represents the proportion of severe punishments changing in time, again divided along the lines of gender. It describes the change as a 'decline of magic' – a conclusion that is very similar to the Weber thesis of rationalization or the demagification of the world.

The 'decline of magic' is, however, no smooth victory for religion and the church.[30] The demagification intended by confessionalization dragged religion down with it, because this was subject to the same secularization as magic: the 'decline of magic' is at the same time the 'decline of religion'.

As part of the results of the social-historical analysis, one can determine in the first place that women were clearly more religious and conformist than men. They were three times less likely than men to be summoned for transgressions. They demonstrated a greater affinity for the church service, catechism, and discipline.

A second result of the analysis was that judges themselves were also frequently among the defendants. Hence they were often accused of lax and uncooperative behaviour or even of being disobedient to magisterial authority. They did not carry out adequately the duties of their

[29] For blasphemy, cursing and swearing see Heinrich Richard Schmidt, 'Die Ächtung des Fluchens durch reformierte Sittengerichte', in Peter Blickle (ed.), *Der Fluch und der Eid* (Zeitschrift für Historische Forschung, Supplement 15, Berlin, 1993), pp. 65–120.

[30] Keith Thomas, *Religion and the Decline of Magic. Studies in Popular Beliefs in Sixteenth and Seventeenth Century England* (London, 4th edn, 1980).

Cursing: Punishments
Vechigen and Stettlen

Average for the whole Period

10.3   Gender differences in cursing penalties

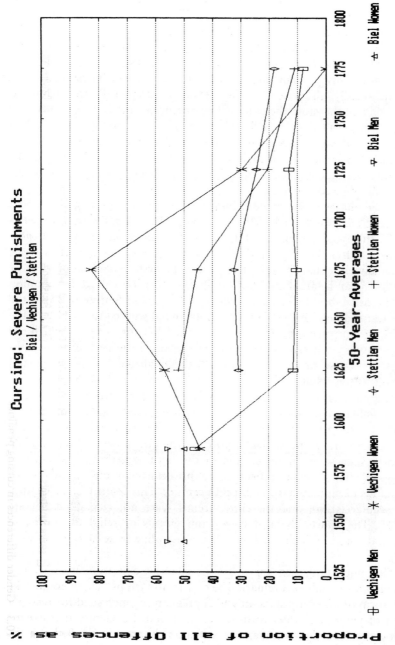

Cursing: Severe Punishments
Biel / Vechigen / Stettlen

Proportion of all Offences as %

50-Year-Averages

⊕ Vechigen Men   ＊ Vechigen Women   ⚡ Stettlen Men   ＋ Stettlen Women   ◇ Biel Men   ⚡ Biel Women

10.4 Long-term trends of severe punishments against cursing

office, as understood by Berne and by the pastor. It can therefore be concluded that the morals courts did not function as an apparatus of the early modern state; they did not follow the prerogatives of a continuous discipline or a concept of improvement.

Third, the offences of religious dissidence or resistance were not the preserve of any one social group, and were in any case not offences of the poor. This did not change over the long term. Surprisingly, but unequivocally, all levels of society retained a certain distance from the Church and therefore the citizenry was predominant.

The concern to put the village inhabitants under church rule only met with partial success. Sunday sermons and communion were already frequently attended in the early seventeenth century. Clearly more problematic were the weekday sermons and catechisms. Figure 10.5 summarizes all religious offences.

Three phases of increased delinquency in the area of religion become apparent: 1600–15, 1640–70/90, 1715–35. In particular around 1640–70/90 the avoidance of the obligations of religious duty increased enormously. After 1735 all indices subsided permanently, and a weak groundswell remained until 1800. While the first, in part minor, peak of 1600–15 can be attributed to the initial problems involved in beginning an intensive moral discipline after the *Chorgericht* Statute of 1587, the greatest peak of 1640–70/90 is possibly linked with consequences of the fall in grain prices and the Swiss Peasants' War of 1653, in which the church was no longer perceived as representing the wishes of the subjects but those of the authorities, with an alienation of church and people as the result.

The phase after 1735 poses the greatest interpretative problems. Are the numbers so small because so few transgressions were committed, or were so few offences investigated because they were regarded as little more than annoyances? The reports of the clergy from 1764 to 1794 clearly suggest an interpretation of the development as a 'decline of religion'. The sources reflect not a breakthrough but a collapse of religious discipline in the eighteenth century. This century is the century of secularization, and therefore, trends were not calculated beyond 1735. The courts changed back from morals or religious courts, to marital courts, which tried to enforce discipline in sexuality and marriage.

This important next aspect of the church's activity was concerned mainly with trials of premarital sexual relationships. These could take the form of paternity suits, in which pregnant women sued for recognition of paternity. Other forms of trials included sexuality that existed altogether outside marriage, even when no children resulted (that is the *Kilten* and *Fensterln*, the nocturnal visits of young men to women, to

10.5 Developments and trends of religious offences

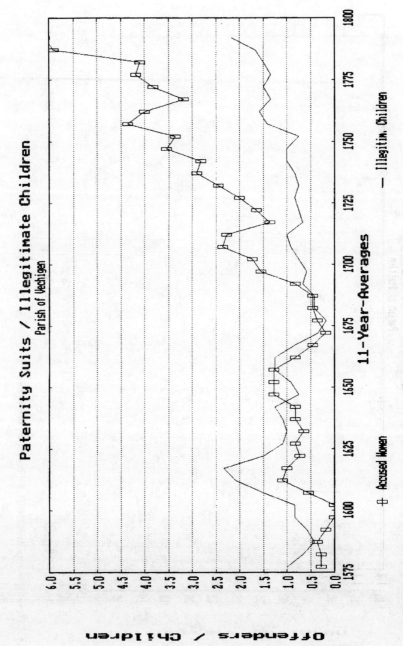

10.6 Number of paternity suits and illegitimate children: parish of Vechigen

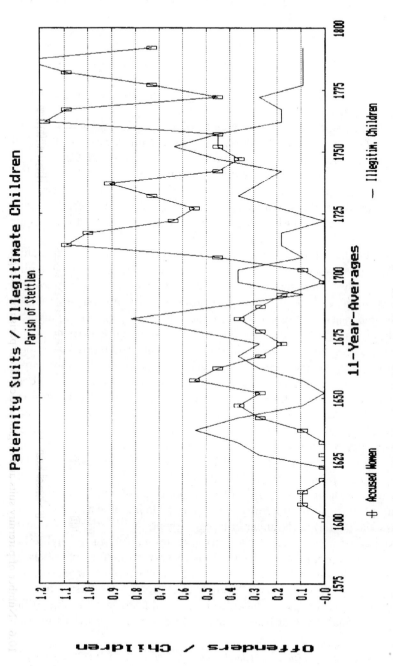

10.7   Number of paternity suits and illegitimate children: parish of Stettlen

which the church naturally objected) and, finally, broken promises of marriage. Pregnant brides, who gave birth eight months or less after marriage, were only prosecuted very late and for a very short period. They were only criminalized between 1690 and 1760 by the *Chorgericht*. This resulted from the fact that the Council of Berne itself regarded the promise of marriage, and the consummation of the relationship, as conclusive for a marriage, with a wedding by contrast being only a confirmation.

With paternity suits the principle of self-disclosure was the rule, mostly by the woman who declared her sin, namely premarital sexual intercourse, and submitted herself to the punishment of the *Chorgericht*. She did this in order to bring the accomplice to justice, who would in any case be sought after and cited, and who would usually receive an equal punishment. Surviving children born out of wedlock were awarded by the courts to the father, not simply paid alimony but placed into his care.

The number of accusations clearly show a decline of moral discipline in the field of sexuality (see Figures 10.6 and 10.7). The overwhelming majority (over three-quarters) of all sexual transgressions were brought to trial in the eighteenth century. Propriety in relationships between the sexes had relaxed. Against this, the total of sexual contacts brought to trial did not increase. Before 1700 approximately twice as many people were tried for *Huren* (fornication) or *Kilten* (illicit nocturnal meetings) as for paternity. After this the numbers of accusations for fornication and paternity came increasingly closer together until they nearly reached a relationship of 1:1. One can interpret this as indicating that until the beginning of the eighteenth century, the *Chorgericht* attempted to stop suspicious sexual contacts before they could lead to a child. The morals courts were practising prophylaxis. That changed later: practically only those cases of fornication that led to pregnancy were punished. From prophylaxis, practice changed to damage control.

The number of lawsuits for breach of betrothal did not increase in the same proportion as paternity suits. The promise of marriage lost its character as a rule. Numbers of engagements before the initiation of sexual contacts in cases of paternity suits fell rapidly in the eighteenth century in comparison to the previous century, from approximately 30 per cent to less than 10 per cent. A change can be inferred from this that can only be described as a 'sexual revolution'.[31] Understanding the process of this change can be aided by a social historical analysis. While the traditional value of roughly over 30 per cent of betrothals in trials

---

[31]   Edward Shorter, *Die Geburt der modernen Familie* (Reinbek, 1977), esp. pp. 258–66, 289–303. English version as *The Making of the Modern Family* (New York, 1975).

for pregnancy remained constant for servants also in the eighteenth century, with craftsmen it lay at barely over 10 per cent. This clear difference determined the trend through the proportional increase in numbers of rural craftsmen. Consequently, it was the rural craftsmen who by their 'lax' sexual behaviour undermined the rule that sexuality leads to marriage. If one distinguishes between 'traditional' and 'proto-industrialized' occupations, it is clear that the 'new' craftsmen, with less than 5 per cent, reveal fewer numbers of betrothals than those practising the 'old' crafts, where the number lay between 20 and 25 per cent.

The apparently far too small number of illegitimate children in the parish baptismal register is just as noticeable (see Figures 10.6 and 10.7). There were many more pregnant women appearing before the *Chorgericht* than there were children of their pregnancies in the parish baptismal register. In particular, in the eighteenth century it is evident that many foetuses conceived outside wedlock and acknowledged by the authorities died in the period from the sixth month of pregnancy until the time of baptism. This was the result of physical or psychological strain, negligence and conscious abortion, or of infanticide. One must concur with contemporary observers and regard 'infanticide', in the widest sense of the word, as a mass phenomenon.

If the goal of moral discipline had been to undermine premarital sexuality and make marriage its refuge, then it failed. The processes of social change were not so much concerned with the history of social disciplining as with the history of the decline of peasant-communal norms.

This change can also be seen in marital disputes. There were very few complaints against women who did not help their husband, care for him, or removed goods and money from the house. Only in a few cases did the *Chorgericht* have to support the dignity of the husband against the wife. Much more common were complaints against men who did not live up to the model of the ideal husband. However, in only 28 per cent of the cases in Vechigen can the source of the complaint be identified without doubt. It is possible that some of the other cases were brought to court by neighbours, until the eighteenth century when the neighbourhood lost its role in regulating morality. Where the complainants can be identified, in approximately three-quarters of all cases, these were women.

The ideology of the well-ordered house (*Hausvater-Ideologie*) cut both ways.[32] On the one hand it supported the marital patriarch, but

---

[32] Especially important for this conclusion are newer studies on marital conflicts: Thomas M. Safley, *Let No Man Put Asunder. The Control of Marriage in the German Southwest: A Comparative Study, 1550–1600* (Kirksville, 1984); Lyndal Roper, *The*

on the other hand it gave the wife the foundation of arguments from which to domesticate her husband. She could draw upon expected standards of performance, above all the expectation to achieve a guaranteed means of support. In connection with this, wastefulness, sloth and alcohol came in for criticism. Severe cases could lead to a ban on public houses, with the accused husband being decried. Disorderly living (*schlechtes Hausen*) was an offence of men. In Vechigen and Stettlen approximately three-quarters of those accused were men (in Vechigen 81 per cent, in Stettlen 74 per cent). In Biel the number of men was hardly smaller at 68 per cent. It is also apparent that in Stettlen the problems of marriage and households were more frequent, relative to the size of the population, than in Vechigen. This is explained by the fact that the community of Stettlen was poorer and more prone to suffering social distress, so economic problems emerged more frequently and led sooner to conflicts. These factors were even more important in connection with alcohol consumption, in particular for men. Stettlen reached levels here which, when coupled with marital strife, were as high as those of Vechigen. Relatively many men were cited for bad household management without a conflict within the marriage being apparent. Thus, in the sense of the thesis of the increasing subjection of social conflict to legal forms (*Verrechtlichungs-These*), bad behaviour – mostly by the men – was corrected in the courts, without the opposing party to a suit having to pick a quarrel and break marital solidarity.[33]

The use of violence in an argument was defined by women as a fundamentally unjustified use of force. Men were accused of violence in 90 per cent of cases in Stettlen and, by comparison, in 74 per cent of cases in Vechigen. Women were, however, more represented in the area of verbal aggression. Every form of violence tended to become a problem and was outlawed through the demand that conflicts should be solved peacefully and with the involvement of the *Chorgericht*. The rights of the man to exercise chastisement were not permitted to exceed strict boundaries. Even when a woman had been 'lawfully' struck, the man was punished for his 'tyrannical' use of force. The relationship between a married couple should be marked by 'friendliness' and 'love'.

Holy Household. Women and Morals in Reformation Augsburg (Oxford, 1989); David W. Sabean, *Property, Production, and Family in Neckarhausen, 1700–1870* (New York, 1990), esp. pp. 88–146; Heinz Schilling, 'Frühneuzeitliche Formierung und Disziplinierung von Ehe, Familie und Erziehung im Spiegel calvinistischer Kirchenratsprotokolle', in Paolo Prodi (ed.), *Glaubensbekenntnisse, Treueformeln und Sozialdisziplinierung zwischen Mittelalter und Neuzeit* (Munich, 1993), pp. 199–235.

[33]   Winfried Schulze, *Einführung in die Neuere Geschichte* (Stuttgart, 1987), pp. 62–5.

The *Chorgericht* usually took the side of the woman. Marital discipline was a field in which women could domesticate their men. This alliance, between the values of the women complaining and the values that the *Chorgericht* had to defend, functioned until the end of the *ancien régime*. The idea of marriage revealed by the Reformed morals courts cannot be described as predominantly patriarchal, but originated from the idea of a Christian marriage based on equality, consensus and co-operation. The thesis (recently increasingly propounded) which proposes that Christian goals launched the end of the idea of partnership appears to be relevant given the evidence presented here.

However, the trends are not clear in this case. In addition to the numbers of marital disputes for Vechigen and Stettlen (see Figure 10.8) some comparison could be drawn from the Aargau, for which there exists an analysis of the surviving data from the seventeenth century. Over the longer term, figures for Vechigen reveal a slight drop in values, and against this, figures for Stettlen and rural Aargau in the seventeenth century clearly reveal a rise. A smooth improvement in behaviour cannot be affirmed before the end of the period for which trends have been calculated (1735).

A change is evident as regards the causes of marital conflict. Economic problems recede in favour of the question of marital sexual fidelity. This could refer to the stronger value placed upon marital fidelity towards the end of the eighteenth century. Parallel to this, the importance of love grew from the seventeenth to the eighteenth century. Lack of love was increasingly a more frequent cause for complaint with both sexes. The wish associated with this, for more love, increased, which strengthens the suspicion that the marital bond had gained a more emotional tone.

Edward Shorter must be treated critically for mystifying the present in an unreliable fashion, in so far as he regarded the period before 1800 as one of coldness and lovelessness, and contrasted it in a romantic manner with a concept of marriage consumed by love in the nineteenth and twentieth century.[34] But one must give him credit for identifying a change in which village, church, and marital power relationships were turned upside down. The approach of capitalism ('proto-industrialization') is potentially crucial here. It strengthened the economic and thus the matrimonial position of women. Nevertheless, the instructional work of the *Chorgericht* was an essential condition without which the emancipation of marriage and love could not have occurred. It helped introduce the idea, albeit clothed in patriarchal language, of the wife as partner.

---

[34] Edward Shorter, *Familie*.

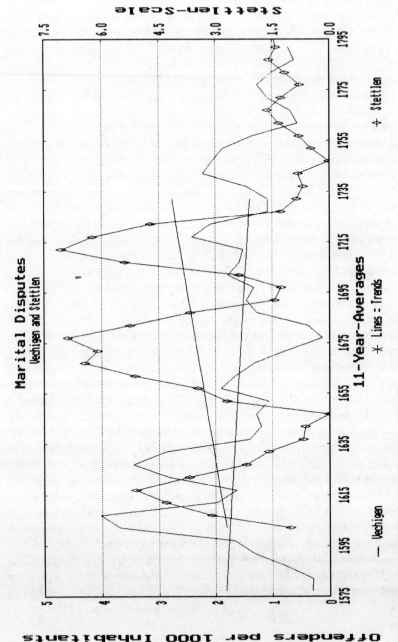

10.8 Trends of marital disputes in Vechigen and Stettlen

The role of the *Chorgericht* in the internal regulation of the community and its constituent parts, the individual houses, is especially clear in the case of marital disputes: there had to be one party that sought a partner in its dispute; the *Chorgericht* could be such a partner is so far as its goals met with those of that party. And, as an overall conclusion, the main goal of all participants was the maintenance of peace and unity. One could describe the basic function of the morals courts, for the whole community and its integral parts, as the regulation of their social stability, and the repair of broken relationships.

The relations within a family were meant to be marked by harmony. Courts also played the role of a mediator in neighbourhood disputes, and sought to re-establish harmony and reconcile neighbours in dispute with each other. Relatively little is known about the meaning of violence in interpersonal conflicts in the early modern period. For this reason we are obliged to extrapolate the role of violence in everyday life from cases of severe offences such as murder and manslaughter. However, we must remain aware of the distortions that have to be accepted in such an approach. This is demonstrated by the very different view offered by the commonplace conflicts between neighbours that were purged before the *Chorgericht*, and the picture presented, for example, by Muchembled's *La violence au village*.[35]

Some information about the social status of the people in dispute exists (with 50 per cent of the women it is possible to ascertain that they were married), and the few details of occupations. From these details, the following conclusions can be reached: violence in disputes among neighbours was more likely to be the offence of household patriarchs or matriarchs than of young men or women. The overwhelming number of married people among the perpetrators permits a further analysis when one compares the names in the marriage register. Some 79 per cent of the names of men involved in neighbourhood disputes are found in marriage rolls. The marriage rolls reveal information about the status of offenders: strangers to the village (non-citizens or *Nichtbürger*) – as far as one can ascertain, part of the lower local classes – were clearly underrepresented, until the situation changed in the second half of the eighteenth century. Above all, the burghers, not the lower levels of society, dominated village conflicts.

Very often the disputes erupted over the theft of provisions or other goods that belonged to the household, also over the children of the parties involved. The infringement of borders or rights of use of water

---

[35] Robert Muchembled, *La violence au village. Sociabilité et comportements populaires en Artois du XVe au XVIIe siècle* (Turnhout, 1989).

or agricultural land weighed heavily on the disputants, as all of these were important for the disputants' existence. The moving of boundary posts, ploughing across field borders, and the diversion of water constituted theft of the most important means of production in agricultural society, the land. Self-defence, or defence of the family, also frequently led to accusations of maledictory magic, that in both communities, however, never broadened into witchcraft trials.

May, June, August and October, possibly also September, were months characterized by the increased frequency of disputes in Berne. The agricultural rhythm of work in the region must bear responsibility for this concentration. Neighbourhood disputes accumulated at the time of work such as harvest and fencing, which brought with it problems of demarcation.

Neighbourhood conflicts involved neighbours. This platitude is not quite as banal as it seems. It contradicts Muchembled's thesis that gangs of village youths dominated the scene, stirred up by alcohol and gambling. What happened in both of these parishes in Berne was quite different: a daily struggle for existence led to various kinds of border disputes.

The *Chorgericht* was not charged with the role of eliminating the causes of conflict. That was the responsibility of the secular courts. The purpose of the *Chorgericht* was the reconciliation of disputes. Neighbours were 'examined, unified, and exhorted to friendliness and neighbourly love'. The phrase 'neighbourly love', which had been disrupted and should be restored, recurred continuously. Neighbourhood and neighbourly love became synonymous. Similar to the concept of friendship (which also means 'relatives'), neighbourhood was a social entity and an ethical value.[36] It could not be compared to any damage, either

---

[36]   See also Heinrich Richard Schmidt, 'Pazifizierung des Dorfes – Struktur und Wandel von Nachbarschaftskonflikten vor Berner Sittengerichten 1570–1800', in Heinz Schilling (ed.), *Kirchenzucht*, pp. 91–128. The same conclusions can be drawn from studies on church discipline in Protestant Europe. See Schmidt, 'Gemeinde' for a European perspective. Also, for Germany, Switzerland: Heinz Schilling, 'Sündenzucht und frühneuzeitliche Sozialdisziplinierung. Die calvinistische presbyteriale Kirchenzucht in Emden vom 16. bis 19. Jahrhundert', in Georg Schmidt (ed.), *Stände und Gesellschaft im Alten Reich* (Veröffentlichungen des Instituts für Europäische Geschichte Mainz, Supplement 29, Wiesbaden, 1989), pp. 265–302; David W. Sabean, *Power in the Blood. Popular Culture and Village Discourse in Early Modern Germany* (Cambridge, 1984), esp. ch. 'Communion and community', pp. 37–60; also Bruce Gordon, 'Kirchenzucht in Zürich am Beginn der Reformation', in Heinz Schilling (ed.), *Kirchenzucht*, pp. 65–90, esp. pp. 79, 85. For France see Alfred Soman, 'Deviance and criminal justice in Western Europe, 1300–1800', *Criminal Justice History. An International Annual*, 1 (1980), 3–28, esp. 18–20; Raymond A. Mentzer, 'Le consistoire et la pacification du monde rural', *Bulletin de la Société de l'Histoire du Protestantisme français*, 135 (1989), 373–89 and his 'Disciplina

material or imaginary, to one's fellow man. Love, peace, unity and friendship all possessed one meaning: the neighbourhood should be marked by Christian love. The love of fellow man was realized through 'neighbourly love'. The requirement to greet neighbours was frequently renewed as an expression of the duty of congeniality. Of constant concern in most cases was not simply the cleansing of conflict, but the elimination of hatred and even of antipathy. Parties in conflict were continuously warned to be good neighbours and not to pass each other silently in the street.

The reconciliation work of the *Chorgericht* aimed at the pure expression of the communion, before which all hatred and all animosity had to be exchanged for love. The love of one's neighbour was the prerequisite for communion. Communion attested to the love and peace that ruled the communicants, and was for this reason a celebration of love and peace.

The relationship between the numbers of citations in the communities where the most evidence survives, in Stettlen and Vechigen, is 1:2.7 – although the difference in the size of the communities is 1:3.8. This reveals that neighbourhood conflicts were more frequent in Stettlen than in Vechigen. The social and economic differences between the communities, described in the introduction, find their expression in the relative offence figures. Stettlen proved to have a clearly higher level of conflict over the whole period than Vechigen, and in addition these conflicts were intrinsically more violent in nature than with the traditional and more stable neighbouring community.

---

nervus ecclesiae: the Calvinist reform of morals at Nîmes', *SCJ*, 18 (1987), 89–115; see also Bernard Vogler, Jean Estèbe, 'La genèse d'une société protestante: Étude comparée de quelques registres consistoriaux Languedociens et Palatins vers 1600', *Annales*, 31 (1976), 362–88, esp. 363. For Scotland see James Cameron, 'Godly nurture and the admonition in the Lord: ecclesiastical discipline in the Reformed tradition', in Leif Grane und Kai Hørby (eds), *Die dänische Reformation vor ihrem internationalen Hintergrund* (Göttingen, 1990), pp. 264–76. For England see John A. Sharpe, '"Such disagreement betwyx neighbours": litigation and human relations in Early Modern England', in John Bossy (ed.), *Disputes and Settlements: Law and Human Relations in the West* (Cambridge, 1983), pp. 167–87; Ralph Houlbrooke, *Church Courts and the People during the English Reformation 1520–1570* (Oxford, 1979), esp. pp. 44–7. For the Netherlands see Herman Roodenburg, 'Reformierte Kirchenzucht und Ehrenhandel. Das Amsterdamer Nachbarschaftsleben im 17. Jahrhundert', in Heinz Schilling (ed.), *Kirchenzucht*, pp. 129–51. For Denmark see Troels Dahlerup, 'Sin, crime, punishment and absolution', in Leif Grane and Kai Hørby (eds), *Reformation*, pp. 277–88, here p. 285. For Sweden see Jan Sundin, 'Control, punishment and reconciliation. A case study of parish justice in Sweden before 1850', in Anders Brändström and Jan Sundin (eds), *Tradition and Transition. Studies in Microdemography and Social Change* (Umeå, 1981), pp. 9–65, esp. pp. 38–44, 56.

Trends in disputes (see Figure 10.9) do not reveal a social disciplining effect. The data from Biel in the sixteenth century reaches only half, or even only a quarter, of the defendants that 'should' have existed when one compares the total of inhabitants. Could the stricter moral discipline in Biel, with excommunication, and the greater temporal and material proximity to the Reformation together explain the stronger effect of discipline? Did success come at the beginning of the attempt to enforce discipline? In Biel, two-thirds of the defendants were women, in Vechigen 40 per cent and in Stettlen 44 per cent – essentially higher proportions to those we are accustomed to for serious offences. Thus women played a greater role in the neighbourhood, a form of public forum, than has usually been supposed.

The tendency towards aggression rose altogether as soon as social distress increased. This is clearly demonstrated when the collapse of grain prices in 1643 threatened the existence of market-oriented peasants who had speculated on the future and taken on credit following the earlier situation of war profiteering. As a result, the number of internal village trials for violence rose sharply on the one hand and, on the other, the potential for aggression was expressed in the great Swiss Peasants' War of 1653 against the state which had intensified the situation through its economic and tax policy. The same relation between aggression and economic problems can be seen in Catholic Lucerne.

The *Chorgericht* was not successful in installing a 'gyro-compass' (David Riesman) which would have made the believers independent of external influences. Indeed the number of trials for neighbourhood disputes declined enormously in the eighteenth century (see Figure 10.9). But this is in my view the result of the diminishing power of the *Chorgericht* and its basis, the religious orientation of social behaviour. Whether there was a social disciplining, understood as a long-term and enduring change in lifestyle, is questionable.

This study proposes that the implementation of Christian ethics depended upon two factors: on Christianity, and on the interests of the community as a whole and of particular groups. These factors operated in a scenario which was strongly influenced by economic pressure. The state could not implement Christianity or social discipline by itself. It was the communities that had to discipline themselves, through themselves.

The goals of the morals courts' activity can be described as friendship, peace and a community in harmony with itself and with God. Moral disciplining was strongly orientated towards the local Christian community. In certain domains, moral discipline broke through the borders set by behaviour through group egoisms. It was demonstrated,

Neighbourhood Disputes
Vechigen / Stettlen / Aargau

11-Year-Averages

Offenders per 1000 Inhabitants

⊞ Vechigen ☩ Stettlen ☩ Aargau (Cases/Year) ☩ Lines = Trends

10.9 Levels and trends of neighbourhood disputes

for example, that the judges as men were able to convey an impulse towards Christianization in marital behaviour that showed the way from patriarchy to partnership. It is also plausible that interests were actively working against the implementation of Christian ethics, so – for example – youth culture tended to protect gambling, dancing, companionship and premarital sexuality against ascetic imperatives.

Except in the case of premarital pregnancies, across the whole period of the investigation of Stettlen and Vechigen, the community of Stettlen – smaller, poorer and more prone to social stress – demonstrated a clear preponderance of offences. Conflicts in marriage and with the neighbours, the readiness of men to be violent, to name some essential areas, were considerably more frequent than in the more traditional and socially more buoyant community of Vechigen. Here economy dominated over morality. Nevertheless the fundamental gradients of development in both communities match to an extraordinary degree, in particular with the culmination of the problems of moral discipline in the middle and second half of the seventeenth century, and then with the sensational reduction of cases in the eighteenth century. The minutes of the morals courts show that the eighteenth century was dominated by processes of secularization, that is, the loss of the religious focus of village society, and of decommunalization, the loss of the communal orientation of the village inhabitants. The *Chorgericht* lost its power to force marital partners or neighbours to be reconciled with each other. It could also no longer suppress illegitimacy. Thus it lost its role as a means of Christian-communal self-regulation.

One can summarize the role played by the *Chorgericht* before 1700, during the phase of confessionalization, as follows:

1. The morals courts were means by which the community regulated itself and re-established broken neighbourhood relations, by which women civilized their men or controlled their aggression, by which adults regulated the sexuality of their offspring, by which a Christian people gained the grace and favour of God, whom they thought of in terms of providence and covenant. The morals courts were not, in the first instance, the means by which the state disciplined its unwilling people.
2. The courts only partially succeeded in disciplining or civilizing villagers, but functioned especially as agents of social regulation.

The bias of all adherents of the Oestreich thesis of social disciplining towards the state prompts them to underestimate, to an extreme degree, all these aspects of the work of the morals courts, which lay within the communities themselves – even in a state–church system like the Bernese one.

Looking back at the Reformation, we can learn something from the study of confessionalization. We should consider the interests and the religious preferences of the ordinary people, those without whom no Reformation could take place. The Reformation began as an appeal by the preachers. It could be heard. But in order to be listened to, there had to be a readiness and a desire to gain a new Christian orientation within the world as a whole in both its spheres, the secular and the sacred. We must try to understand better the parameters of this reception by ordinary people, in order to comprehend the social depth of the Reformation. These parameters could be found in the social needs for orientation and regulation. From this point of view there is no difference to be found between the Reformation era and the period of confessionalization. The Reformation, in the sense of the religious involvement of society, did not end in the sixteenth, but in the eighteenth century. And this long Reformation must be examined from the perspective of the lowest levels of society.

CHAPTER ELEVEN

The Reformation in Poland and Prussia in the sixteenth century: similarities and differences

Janusz Małłek

In the years 1838 and 1840 the work of Count Valerian Krasiński dealing with the history of the Reformation in Poland appeared in print in London.[1] Count Krasiński, a Calvinist, found himself in England and then in Scotland as an exile after the November Uprising in 1830–31. He was also the author of a book of lectures on the religious history of the Slavonic nations.[2] Krasiński's work, *The Reformation in Poland*, was the first modern synthesis of the religious history of the Polish Reformation. Paradoxically, it saw the light of day not in Poland, but in England and in English, while its Polish translation only appeared in print some 60 years later.[3] The author himself died in Edinburgh in 1855 and was buried there. I mention these facts for there is something symbolic in the fact that we are gathered here for a conference in St Andrews, at no great distance from Edinburgh, 150 years after the publication of interest to us, in order to consider the history of the Reformation in East-Central Europe which Count Krasiński revealed to English and Scottish readers of the nineteenth century.

In 1982 at a conference of historians of the Reformation in Wittenberg I delivered a paper, 'Ducal Prussia and the Reformation in Poland'.[4] The conclusion of that paper was that there exists a close link between the development of the Polish and Prussian Reformations. Therefore, when I was offered the opportunity to outline the problems connected with the history of the Polish Reformation within the framework of the

---

[1] V. Krasiński, *Historical Sketch of the Rise, Progress and Decline of the Reformation in Poland* (2 vols, London 1838, 1840).

[2] V. Krasiński, *Lectures on the Religious History of the Slavonic Nations* (Edinburgh and London, 1896).

[3] V. Krasiński, *Zarys dziejów powstania I upadku reformacji w Polsce*, J. Bursche (ed.) (Warsaw 1903, 1905).

[4] J. Małłek, 'Das Herzogtum Prussen und die Reformation in Polen', in *Probleme der Reformation in Deutschland und Polen* (Studien zur Geschichte der deutsch-polnischen Beziehungen, Heft 8, Rostock 1983), pp. 23–40.

present conference, the connection between it and the history of the Prussian Protestant Church seemed indispensable to me. The title of this chapter is the consequence of such argumentation. However, it requires further explanation.

In the sixteenth century Prussia no longer formed one territory, for there existed Ducal Prussia, a fief of Poland and also Royal Prussia, otherwise known as Polish Prussia, which became part of the Polish nation first in 1454 and definitely from 1466. However, Royal Prussia retained political autonomy until 1569. This had its repercussions in the organization of the Church. The Protestant (Lutheran) Church in Royal Prussia remained, in principle, outside the structure of the Protestant Church in Poland. It is true that Gottfried Schram in his thorough thesis on the Polish Reformation, 'Der Polnische Adel und die Reformation 1548–1607' treats Royal Prussia on a par with the other provinces: Little Poland, Red Ruthinia, Great Poland, Mazovia or Lithuania.[5] But there is nevertheless much to be said for differentiating it. The close ties of the Lutheran Church in Royal Prussia with the Church of that confession in Ducal Prussia are a fact, although they did not constitute an organizational whole and we should treat them separately. In any case it is difficult to talk about an 'all Prussian' Protestant Church in the sixteenth century.[6]

To this day historians of the Reformation are not able to give a full answer to some elementary questions concerning the character and especially the reasons for the decline of this religious movement in Poland. Research to date has only sporadically resorted to comparative methods, which may or may not always be useful. The present chapter is an attempt, albeit on a modest scale, to apply this comparative approach. Limiting ourselves to the comparison of the development of Protestantism in the kingdom of Poland and Lithuania and in Royal and Ducal Prussia in the sixteenth century, we concentrate on a few questions, such as the attitude of society to the Reformation, stages in its development, the organizational structure of the new Church and its attitudes to other confessions.

Let us start with the country which first embraced the Reformation, namely Ducal Prussia. The Prussian Duchy became the first Lutheran state in Europe. As early as 6 July 1525 Prince Albrecht Hohenzollern ordered the propagation of the 'pure Word of God' in his domain. The introduction of the Reformation 'from above' also met with an enthusi-

---

[5] G. Schramm, *Der polnische Adel und die Reformation 1548–1607* (Wiesbaden, 1965) pp. 116–36.

[6] P. Tscheckert (ed.), *Urkundenbuch zur Reformationsgeschichte des Herzogtum Preussen* (Leipzig, 1890) 2, no. 371; and a discussion of the mandate, 1, pp. 118–19.

astic reception 'from below', especially in Koenigsberg where the churches were full of people listening to the new teachings.[7] The acceptance of the teachings of Luther was assisted by the fact that a considerable section of the inhabitants of the Prussian towns used the German language. Cases of resistance were sporadic and, besides, inspired by the former Teutonic Knights. Progress was made most carefully in the countryside where changes in the liturgy were introduced gradually so as not to upset the faithful. As early as 1530 the Augsburg Confession was accepted as binding. The outstanding scholar of the Reformation in Ducal Prussia, P. Tschackert was of the opinion that after the visitations and introduction of church regulations in 1544 the Prussian Duchy became completely Lutheran.[8] The next stage in the history of Protestantism in Ducal Prussia is connected with the disputation during 1549–52 between orthodox Lutheranism and Osiandrism, which was supported by Prince Albrecht. Lutheranism came off well from this encounter and in 1567 sanctioned its confession with the act 'Repetitio corporis doctrinae'. The appearance of Calvinism, its main rival, preceded by the Brandenberg Elector did not unsettle the position of Lutheranism in Ducal Prussia. Only in 1817 did the creation of the united church (Lutherans and Calvinists) bring in a new confessional standard in Prussia. With certain interruptions, the Lutheran Church in Ducal Prussia had an episcopal regime until 1587. Later a consistorial regime was set up in its place. The Prussian Duchy was a haven for Protestants from the whole of Europe and especially from Poland. Schwenkfeldians, Mennonites and the Czech Brethren all settled here. On the other hand, Catholics were unwillingly tolerated here and were not allowed into the civil service or into university. In Prince Albrecht's visitation instructions of 31 March 1526, article seven already stipulates the dismissal of all priests who do not accept the principle of faith.[9] In the Prussian Duchy the principle of 'cuius regio, eius religio' was brought in to its full extent. In all likelihood, nowhere else in Europe was 'Lutheran confessionalisation' established so early.

Reformation in Royal Prussia, on the other hand, did not have such advantageous conditions for development. At the beginning the Reformation in Toruń (Thorn), Elbląg (Elbing), and Gdańsk (Danzig) was received as warmly as in Koenigsberg. However, King Sigismund the Old's bloody suppression of social and religious revolt in Danzig in 1526 held back the expansion of an official Reformation for a quarter of a century. It continued to develop in a more restrained fashion, in

[7]   Ibid., 2, no. 30.
[8]   Ibid., 1, p. 223.
[9]   Ibid., 2, no. 460 and discussion 1, pp. 133, 134.

secret. Only in the 1540s at the end of Sigismund's reign did it make further progress. The accession to power of Sigismund Augustus in 1548 diametrically changed the situation of Protestants in Royal Prussia and in the whole Polish–Lithuanian nation as well. At that time, two camps clearly stood out in Royal Prussian society: Protestant and Catholic. In May 1556 at the regional council of Royal Prussia (comprising the nobility, and representatives of the large and small towns) it was declared that they did not want the 'new' religion, which they were accused of seeking, but the proclamation of the 'pure Word of God proclaimed by the Prophets, by Jesus Christ our Lord, by the Apostles and their rightful successors', but without erroneous human additions – this concerns the sacraments and especially the Lord's Supper. They believed that neither the Pope, nor church councils nor canons had the right to bring changes into the true, orthodox Catholic Church which persisted in the Augsburg Confession. The Catholic camp answered this declaration through the Bishop of Varmia, Stanislaus Hozjusz, saying that this was false teaching. Then two Lutheran voivodes, Achacy Cema from Marienberg and Fabian Cema from Pomerania replied that, after all, this 'false teaching' had taken root for good in Royal Prussia in the last 30 years and that it was not possible to eradicate it in three months – as the bishops seemed to desire.[10]

At that moment it was difficult to forecast which confessional option, Protestantism or Catholicism, would be victorious in Royal Prussia. For the time being the initiative lay with the Protestants who were striving for legal recognition of their confession. As early as 1557–78 the large Prussian towns, Toruń, Elbing and Danzig, obtained religious privileges allowing communion to be taken in two forms, but only for the period of one year, i.e. until the beginning of the next *seym* or the beginning of the national council. Therefore there was no recognition of full religious freedom in the privileges conferred. The Augsburg Confession was not mentioned once, but the royal agreement to communion in both kinds, representing a fundamental part of the teachings of Luther, nevertheless opened the way for further decisions. Once granted, a right was difficult to take back. Following the example of the large towns, small towns also began to strive for religious privileges, with, moreover, positive results. In turn, the nobility from Royal Prussia could cite the decision of the Piotrków *seym* of 1555 which accepted the proposal of a confession close to the Augsburg Confession.

The next 20 years were unusually advantageous for the development of Protestantism in Royal Prussia. According to W. Neumayer's calcula-

---

[10] H. Neumeyer, *Kirchengeschichte von Danzig und Westpreussen in evangelischer Sicht* (Leer, 1971), 1, p. 86.

tions in 1580 there were 162 evangelical parishes here, including 114 in the country.[11] Their number more or less corresponded to the number of Catholic parishes. The Catholic Church was predominant in the countryside and the Lutheran Church in towns. The Lutheran Church did not create a centralized church organization in Royal Prussia, whereas the Catholic Church did. There were no Protestant bishops here, nor synods for the whole province. The large towns took the lead in religious life. This balance of power between Protestants and Catholics, in fact, guaranteed mutual tolerance. Even the reduction of the number of Protestant parishes by 70 during the period of Counter-Reformation did not change this state of affairs.[12] Sporadic disputes arose at that time but in general Catholics and Protestants lived fairly peaceably side by side until 1724.

The Reformation embraced the Crown and Lithuania with some delay. Its development was blocked from the very beginning by the anti-Lutheran edicts of Sigismund I from as early as 1520. Moreover, in the opinion of G. Schramm, the reception of the writings of Luther and other reformers published mainly in German only found favourable conditions at the beginning in the towns, Cracow, Posen or Vilnius, among the section of the townspeople who knew this language.[13] A distinct expansion of the Reformation in Poland took place as early as the 1540s, when fear of repression on the part of the old and sick king steadily diminished. In 1542 the Cracow burgher J. L. Decjusz informed the Prussian Prince Albrecht in letters that in Cracow thousands of people assembled every day at sermons preached in the spirit of the Reformation[14] and that the 'pure' way of teaching the Gospel was carried out in many places, even in the presence of Archbishop Piotr Gamrat.[15] Graduates from the university in Wittenberg gave a new impetus to the Polish Reformation. In the years 1523–46, when Martin Luther was lecturing at the university, about 100 Poles passed through the 'Leucorea' rooms.[16] Despite strict royal edicts prohibiting people

---

[11]   Ibid., p. 96.

[12]   Ibid., p. 97ff.

[13]   G. Schramm, 'Reformation und Gegenreformation in Krakau', *Zeitschrift für Ostforschung*, **19** (1970) 3–41.

[14]   *Elementa ad ffontoim editiones* Carolina Lanckorońska (ed.), (Rome, 1980) XLIX, no. 440, p. 42, Cracow, 27. 12. 1542 'es horen allein einen man teglich vil tausand menschen, under den auch beider standt die grossen prelaten und hern ... '.

[15]   Ibid. no. 420, p. 3, Cracow 8. 1. 1542 'bey uns das wort Gots und evangelio polnisch an vil orten lauter, rein und myt vil gutter hoffnung, auch her ertzbischoffs gegenwertigkeyt predigt ... '.

[16]   J. Małłek, *Preussen und Polen. Politik, Stände, Kirche und Kultur vom 16. bis 18. Jahrhundert* (Stuttgart, 1992) p. 172.

from going abroad to Lutheran universities one can trace a fashion in Poland for studying at Wittenberg. Later advocates of the Polish Reformation were graduates of Wittenberg, for example, Abraham Kulwieć, Stanisław Rafajowicz, Stanisław Lutomirski, Stanisław Murzynowsky, Eustachy Trepka, Marcin Krowicki, and many others. In the years 1533–35 Andrzej Frycz Modrzewski, the great irenist and author of *De republika emendanda*, lived with Philip Melanchthon. After the death of Luther in 1546 and the occupation of Wittenberg by the imperial army in 1547, that university lost its attraction for young Polish dissenters. Its task was taken over by the university established in Koenigsberg in 1544 which was also Lutheran. During the period 1544–50, 69 students from Poland studied here; in contrast, in 1551–55, 29 students, in 1556–60, 25 students, and in 1561–65, 24 Polish students matriculated in Wittenberg.[17] Furthermore, Koenigsberg provided Polish Protestants with the first translation into Polish of the New Testament, the Catechism, Postil and Psalter. From 1545 to 1552 more publications in Polish, most with a religious content, saw the light of day in Koenigsberg than in Cracow.

Sigismund Augustus's accession to power in Poland in 1548 diametrically changed the situation of Polish Protestants. At the beginning the king had two Protestant preachers at his side and dissenters cherished the hope that he would follow in Henry VIII's footsteps by creating a national church. In the 1550s Protestantism spread with unprecedented vigour, especially among the noble élite. The idea of not paying tithes and of acquiring independence from the verdicts of the ecclesiastical courts, a clearly anticlerical agenda therefore, fell on favourable ground here. Already in 1555 at the *seym* in Piotrków 113 deputies from the Lower Chamber, pointing out that they were expressing the opinion of the whole of the nobility, demanded from the king 'that the Word of God be proclaimed in the pure way according to the teachings of Jesus Christ and the Apostles and similarly concerning dispensing the sacraments'. Simultaneously the deputies submitted the confession written by Stanisław Lutomirski which was an adaptation of the Augsburg Confession. They also demanded the convening of a national church council.[18] When Prince Albrecht the Prussian received news of this fact, he wrote to his deputy in Piotrków, Asverus Brandt, that they must thank Almighty God that the Word of God was also beginning to spread in the

---

[17] M. Pawlak, *Studia uniwersyteckie młodzieży z Prus Królewskich w XVI–XVIII w.* (University studies of young people from Royal Prussia in the sixteenth to the eighteenth centuries), (Toruń, 1988), table 7.

[18] J. Małłek, *Preussen und Polen.* pp. 176–88.

Kingdom of Poland.[19] In the opinion of witnesses to the events and also of historiography, the Piotrków *seym* of 1555 was the high point of the Polish Reformation. The Protestant theologian Jacobus Sylvius, beginning the official record of heretical synods, wrote that in 1550 the Reformation had embraced both parts of Poland (Little Poland and Great Poland) 'lux Evangeli Jesu Christi Publice inclarescere ceopit in utraque Polonie'.[20] In Little Poland in 1548–72 the proportion of Protestant deputies to Catholic ones was 65 to 27.[21] The years 1556–60 were an unusually important stage in the history of the Polish Reformation, linked with the activity of the most outstanding Polish reformer Jan Łaski. Everything points to the fact that the influence of Łaski was of primary importance in moving the mainstream of the Polish Reformation away from Lutheranism in the direction of Calvinism. The 'democratic' organization of the Calvinist Church was closer to the wishes of the Polish nobility than the more centralized structure of the Lutheran Church. This organizational solution gave the nobleman considerable influence on the choice of vicar. Moreover, the shift of the focus of reformation thought from Wittenberg to Calvin's Geneva after Luther's death meant that Polish youth began to consider Calvinist universities to be more attractive than Lutheran ones and therefore preferred universities in Basle, Strasbourg, Heidelberg and, a little later, in Leiden. Basle alone saw 124 Poles matriculate in the sixteenth century while 145 Polish students matriculated in Heidelberg.[22]

These direct contacts of Poles with Calvin and Calvinist universities had a great influence on a considerable section of the Polish reformist camp declaring itself for this confession. Already in the 1560s one can talk about Little Poland, Ruthenia and Lithuania as being on the side of Calvinism, whereas Great Poland remained faithful to the Lutheran confession and the Czech Brethren. Mazovia alone underwent only a slight influence of the Reformation. In 1562 the Protestant movement suffered a separation in Poland into the so-called great church – Calvinist, and small church – Polish Brethren or Arians. The move of the most outstanding theologians to the small church considerably weakened the Protestant movement. However, the 'Sandomierz Consensus', agreed upon in 1570, provided for mutual toleration of the liturgy and the

---

[19]   *Die Berichte und Briefe des Rats und Gesandten Herzog Albrechts von Preussen Asverus von Brandt, Bezzenberger,* (Leipzig, 1921), 4, no. 201, p. 507.

[20]   *Atka synodów różnowierczych w Polsce,* M. Sipayłło (ed.), (Warsaw, 1966), 1, p. 1.

[21]   I. Kaniewska, *Małopolska repezentacja stanowa za czasów Zygmunta Augusta 1548–1572.* (Warsaw, 1974), p. 156.

[22]   M. Pawlak, *Studia uniwersyteckie* tables 15 and 28.

interpretation of communion of the Lutherans, Calvinists and Czech Brothers, slowing down the process of erosion and increasing their strength. Consequently the Protestants were able to obtain a guarantee of religious tolerance at the Warsaw Confederation of 1573. Moreover, at the time they represented a significant political power in the country. As many as 50 per cent of the senate members were Protestant in 1569.[23] At the time of the greatest expansion of the Reformation in Poland (1570–80) about 1 000 Protestant churches were functioning here, of which about half belonged to the Calvinists.[24] In 1591 one in six parishes in Poland was non-Catholic.[25] From then on there was a sudden decline in the movement, characterized by numerous conversions to Catholicism. Valerian Krasiński, mentioned at the beginning, detected a reason for the decline of the Polish Reformation in the consistent activity of the Jesuit order and the excessive compliance of the Protestants. The matter is undoubtedly more complicated than this, and has thus far not found a full explanation in the historiography.

The Protestant Church in Poland created certain organizational models for itself which were expressed in the division into districts and the fairly regular convening of synods. The minutes of the synods have been preserved, a particularly valuable source for reconstructing their activity. G. Smend published them for the Lutheran Church in Great Poland[26] and M. Sipayłło in a three-volume edition for the Calvinist Church and the Czech Brethren in the whole of Poland.[27] Despite spectacular successes in the 1550s and the next decades of the sixteenth century the Protestants in Poland were the weaker partners in relation to the Catholic Church. In general, they were advocates of religious tolerance. In support of this thesis we can mention two facts. At the conference of dissenters in Buzenno on 16 June 1561 it was declared that no one was to be forced to take the sacraments or forced to swear allegiance to this or that confession.[28] In turn, at the synod in Wągrowiec on 25 to 30 December 1565, it was declared that 'in God's true church one cannot control the faith of another, nor be constrained to it'.[29]

---

[23] H. Merczyng, *Zbory I senatorowie w dawnej Polsce*, (Warsaw, 1905), p. 143.

[24] S. Litak, 'Kościół Polski w okresie reformacji i odnowy potrydenckiej' (The Polish church in the period of the Reformation and the post-Tridentine restoration), in H. Tüchle (ed.), *Historia Kościoła* (The History of the Church), (Warsaw, 1986), 3, p. 361.

[25] H. Merczyng, *Zbory I senatorowie*, p. 143.

[26] G. Smend, *Die Synoden der Kirche Augsburgischen Konfession in Grosspolen im 16. und 17. und 18. Jahrhundert*, (Poznań, 1930).

[27] *Akta synodów róznowierczych*, compiled by M. Sipayłło, (3 vols, Warsaw, 1966, 1972, 1983), 1 (1550–59), 2 (1560–70), 3 (1571–1632).

[28] Ibid., 2, p. 104.

[29] Ibid., 2, p. 198.

To conclude, comparing the lines of development of the Reformation in Ducal Prussia, Royal Prussia and in the Crown and Lithuania allows us to draw some conclusions in the matters which we mentioned at the beginning. First, the involvement of society in the Reformation movement was an indispensable but not predetermining condition for success. In Ducal Prussia, Royal Prussia and in Poland and Lithuania alike, a significant section of society supported reform, although in different periods. The results were however different.

Second, the position of the authorities, be it as advocates or as opponents of change, was particularly important in the dispute between the old and new Church and could predetermine the success or failure of the Reformation. In Ducal Prussia, Prince Albrecht played a significant part in deciding the confessional fate of the Duchy and its inhabitants. On the other hand, Sigismund the Old torpedoed the changes while Sigismund Augustus left them to run their own course.

Third, the acceptance of a single confession guaranteed greater possibilities of development (as for instance in Ducal Prussia and Royal Prussia with Lutheranism, at least in the sixteenth century). In Poland, the division of the Protestant movement into Lutheran and Calvinist confessions and the Czech Brethren, and later the separation of the Polish Brethren, had a weakening effect on the development of the Reformation movement.

Fourth, not attaching enough importance to the creation of uniform organizational structures could also weaken the Reformation movement. Such structures were created in Ducal Prussia (by bishoprics and then a consistory), in Royal Prussia they were independent enclaves (so-called *Geistliche Ministeria*) and in Poland–Lithuania, and later in the Republic, they took on the character of a loose union (the division of the country into districts or joint synods).

Finally, religious tolerance or 'confessionalization' was a commentary on the position of the old or new Church in the country. Thus there was 'Lutheran confessionalization' in Ducal Prussia, equilibrium in the form of religious tolerance in Royal Prussia, although in the bishopric of Varmia we meet 'Catholic confessionalization', and lastly in Poland–Lithuania religious tolerance was used as a 'defensive shield' by Polish Protestants who were less accepted by Polish Catholics.

The conclusions presented have by the nature of things, a broad, simplified and impressionist character. There are significantly greater possibilities in applying the comparative method in detailed analysis, particularly in the analysis of socio-religious structures. For example, one could compare the parish network in individual countries or establish the rhythm and intensity of the Reformation movement on an appropriate scale. It would also be possible to apply *tertium comparationis* for the historical processes of the Reformation, but it would probably have to be a separate measure for each confession; that is to say that choosing, for example, Ducal Prussia as a classical Lutheran country, we could compare it with Sweden, Denmark or the Lutheran countries of the Empire, but this country would not necessarily be a good point of reference for Calvinist Holland.

At the conference of the International Committee for the Comparative History of Churches deliberating in Warsaw in 1971 particular attention was paid to the use of cartography in comparative analyses of socio-religious structures.[30] In Poland, under the supervision of Professor Jerzy Kłocowski from the Catholic University of Lublin, an atlas of Christianity in Poland is being prepared which also includes Protestant communities. At the present stage of research on Polish Protestantism the observation of at least the similarities and differences between the process of development in Poland–Lithuania and either neighbouring countries (Ducal Prussia) or countries making up the republic (Royal Prussia), could be a starting-point for a more in-depth analysis.

---

[30] *Colloque de Varsovie 27–29 Octobre 1971 sur La Cartographie et L'Histoire Socio-Religieuse de l'Europe jusqu'à la fin du XVIIᵉ siècle, Miscelannea Historiae Ecclesiasticae* (Louvain, 1974) 5.

CHAPTER TWELVE

Late Reformation and Protestant confessionalization in the major towns of Royal Prussia

Michael G. Müller

The history of the Reformation in Danzig, Elbing and Thorn, the major towns in the Polish province of Royal Prussia, seems in many ways characterized by factors specific to the region. Although representing a predominantly German-speaking community, the Protestants of the three towns did not consider themselves part of the German Reformation and never became immediately associated with the Lutheran churches across the borders in the Holy Roman Empire and the Duchy of Prussia prior to the mid-seventeenth century. With respect to its political status as well as in terms of the social and cultural profile of its élites, Protestant Prussia remained clearly distinct not only from its German neighbours but also from its Polish–Lithuanian hinterland. Unlike their co-religionists in other provinces of the Polish–Lithuanian monarchy, the Prussian burghers soon put into place strong Protestant Church organizations on a local basis on to the German model without, however, following the German example of institutionalizing interurban ecclesiastical relations, let alone establishing a united *Landeskirche*. In spite of close links with the ecclesiastical milieus of the Polish–Lithuanian, Bohemian and German Protestants, Prussian Protestantism maintained a particular confessional status of its own at least until the first half of the seventeenth century. In short, the urban Reformation in Royal Prussia was neither simply a part of the history of the German or the Polish Reformation, nor could it be considered as immediately representative of contemporary developments in the broader region to any large extent.

The case of Royal Prussia deserves our attention all the more, however, with respect to the role of the province and its towns in 'mediating' between the German Reformation and the Protestant movements in East-Central Europe. Not only were the Prussian burghers among the first to introduce the Reformation to the realm of the Polish kings, and to disseminate the teaching of Luther and Melanchthon in the Polish–Lithuanian world. But more importantly, once their church organizations were firmly established on the basis of the privileges granted after 1557, the three towns also rapidly gained importance as institutional and theological centres of Protestant life. Eventually they extended their ecclesiastical influence far beyond the province – both into Poland–Lithuania and the Habsburg lands and, as a secondary effect, into Protestant Germany as Prussian theology became increasingly perceived as representing an alternative to Protestant confessionalism within the Empire.

A closer examination of the early development of Protestantism in the towns of Royal Prussia might therefore provide at least some more than merely regional insights into the history of the Reformation in East-Central Europe. On the one hand, the Prussian case lends itself to an analysis of the relationship between Protestantism and 'German culture' in the regions bordering the Empire. Was urban Reformation here, as has commonly been suggested, both in theological and cultural terms essentially a German affair? Or should one much rather speak of an interactive relationship – resulting in the emergence of a genuinely distinct religious culture in the regions of late Reformation? And not least, how did Protestant life and ecclesiastical policies overlap with, and affect, existing social and political relations in the region? That is, was the Reformation, as most historians claim, bound merely to reinforce existing cultural and social cleavages? Or did Protestantism also provide for the emergence of new loyalties that might have cut across older identity patterns?

On the other hand, Royal Prussia represents a particularly interesting object for the study of the dynamics of Protestant confessionalism outside the Holy Roman Empire, and under the specific conditions of a late Reformation. It allows us to examine to what extent the phenomenon of *Spätreformation* implied that the Protestant communities east of the Empire actually remained under the influence of theological and ecclesiastical models that had been developed elsewhere earlier on. Or to put it differently, the case of Royal Prussia might help to establish whether the developments in the regions secondarily influenced by the Reformation essentially reproduced the chronological pattern of confessionalization in the West, or whether they reflect a substantially diverging dynamic.

It is in this light that the present article attempts to discuss the major characteristics of the process of Reformation and of Protestant confessionalization in the towns of Royal Prussia, roughly between the mid-sixteenth century and the breakthrough of the Polish Counter-Reformation.[1]

---

[1] For a more comprehensive account see Michael G. Müller, *Zweite Reformation und städtische Autonomie im Königlichen Preussen. Danzig, Elbing und Thorn in der Epoche der Konfessionalisierung* (Berlin, forthcoming 1996).

Any study of the ecclesiastical history of Royal Prussia since the Reformation has to take into account that it refers to some of the most controversial issues of Polish and German regional historiography.[2] Undoubtedly, the history of urban Reformation in the province belongs not only to the best documented but also to the most intensely researched aspects of German ecclesiastical history. But, paradoxically enough, it also constitutes a field of research where distorted factual information, and misleading interpretations, have rendered solid scholarly analysis unusually difficult until very recently. The main reason for this is that virtually since the beginning of scholarly historiography, and almost without interruption, the origins of Prussia's religious, or rather confessional profile have been at the centre of a highly politicized debate. In its origins, in the sixteenth and seventeenth century, this debate was primarily rooted in interconfessional rivalry between German Lutherans and their (German as well as Polish and Bohemian) Calvinist opponents.[3] Later it also acquired a national dimension as the religious question became an issue of Polish–German dispute over the ethnic and cultural identity of the Prussian province. German nationalist historiography started to use the argument of an allegedly uninterrupted German Lutheran tradition in the province from the 1550s onwards in order to substantiate political claims of the German national state with respect to Prussia.[4]

It is, however, not the phenomenon of politicized controversy as such that seems exceptional and noteworthy, but much rather the fact that, in this case, it resulted in a gradual consolidation of a largely biased view of the problem, giving a sort of protected status to the Lutheran interpretation of events since the mid-sixteenth century. In fact, Lutheran rewriting of church history, or to put it more fashionably, Lutheran 'reinvention' of tradition, had started as early as the mid-1650s, in the context of the attempts to consolidate the recent victory of Lutheran confessionalism over the once dominant Calvinist orientation of Prussian Protestantism. Both town councils and Lutheran ministers

---

2   Marceli Kosman, 'Reformacja i kontrreformacja', in Jerzy Krasuski et al. (eds), *Stosunki polsko-niemieckie w historiografii* (Poznań, 1974), I, pp. 362–409; Stanisław Salmonowicz, 'Preussen königlichen Anteils und das Herzogtum Preussen als Gebiete der Begegnung zweier Kulturen vom 16. bis 18. Jahrhundert', in *Schlesien und Pommern in den deutsch-polnischen Beziehungen vom 16. bis 18. Jahrhundert* (Braunschweig, 1982), pp. 66–86.

3   The most famous contemporary account, from a distinctly Lutheran perspective, was that by Christoph Hartknoch, *Preussische Kirchen-Historia* (Frankfurt am Main and Leipzig, 1686).

4   A recent example is Heinz Neumeyer, *Kirchengeschichte von Danzig und Westpreussen in evangelischer Sicht* (Leer, 1971), I.

in Royal Prussia took a vivid interest in eliminating the traces of a 'non-orthodox' Protestant tradition that was increasingly perceived as religiously and politically embarrassing. This involved not only strict censorship of urban historiography,[5] but also a thorough 'cleansing' of council records.[6]

Modern regional historiography subsequently endorsed the Lutheran reading of events, at least *de facto*, as the emphasis of scholarly controversy shifted from strictly ecclesiastical matters to the question of competing 'national' cultures. While German historians continued to reproduce the dominant narrative of a teleological and essentially unchallenged development of Lutheran, i.e. 'German', culture in the towns of Royal Prussia in ever more simplified versions, the primary concern of Polish historiography was to highlight the continuity of Catholic, i.e. 'Polish', life in the province rather than to engage in discussions over what were increasingly perceived as scholastic problems of Protestant Church history. As a result, both historiographies contributed to a general denegration of the role of confessional counter-currents to Lutheran orthodoxy in the Prussian Reformation and, therefore, to corroborating a quite anachronistic identification of Protestantism with German Lutheran culture. The most recent comprehensive history of Danzig published by the Polish Academy of Sciences in the 1980s may serve as an example. Criticizing earlier nationalist misjudgements on both sides, the authors suggest that Polish historians should also duly acknowledge the fact that Danzig's German-speaking burghers quite 'naturally' adhered to the Lutheran Reformation and that the consolidation of the new faith 'inevitably' reinforced their German cultural identity.[7]

Even a brief examination of the sources, however, leads to quite different conclusions. The only argument that could reasonably be put forward in support of the 'German hypothesis' would be that the prov-

---

[5] As in the case of Reinhold Curicke, a Danzig Calvinist, whose history of Danzig could only be published after his death, and after the detailed account of the ecclesiastical conflicts in Danzig around 1600 had been eliminated from the manuscript: Reinhold Curicke, *Der Stadt Dantzig historische Beschreibung* (Danzig and Amsterdam 1687, Reprint Hamburg, 1979); unfortunately the reprint does not account for the missing chapters either, although these were included in at least some copies of the first Amsterdam edition.

[6] For a clearly identifiable case of ex-post censorship see the Danzig 'Ordnungsrezesse' (Council minutes) for the year 1605, Archiwum Państwowe Gdańsk (APGd.) 300, 10/18.

[7] Edmund Cieślak, (ed.), *Historia Gdańska* (Gdańsk, 1982), II. In a similar sense Janusz Tazbir, 'Społeczny i terytorialny zasięg polskiej reformacji', in *Kwartalnik Historyczny*, 82 (1975), 723–35.

ince's first encounter with Reformation was actually the challenge by the wave of Protestant *Bürgerkämpfe* that had spread from German territories eastward in the course of the 1520s. Like many German towns at an earlier stage, and like Reval and Riga later on, the Prussian towns faced popular unrest fuelled by anticlericalism, hatred of the rich and the desire for a restoration of true urban freedom as associated with the medieval past. These popular movements were largely based on Protestant experiences in Germany, and supported by theologians maintaining closer links with Wittenberg.[8] However, after the 'Reformation from below' had been subdued in Royal Prussia – by royal intervention, but with the whole-hearted support of the urban élites – almost no traces of the ecclesiastical movement survived. That is to say, if Protestant thought had taken root at all in the towns of Royal Prussia following the episode of 1525–26, it was merely in the form of some kind of crypto-Protestantism – inspired mainly by developments in neighbouring Königsberg. In any case, in terms of church organization and theological orientation the Reformation had to be introduced once again when the Prussian towns were granted individual privileges formally confirming their adherence to the *Confessio Augustana* after 1557.

In the perspective of the late 1550s, the matter of establishing ecclesiastical relations with the Protestant world outside the province presented itself already in a different light. The German Protestant churches consolidated on the basis of the *Religionsfrieden* remained a major point of reference in many respects. But Germany's Protestant territories no longer simply presented themselves as the natural homestead of the Reformation, nor as the only obvious allies for the German-speaking Protestant burghers outside the Empire. On the contrary, German Protestantism in the meantime had become increasingly associated with theological discord and religiously inspired social and political unrest – an experience that the latecomers to the Protestant community were most eager not to repeat. Prussian magistrates followed the events surrounding the Osiandrian dispute across the border with Ducal Prussia with considerable unease as well as the progress of Flaccian mobilization in some of the Lutheran territories in the Empire. And they hastened to turn down Lübeck's proposal that the Prussians should join the efforts of the Hanse to establish a common church organization on the basis of Lutheran orthodoxy. As a member of the Danzig Council phrased it in the 1570s, if the Prussian towns did not wish to become involved in endless struggles with obstinate ministers and rebellious

---

8 Janusz Małłek, 'Marcin Luter a reformacja w Prusach Książęcych i Prusach Królewskich', *Rocznik Teologiczny*, 25 (1983), 2, 91–100.

burghers, they should avoid, above all, siding with one of the confessional parties in the Empire and thereby unnecessarily engaging in what appeared to be 'quarrels among foreign churches' (das gezänke ausländischer Kirchen).[9]

Indeed, the Prussian towns did try to follow this advice carefully when laying the foundations for their church organizations. The first church order to be issued in a Prussian town, the 'Notula Concordiae' drafted by jurists in the service of the Danzig Council and implemented in Danzig in 1562, was obviously an attempt to keep the risk of becoming affected by Germany's confessional controversies to a minimum. Drawing primarily on the writings of moderate Swiss theologians as well as on those of John a Lasco, the authors of the 'Notula' opted, on the theological level, for a moderate interpretation of the Augustana that was to accommodate, if not all, then at least the more conciliatory variants of both Swiss and Lutheran theology. At the same time, the 'Notula' outlined a model of church organization that, being firmly based on the idea of a hierarchical relationship between magistrates and ministers, was to be understood as excluding competing Lutheran projects referring to the three-kingdom doctrine.[10] Moreover, the decision to refrain from establishing a territorial church even in the form of a Prussian tripolitana, and to insist, instead, on individually regulating the towns' ecclesiastical status, was clearly aimed at maintaining freedom of manoeuvre in confessional matters, but also at clearly distinguishing the Prussian churches from the neighbouring German Landeskirchen.

With respect to the recruitment of ministers, however, such clear demarcation proved impossible. Compromises had to be made, since for almost another generation to come, the province itself was unable to provide the theological personnel for the rather sizeable urban churches. The well-established links with the German-speaking world offered little help in this respect, since both neighbouring Ducal Prussia and the leading Hanseatic towns represented precisely the orthodox Lutheran profile that the Prussian magistrates were eager to avoid. They therefore made remarkable efforts to establish a network of ecclesiastical contacts with those among the German universities and territorial churches that, in confessional terms, were most likely to support their attempts to recruit 'peaceful and learned ministers' of moderate theological views. Since the only theological milieus in the neighbouring German territo-

---

[9] For a detailed account of the debates and the decisions of the Danzig Council, Jacob Fabricius, Historia Notulae, APGd. 300 R/Pp 2.

[10] The text of the Notula: APGd. 300R/Pp q. 1, 3r.–21v. For its origins and contents, Curicke, Stadt Dantzig, pp. 202–310; Gustav Koetz, 'Die Dantziger Concordienformel über das heilige Abendmahl', (PhD dissertation, Königsberg, 1901).

ries to meet such expectations were the remaining centres of Melanchthonian teaching, the Prussian towns associated themselves primarily with the Philippist churches of Saxony, Silesia and Pomerania.[11] Thus, it cannot be denied that the general pattern of recruitment reflected a strong German orientation that was, in fact, to persist until the Prussian churches became more firmly established. This was, however, a matter of organizational pragmatism rather than of theological or ecclesiastical affinity.

What had been a latent division between the Protestant churches in Danzig, Elbing and Thorn and the Lutheran milieu in the Empire, became much more visible however, as roughly from the mid-1570s onwards, the towns' ecclesiastical policies shifted towards establishing closer links with the Polish Protestant world. Several factors had contributed to bringing this reorientation about. It was, on the one hand, an immediate reaction to the confessional tensions in the Empire after the proclamation of the Lutheran *Formula Concordiae* indicating that the process of polarization was once again accelerating.[12] On the other hand, it accounted for the fact that, at the same time, the developments in Poland–Lithuania seemed to go in the opposite direction, as the different Protestant churches made efforts to implement a pragmatic supra-confessional co-operation on the basis of the *Consensus Sendomirensis* of 1570, and to establish firmer links with other Protestant milieus.[13] However, even the shift in ecclesiastical orientation reflected a change in the relationship between the three Prussian towns. As Thorn and Elbing gradually emancipated themselves from Danzig's leadership in matters of ecclesiastical policies, they started to establish ecclesiastical networks of their own that, to a much larger extent than in the case of Danzig, were to rely on the towns' traditionally close contacts with their non-German hinterland.

The immediate reason for the towns' redefinition of their ecclesiastical position was, however, the need to react to the erosion of inter-Protestant dialogue in Germany itself and, in particular, to the crisis of Philippism.[14] Moderate Melanchthonian theology had been on the re-

---

11   For a more detailed analysis of recruitment patterns, on the basis of prosopographic studies, Müller, *Zweite Reformation*, ch. 2.4.

12   Inge Mager, 'Aufnahme und Ablehnung des Konkordienbuches in Nord-, Mittel- und Ostdeutschland', in *Bekenntnis und Einheit der Kirche. Studien zum Konkordienbuch*, (Stuttgart, 1980), pp. 271–301.

13   Kai Eduard Jordt Jörgensen, *Ökumenische Bestrebungen unter den polnischen Protestanten bis zum Jahre 1645*, (Copenhagen, 1942).

14   For the structural changes underlying the 'crisis of Philipism' in the Empire see Heinz Schilling, 'Zweite Reformation als Kategorie der Geschichtswissenschaft', in Heinz Schilling (ed.), *Das Problem der Zweiten Reformation*, (Gütersloh, 1986), pp. 387–437.

treat in Germany since the late 1560s, and was practically deprived of its ecclesiastical basis after the dispute between Ernestinian and Albertinian theologians in Saxony had led to the expulsion of the Philippists from the territory in 1574. One of the consequences was that the Prussian churches lost the theological backing and the institutional support for their own policy of confessional compromise. At that stage, the towns could have maintained their links with Protestant churches in the neighbouring German territories only under the condition that they revised their confessional position accordingly, by opting for a clear Lutheran course.

Indications of growing tension had, in fact, become visible as early as 1571. When confronted with urgent appeals by Lutheran theologians in Germany to endorse the Lutheran interpretation of exorcism, magistrates and ministers in Danzig decided for the first time to acknowledge formally a diverging theological position, and to refer openly to the *Consensus Sendomirensis* in order to legitimize their option. Since the 'theologians and lay patrons of the Polish church assembled in Sandomierz' in 1570 had unanimously condemned exorcism, Danzig argued in response to the Lutheran requests that the Prussian churches did not feel free to proceed otherwise.[15] A number of similar incidents occurred over the following years. But it was only towards the end of the decade that the Prussian magistrates decided to put an end to smouldering conflict by clearly demarcating the confessional status of their towns against that of the Lutheran churches in the Empire. By 1578 all three towns had introduced the *Corpus Doctrinae Melanchthonis*, and in 1580 they formally rejected the Lutheran *Formula Concordiae*.[16]

The timing of Prussia's emancipation from the German Lutheran churches should, however, also be seen against the background of developments in Poland–Lithuania. It was also in the course of the 1570s that the Protestant churches united by the *Consensus Sendomirensis* started to be seen from the Prussian perspective as offering a valid alternative to the former alliance with the German Philippists. This was certainly true in theological terms, since the *fraterna coniunctio* between the Augsburg, Swiss, and Bohemian Protestants of 1570 was based precisely on the principles of supra-confessional pragmatism that had been adopted by the Prussian towns one decade earlier. It seemed sufficiently flexible to accommodate a cautious 'clarification and improvement' of the Confession of Augsburg as more urgently advocated

---

[15] Fabricius, *Historia Notulae*, 189r.
[16] Curicke, *Stadt Dantzig*, p. 327.

by Philippist theologians in Prussia as a response to Lutheran orthodoxy.[17] At the same time, the confessional formula of Sandomierz was
balanced and pragmatic enough to avoid committing the Polish churches
to an overtly anti-Lutheran course. Clearly distinguishing the proposed
fraterna coniunctio from the much more ambitious project of a church
union, the *Consensus Sendomirensis* emphasized the idea of containing
theological disputes rather than of promoting a common interpretation
of the Gospel. And unlike their Lutheran critics, the authors of the
Consensus retained the Philippist view that the Lutheran churches duly
belonged to the larger Protestant community committed to the
Augustana.

Apart from theological considerations, however, pragmatic requirements spoke increasingly in favour of establishing closer links with the
Polish–Lithuanian churches. Since the beginning of the 1570s, Thorn
and Elbing in particular had developed their own initiatives in this
direction. The most acute problem was still the recruitment of ministers, essentially affecting all three towns alike. While the need for external recruitment persisted, the chances of finding adequate candidates of
moderate views among the German Lutheran theologians of the Empire
had rapidly diminished. Moreover, in all three cases religious tension
within the towns seemed to grow as the magistrates' concept of a
confessionally neutral ecclesiastical policy was increasingly challenged
by a minority of determined Lutherans among the urban clergy. However, the towns responded to this situation in different ways. While in
Danzig the magistrates tried to increase their control over selection
procedures, and to contain theological dispute among the ministers by
administrative means,[18] Thorn and Elbing tended rather to solve the
problem by changing the patterns of recruitment.

In the case of Thorn, this was largely facilitated by the high degree of
the town's integration with the Polish hinterland. Particularly after the
late fifteenth century, not only had Thorn developed much closer commercial relations with the western and southern regions of Poland than
any other Prussian town, but it also hosted a sizeable Polish population
of which a significant part belonged to Polish Protestant parishes.[19]

---

[17]   For the debates in Danzig in which Jacob Fabricius represented the Philippist
majority among the town's ministers his own detailed account, Fabricius, *Historia Notulae*,
135v.–180v.

[18]   After a number of major disputes in the course of the 1580s, the magistrates in
1586 finally issued a 'decretus de non calumniando' that provided the basis for a more
rigid control over the ministry; Ordnungsrezesse APGd. 300, 10/9, 302r.–304r.

[19]   For an overview of the developments in Thorn see the chapter on the Reformation
in Marian Biskup (ed.), *Historia Torunia*, (3 vols, Toruń, 1994), II, p. 2.

Access to Polish Protestant circles outside the province was therefore easy, and the town could soon count highly qualified theologians from other Polish provinces among its ministers. Mostly they were recruited from among the Bohemian theologians and their Polish followers.[20] But the milieu of the moderate Lutherans in Great Poland also contributed, at least in the earlier stages, to filling the ranks of Thorn's ministry. The most prominent among them was Erasmus Gliczner from Poznan, one of Thorn's leading theologians since 1567, and co-author of the *Consensus Sendomirensis* of 1570.[21]

In spite of the significant influence of Polish theology on the town's ecclesiastical profile, Thorn was however to remain an essentially bi-confessional Protestant community for some time to come. As in the two other towns, German Lutheran opposition among the ministers persisted, and relations between German and Bohemian theologians remained tense. It was only after the mid-1570s that the balance between the two theological groupings shifted. With the support of exiled German Philippists the Bohemian theologians eventually gained a dominant position over their Lutheran opponents, and their increasingly important ecclesiastical activities outside the province contributed to a consolidation of this position. With the appointment of Piotr Artomius as the town's senior Bohemian minister in 1583, the church of Thorn, in fact, acquired the status of Poland's leading centre of Bohemian theology.[22]

In the case of Elbing, the process of ecclesiastical reorientation appears somewhat less conspicuous – not least because sources covering the earlier history of Elbing's Protestant church are scarce. Nevertheless the developments in Elbing seem to fit into the general pattern in at least two respects. The influence of non-German Protestant circles on religious life in the town increased significantly in the course of the 1570s, and a theological opening towards the churches of the *Consensus Sendomirensis* was part of this process. Unlike in the case of Thorn, however, the transformation of the town's confessional profile did not apparently occur as a result of joint action by ministers and magistrates, but rather in response to the religious demands of a new social group: the Scottish Presbyterian merchants who, after their arrival at Elbing in 1577, soon

---

[20] Peter Arndt, 'Die reformierten Geistlichen im Stadt- und Landkreis Thorn 1586–1921', *Mitteilungen des Copernicus-Vereins*, 47 (1939), 1–51.

[21] Theodor Wotschke, 'Erasmus Gliczner', *Aus Posens kirchlicher Vergangenheit*, (1917–18), 1–14.

[22] J. E. Wernicke, *Thornische Presbyteriologie*, Archiwum Panstwowe Toruń (APT) Kat. II, X–27; Stanisław Salmonowicz, 'Piotr Artomiusz (Krzesichleb), 1552–1609', Marian Biskup (ed.), *Wybitni ludzie dawnego Torunia*, (Warsaw, 1982), pp. 45–9.

established themselves as an influential urban élite. While Scottish theologians did not join the town's ministry until a generation later, the presence of a Presbyterian community had an immediate influence through the fact that it apparently encouraged the anti-Lutheran attitude of the Philippist ministers, and that the magistrates could not ignore the need to accommodate the spiritual needs of the new élite. In any case, it was certainly not mere coincidence that Elbing witnessed a major redefinition of its confessional status in the years immediately after 1577. The senior German ministers now expressed their pro-Calvinist views much more freely than in previous years, and a closer co-operation with both Bohemian theologians and Lithuanian Calvinists paved the way for a rapid rapprochement with the Polish Protestant churches.[23]

Although the towns had adopted quite different strategies for dealing with the confessional tensions within their churches, the outcome of the process of confessional repositioning was essentially the same everywhere. All three towns had eventually separated in a more or less formal way from the leading Lutheran churches in the Empire, and ecclesiastical peace had been consolidated on the basis of what councils claimed to be a conciliatory interpretation of the Confession of Augsburg – and what was a provisional consensus over mutual toleration among the confessions represented by the *Consensus Sendomirensis*. It is therefore hardly surprising that a more formal redefinition of the towns' relationship with the churches of the *Consensus* was soon to follow. After 1590, the Prussian magistrates started to characterize 'the churches of our Prussian province' as being explicitly 'Reformed', and to stress that Royal Prussia should be considered an integral part of the Polish–Lithuanian lands united under the *Consensus*.[24] And in 1595 the three towns also formally adhered to the compromise of Sandomierz after a separate, and initially secret, declaration to this effect had been negotiated between the magistrates and the magnate protectors of the Polish–Lithuanian Protestant churches during the synod of Thorn.[25]

---

[23]   Alexander Nikolaus Tolckemit, *Elbingisches Lehrer Gedächtnis*, (Danzig, 1753), 171 ff; Otto Heuer, 'Von den Anfängen der reformierten Gemeinde in Elbing', *Mitteilungen des Copernicus-Vereins*, 47 (1939), 86–101.

[24]   Michael G. Müller, 'Dicursus in der Religions Sache der Preussischen Städte. Ein Dokument zur Geschichte von Konfession und Politik im Königlichen Preußen des 16. Jahrhunderts', in Kazimierz Wajda (ed.), *Między wielką polityką a szlacheckim partykularyzmem*, (Toruń, 1993), pp. 177–87.

[25]   The text of the declaration can be found in APGd. 300 R/Pp 82, 617–19; a copy also exists in the manuscript collection of Warsaw University Library BUW Rkp. No. 590 (Syn. 3). For an account of the negotiations, Gottfried Lengnich, *Geschichte der Preussischen Lande Königlich Polnischen Anteils*, (9 vols, Danzig, 1722–48), IV, Doc. 138–40.

Considering the initial phase in the development of Prussian Protestantism, it is therefore safe to say that the process was determined by the supranational dynamics of confessionalization rather than by an allegedly 'natural' affinity of Prussian Protestantism towards the German world. The fact that Prussian and Polish–Lithuanian Protestants shared the experience of a later Reformation, and developed very similar attitudes towards the challenges of Protestant confessionalization, proved far more important than the existence of traditional ties with Germany's Lutheran churches. Protestant life in Royal Prussia thus did not only become an integral part of the Polish Reformation, but the ecclesiastical bonds between the province and other Protestant lands of the realm were also instrumental in consolidating further the relations between the German-speaking urban élites and parts of the Polish–Lithuanian aristocracy. The effects of this development on Prussia's relationship with Germany, on the other hand, were twofold. While the dependence of the Prussian towns on support by the consolidated German *Landeskirchen* rapidly diminished, the Prussian model became increasingly perceived as an alternative to that of Lutheran orthodoxy. In comparison with many Protestant churches in the Empire the Prussians had, at least for the time being, been remarkably successful in containing the centrifugal powers of confessionalism, and growing numbers of moderate German theologians looked towards Prussia for protection and support to be provided by the tolerant and wealthy urban communities.

During the following brief period between 1595 and 1610 the Protestant churches in Royal Prussia were to reach the height of their development as the centres of Protestant culture in the broader region. This was largely due to the fact that the consolidation of the urban churches as theological and organizational centres of Protestant culture coincided with the beginning of the crisis of Protestantism elsewhere in East-Central Europe. While the ecclesiastical Counter-Reformation made rapid progress, persisting inter-Protestant conflicts, particularly over relations with the Antitrinitarians, weakened the Protestant position from within. And crucially, the Protestant movement was about to lose its political momentum as aristocratic opposition against monarchical rule that had mobilized the estates in support of the Reformation almost everywhere in East-Central Europe was either suppressed or, as in the case of Poland–Lithuania, accommodated by extending the political privileges of the noble Estate.[26] Given the fragile institutional basis of

---

[26] The best account of the main developments in Poland–Lithuania in this period still is Gottfried Schramm, *Der polnische Adel und die Reformation 1548–1607* (Wiesbaden, 1965).

the Reformation, this rapidly led to a situation where, in many regions, the very existence of Protestant churches seemed to be threatened. Protestant hopes therefore turned increasingly towards Royal Prussia, encouraging the towns to claim, and actually play, the role of defenders of the new faith.

In terms of church organization, the Prussian Protestants were obviously in a much better position than their co-religionists in the neighbouring Polish and Lithuanian lands where the Reformation had never been consolidated in a territorially-based institutional framework. Unlike in the Empire, the status of the Protestant congregations in the realm relied exclusively on the individual's freedom of belief as formalized in the *Pax Dissidentium* of the Warsaw Confederation; no legal provision was made for the institutional coexistence of confessional churches, let alone for the protection of minority Protestant congregations. Therefore, in most regions Protestant life remained dependent on the commitment by individual magnate protectors or local noble communities, and wherever the protectors withdrew from the Protestant cause the organizational structure of the congregations in most cases declined rapidly.[27] The only exception to this rule was Royal Prussia where at least the size of the Protestant communities if not their legal status provided for a degree of institutional stability that made the urban churches comparable to a German *Landeskirche*. In Danzig, Elbing, and Thorn political and financial support for the sizeable Protestant ministries was never at risk, and as the councils of all three towns had engaged in systematically transferring the control over institutions to the new church since 1558, the constitutional practice of individual toleration managed to contain Catholic counter-action effectively in this case. Although firmly backed by the king and the episcopate, the activities of the Catholic clergy remained strictly confined to administering those few churches, monasteries and schools that had been reclaimed as royal or monastic property since the 1570s.[28]

As a result, Royal Prussia became increasingly attractive as an expanding labour market for Protestant theologians from other parts of Central Europe. After 1590, the number of foreigners seeking and

---

[27] Michael G. Müller, 'Protestant confessionalization in the towns of Royal Prussia and the practice of religious toleration in Poland–Lithuania', in Ole Peter Grell and Robert W. Scribner (eds), *Tolerance and Intolerance in the European Reformation*, (Cambridge, 1996).

[28] For an analysis of Protestant–Catholic relations see the more recent literature on Thorn: Stanisław Salmonowicz, 'Religiöses Leben in Torun im 16. und 17. Jahrhundert', in Marian Biskup (ed.), *Probleme der Reformation in Deutschland und Polen*, (Rostock, 1983), pp. 41–55; *Historia Torunia*, II.2, 178–88.

finding employment with Prussian churches and schools increased, as did the proportion of non-German theologians coming from more distant regions such as southern Poland, Moravia or Hungary. On the other hand, the towns increasingly became regarded as major points of support, if not institutional centres, for the non-German Protestant communities outside the territory. The most prominent example is that of Thorn where ever since the time of Piotr Artomius the town's senior Bohemian theologian simultaneously acted as the Senior of all Polish–Bohemian presbyters.[29]

Moreover, the three Prussian towns acquired an outstanding position as centres of Protestant learning, as a result of the far-reaching educational reforms undertaken by the Calvinist urban élites after the 1570s. The ambitious plans for establishing a 'Reformed University for the Prussian Lands', energetically pursued by Thorn's Calvinist Bürgermeister Heinrich Stroband since 1594 were finally abandoned – mainly, it seems, because of political rivalry between the Prussian towns. But the simultaneous efforts to transform the towns' *Gymnasia* into academic schools proved ever more successful, and resulted in the towns' acquiring an outstanding reputation as centres of humanistic learning. The share of foreign students in Royal Prussia, including Polish and Lithuanian, and occasionally even Hungarian magnates grew steadily, as did the number of distinguished European theologians who, like Jan Comenius at Thorn or John Dury at Elbing, committed themselves to teaching at Prussian *Gymnasia* – attracted both by their academic reputation and by their liberal confessional profile.[30]

Finally, the integration of Royal Prussia into the Protestant community based on the *Consensus Sendomirensis* also had a political dimension. It paved the way for a close co-operation between the Prussian towns and the dissident Estates of Poland–Lithuania, including the orthodox nobility, thus enabling the urban élites to play a much more active role in the Commonwealth's political life than in previous periods. Once the Prussian churches had formally adhered to the *Consensus* in 1595, the towns became immediately involved in the efforts of the dissident aristocracy to mobilize the estates in defence of republican freedom against monarchical and papal tyranny, and they were also granted protection and parliamentary backing in return. Throughout

---

[29] See footnote 22.

[30] Stanisław Tync, 'Próba utworzenia akademii protestanckiej w Prusach Królewskich w 1595 r.', *Reformacja w Polsce*, 4 (1926), 46–59. For an overview of the rich literature dealing with the academic *gymnasia* Stanisław Salmonowicz, 'Jesuitenschulen und akademische Gymnasien in Königlich Preußen (16.–18. Jh.)', *Zeszyty naukowe wydziału humanistycznego uniwersytetu Gdańskiego*, 15 (1985), 15–27.

the following decade, the dissident senators and noble deputies eagerly supported the Prussian towns' appeals to the provincial Diets and to the *Sejm*, and when the king threatened to execute a court sentence against the town of Danzig in 1603, the Voivode of Brest publicly declared that the dissident estates would rather 'risk their blood' than tolerate the violation of the freedom of their Prussian co-religionists.[31]

Even much distinctly than in the preceding period, in its second phase the process of Protestant confessionalization in Royal Prussia had thus developed a dynamic of its own. On the one hand, this was the result of the towns' confessional emancipation from the Empire, formally completed in 1595. Being no longer under the immediate pressure of what, in the case of German Protestantism, was increasingly experienced as a mutually paralysing process of confessional polarization, the well-established Prussian churches were at the centre of a broader movement towards post-confessional renewal. This encompassed both the theological debate and the attempts at an all-embracing *reformatio vitae* in the spirit of humanism, and it reflected the specific intellectual and socio-political context of the Reformation in East-Central Europe. On the other hand, the developments in Prussia in the 1590s have to be explained against the background of the province's rapidly advancing integration into the Polish–Lithuanian Commonwealth. Both theological affinity and common political interests led to a closer co-operation between German and Polish-speaking Protestants in the Commonwealth, and this co-operation became more significant as the pressure on the Protestants in Poland–Lithuania increased overall. In all, the period of Royal Prussia's most active role as a centre of central European Protestantism was simultaneously that of the weakest links between the province and the Protestant churches of the Empire.

Virtually all these developments since the mid-1590s were, however, dramatically reversed during the subsequent decades representing the third and last phase in the process of confessionalization in Royal Prussia. At the roots of the crisis were inner-urban tensions between the dominant Reformed élites and Lutheran opposition that, after 1604, led to open conflict over the towns' confessional status and, eventually, to a rather abrupt reorientation of the Prussian churches towards Lutheran orthodoxy. As a result, the province came once again under the immediate ecclesiastical influence of German Protestantism while, on the other

---

[31]   Michael G. Müller, 'Wielkie miasta Prus Królewskich wobec parlamentaryzmu polskiego po Unii Lubelskiej', *Czasopismo Prawno-Historyczne*, 45 (1993), 257–67. The initiative by the Voivode of Brest is documented in reports by officials of the Thorn magistrates covering the town's negotiations with Protestant leaders in 1603 and 1604, APT Kat II, XIII–10.

hand, the ties with the Polish–Lithuanian hinterland gradually loosened.

Three factors can primarily be held responsible for bringing about these changes. Although representing merely a minority among the towns' ministers, the pro-Lutheran theologians had been able to preserve a separate status within their churches that, under different circumstances, served as a basis for mobilizing forces against the Reformed majority. In accordance with the *Consensus Sendomirensis* the Prussian towns had, in fact, never questioned their adherence to the Confession of Augsburg, and as popular pressure to re-establish orthodoxy eventually increased, the Lutheran ministers were in a legal position to claim theological leadership.[32]

Parallel to theological opposition, popular resistance against Reformed confessionalization had developed in the context of disputes over church rites. A deeply rooted conservatism of popular religiosity made the common man highly receptive to Lutheran polemics against attempts by the Reformed ministers to introduce ritual changes, however cautious, and popular action against such changes, stirred by Lutheran theologians, had occurred as early as the 1580s.[33]

Finally, political interests came to bear as inner-urban opponents to patrician rule exploited the confessional issue for their purposes, and the Polish king encouraged such attempts in order to neutralize the towns' support for the dissident estates.[34]

The crisis became imminent when Lutheran mobilization against alleged Calvinist abuses led to an open revolt against the council of Danzig in 1605. A group of Lutheran burghers led by some of the wealthiest, and most influential rivals of the ruling patrician families formally accused the Danzig Council of violating the royal privileges defining the town's religious status, and appealed to the king for intervention. The subsequent investigations by royal commissioners and legal proceedings against the Council at the royal tribunal in Cracow lasted two years without leading to conclusive results. However, the pressure on the town resulting from the legal and political escalation of the conflict was strong enough to convince the councillors in Danzig,

---

[32] The underlying theological and juridical debate can most accurately be reconstructed on the basis of Fabricius, *Historia Notulae*. It was written in 1604, in order to provide legal evidence as well as theological arguments as a defence against the Lutheran attempts to reinterpret the confessional status of the Prussian towns.

[33] The individual events, in the case of Danzig, are reported in detail by Reinhold Curicke, *Verbesserter historischer Auszug von Verenderung der Religion in Dantzig.* (Danzig, 1652); see also idem, *Stadt Dantzig*, 335 ff.

[34] For the broader context Müller, *Zweite Reformation*, ch. 3.2.

and subsequently also in Thorn and Elbing, that the crisis could only be overcome by neutralizing Lutheran opposition through a major read-justment of their ecclesiastical policies. In Danzig the conflict came to an effective end after the Council had co-opted a number of pro-Lutheran patricians, and the town's ministry had been formally in-structed to observe strictly the 'pure' *Augustana*. What followed was a rapid, and remarkably smooth, transition of the whole church towards an explicitly Lutheran position; although almost all members of the ministry remained in office, within a decade all but two of the town's parishes had abandoned Calvinist or syncretist practices. Developments in Thorn and Elbing followed a slightly different pattern. While avoid-ing a clean break with Calvinist tradition, the councils used their con-trol over the recruitment of ministers to shift the balance gradually between the Protestant confessions in favour of the Lutherans. It was through the change of generations that the ecclesiastical reorientation towards a Lutheran profile was achieved.[35]

The consequences of Prussia's confessional reorientation on the exter-nal relations of the province soon became apparent. Cutting the links between the Prussian towns and the churches of the *Consensus Sendomirensis* not only weakened the Protestant camp in Poland–Lithua-nia as a whole, but also accelerated the ecclesiastical and, not least, political isolation of the province from the rest of the Polish–Lithuanian Commonwealth. Prussian Protestantism, both inside and outside the province, now became increasingly perceived as an essentially German affair, and as the confessional issue thus acquired a national connota-tion, the towns could no longer prevent its being exploited in the context of political attempts to undermine urban autonomy in Prussia.

The question was once again on the agenda when the outbreak of Polish–Swedish hostilities in 1617 put the province in a strategically crucial position. In fact, all three towns remained entirely loyal to the Polish crown throughout the subsequent wars between the two Vasa monarchies over the possession of Livonia and the succession to the Swedish throne, and their involvement in the conflict was of an essen-tially passive nature. However, the very fact that Danzig was eventually forced to open its port to the Swedish fleet, and that Elbing and Thorn proved unable to resist the Swedish siege and occupation, were enough

---

[35]   The events in Danzig are well documented through Lutheran sources, in particular the reports by the leaders and representatives of the Lutheran opposition on their negotiations with the court and the royal commissioners in 1605 and 1606, APGd. 300 R/Pp 16. For developments in Thorn and Elbing see *Historia Torunia*, II.2, 273ff.; Marian Pawlak, *Reformacja i kontrreformacja w Elblągu w XVI–XVIII w.*, (Bydgoszcz, 1994), 50 ff.

to mobilize anti-Prussian feelings that were soon to find a religious expression. In attempts to explain the sweeping military success of the repeated Swedish invasions of Prussia, and to justify growing political and fiscal pressure on the Prussian towns, Polish propaganda blamed the Prussian burghers for collaborating so readily with their Lutheran co-religionists in Sweden. And such allegations were seemingly supported by the fact that the Swedish invaders themselves underlined the religious motivation of their military presence – not least by persecuting the Catholic minorities in the Prussian towns, allegedly in defence of the Lutheran population. In any case, by the end of the Swedish Wars the religious alienation between the German-speaking Prussian towns and the 'Polish nation' had, in the Polish perspective, become irreversible. The Lutheran burghers were, from now on, considered as being by definition excluded not only from the religious but also the political culture of Polishness.[36]

Simultaneously, the self-perception of the urban population of Royal Prussia started to change. While the ecclesiastical links with the Polish–Lithuanian Protestants weakened and the political cleavages between 'German' towns and 'Polish' noble estates became more prominent, a new identification of Prussian Protestantism with a German cultural identity also seems to have been established from within. This did not refer, for the time being, to the political sphere; at least until the late eighteenth century the territorial identity of Royal Prussia, including the towns, remained firmly associated with the Polish–Lithuanian Commonwealth. In the religious context, however, the realignment of Prussian Protestantism with the German Lutheran churches after 1605 was immediately reflected in a growing sense of belonging to the German Protestant world.[37]

In any case, for the period from the early seventeenth century onwards the thesis of the 'German profile' of the Reformation in Royal

---

[36] For the broader political context Gerard Labuda, (ed.), *Historia Pomorza*, (3 vols, Poznań, 1976), II, p. 1. The role of the confessional issue in the political relations between the Prussian towns and the crown is extensively discussed by G. Lengnich, *Geschichte der preussischen Lande* ... , vols 5 and 6. An interesting case study of royal intervention in Danzig on confessional grounds in the second half of the seventeenth century is Edmund Cieślak, *Walki społeczno-polityczne w Gdańsku w drugié połowie XVII wieku. Interwencja Jana Sobieskiego*, (Gdańsk, 1962).

[37] There is clear evidence for this in Hartknoch, *Preussische Kirchen-Historia*. Some reflections on the problem can be found in Janusz Małłek, 'Die Entstehung und Entwicklung eines Sonderbewußtseins in Preußen', *Zeitschrift für Ostforschung*, 31 (1982), 48–58; Karin Friedrich, 'Better in perilous liberty than in quiet servitude ... the idea of freedom in the writings of two Protestant burghers in seventeenth century Royal Prussia', in Kazimierz Wajda (ed.), *Między wielką polityką a szlacheckim partykularizmem*, (Toruń, 1993), pp. 71–86.

Prussia seems to hold true. After having been challenged by opposition from within, and deprived of its influence beyond the territory, the 'Prussian model' of a supra-confessional Protestantism ultimately lost its basis. It was replaced by the German model of Lutheran confessionalism and, as a result, the Protestant churches of the province were confined to an increasingly marginal role within the Protestant world.

CHAPTER THIRTEEN

Patronage and parish: the nobility and the recatholicization of Lower Austria

Rona Johnston Gordon

By the mid-sixteenth century there was little allegiance to the rites and authority of the Roman Catholic Church apparent in Lower Austria; by the end of the seventeenth century the archduchy was a centre of reformed Catholicism typified by highly demonstrative lay participation.[1] There is general agreement that this transformation took place; the nature of the process and in particular its timing are, however, debated. Historians were initially eager to praise the impact of the Jesuit presence in Vienna from the 1560s and insisted on a dramatic reversal of Protestant fortunes with the accession of Rudolf II in 1576, bringing to an end the conciliatory attitude of Maximilian II.[2] More recent work, however, has demonstrated the ambivalent attitude of Rudolf II towards the Catholic faith and his animosity towards the hierarchy of the Roman Catholic Church whose revival in his lands he was presumed to have furthered.[3] Doubts about the effectiveness of these early developments in the period 1576 to 1609 are reinforced by the continued presence of Lutheran preachers in Lower Austria and their official expulsion as late as 1627. In 1628 it was deemed necessary to order all Lower Austrian subjects – except the members of the noble Estates, an essential exception to our story – to attend Catholic services

---

[1] On the nature of Catholicism in the hereditary lands see in particular Anna Coreth, *Pietas Austriaca: Ursprung und Entwicklung barocker Frömmigkeit in Österreich* (2nd edn, Vienna, 1982) and R. J. W. Evans, *The Making of the Habsburg Monarchy 1550–1700* (Oxford, 1979), chs 4 and 5.

[2] On the early Jesuit presence in Vienna, Bernhard Duhr, *Geschichte der Jesuiten in den Ländern deutscher Zunge* (3 vols, Freiburg i. Br. and Regensburg, 1902–21), I. pp. 45ff. This interpretation can be identified, for example, in the work of Victor Bibl including 'Erzherzog Ernst und die Gegenreformation in Niederösterreich, 1576–1590', *Mitteilungen des Instituts für Österreichische Geschichtsforschung*, Ergänzungsband 6 (1901), 575–96 and *Die Einführung der katholischen Gegenreformation in Niederösterreich durch Kaiser Rudolf II* (Innsbruck, 1900).

[3] R. J. W. Evans, *Rudolf II and his World* (Oxford, 1975), pp. 84–115.

and to celebrate the Catholic rites. The foundations of the edifice of Austrian baroque Catholicism were laid slowly and in a very piecemeal fashion.

It is this piecemeal development which is examined here, in relation to authority over the parishes in the diocese of Passau in Lower Austria. Catholic contemporaries were convinced that the lack of allegiance to the true Catholic way was the fault of the regular and secular clergy who were meant to provide the laity with an exemplary, righteous way of life, to instruct them in the teachings of the Catholic Church and to administer the sacraments. It was held that the laity in their ignorance had been led astray by the inability of the clergy to provide this leadership; instead false Lutheran teachings had been able to gain a hold on their minds and there was no allegiance to the authority of the Roman Catholic Church to counter the presence of a Lutheran ministry. While the resurgence of the medieval monasteries and the emergence of the new orders were to play a central role in establishing the vitality of reformed Catholicism in the province,[4] until the 1630s it was often at the level of the parish that the confessional battle for most of the laity was fought: in the selection of priest or pastor, the content and intent of his spiritual duties, his lifestyle and maintenance, the fabric of the church and the behaviour – and indeed the minds – of his parishioners both within and outside the church. This authority was in various hands, both secular and ecclesiastical, such as the Emperor, many town councils, the monasteries, the Bishops of Vienna and Passau and their Cathedral chapters. The large number of monasteries in Lower Austria could in theory play a highly influential role in the parishes, but this impact was limited by the decline amongst the regular clergy which had set in by the mid-sixteenth century.[5] Above all, many localities, in particular the rural districts, were under the authority of the nobility as local landowners. Control of the presentation and performance of the parish priest was central to the reform programmes drawn up in Passau and Vienna and therefore in turn became a central issue in the debate over political authority in the province.

The jostling for position between Estates and prince in the sixteenth and early seventeenth centuries throughout the hereditary lands has been charted and resulted in a triumvirate of prince, nobility and church by the later seventeenth century.[6] In Lower Austria this process can be

---

[4] The most accessible discussion is provided in Evans, *Making of the Habsburg Monarchy*, pp. 123–33.

[5] Floridus Röhrig, 'Protestantismus und Gegenreformation im Stift Klosterneuburg und seinen Pfarren', *Jahrbuch des Stiftes Klosterneuburg*, neue Folge 1 (1961), 106–43.

[6] Evans, *The Making of the Habsburg Monarchy*, see also the essays in R. J. W.

identified in the debates of the noble Estates in the *Landhaus* in Vienna, the execution of their tax-raising powers and their demands which were often made in terms of confessional freedom.[7] This process also had repercussions outside the Viennese capital, for all those living in the province. In their rural estates the nobility were the immediate authority over the lives of their subjects including the exercise of low, and in some cases high, justice. Orders from Vienna and Prague could simply be ignored and the principle of *cuius regio eius religio* was applied instead on this local scale. At the same time the towns, basking in the combination of their increasing economic strength and relative autonomy had adopted a distinctively Protestant identity and sided with, and indeed relied upon, the support of the noble Estates in disputes with the ruler, the immediate authority over the princely towns.[8] The independence of the nobility and the towns had to be incorporated into the political realignment which emerged from the Thirty Years War.

The defining characteristic of the Lower Austrian nobility in the sixteenth century was their almost complete defection to the Lutheran camp.[9] Comment on this development has often been unfavourable: both contemporaries and historians condemned the nobility throughout the Empire for adopting Protestantism simply in order to justify the seizure of church property from the monasteries and the parishes; in turn the reconversion of the Lower Austrian nobility to Catholicism can then be viewed as a self-motivated step into the obvious financial and status benefits of Habsburg patronage in the following century.[10] The nobility retained control of Lutheranism in the province for, despite the

---

Evans and T. V. Thomas (eds), *Crown, Church and Estates. Central European Politics in the Sixteenth and Seventeenth Centuries* (London, 1991).

[7] For example, Hans-Günther Erdmann, 'Melchior Khlesl und die niederösterreichischen Stände' (dissertation, University of Vienna, 1948).

[8] This process is, for example, evident in Gustav Reingrabner, 'Die Reformation in Horn', *Jahrbuch der Gesellschaft für Geschichte des Protestantismus in Österreich*, 85 (1969), 20–95 and in Richard Hübl, *Die Gegenreformation in St. Pölten* (St Pölten, 1966).

[9] Gustav Reingrabner, *Adel und Reformation. Beiträge zur Geschichte des protestantischen Adels im Lande unter der Enns während des 16. und 17. Jahrhunderts* (Vienna, 1976) also Gustav Reingrabner, 'Der evangelische Adel in Niederösterreich – Überzeugung und Handeln', *Jahrbuch der Gesellschaft für Geschichte des Protestantismus in Österreich*, 90/91 (1975), 3–59.

[10] See, for example, the judgement of Theodor Wiedemann, 'As in Germany, so too in Austria the nobility were converted to the new teachings only by desire, longing and love for church property. Love of the Gospel and longing for the purified word of God were only external propaganda, designed to cover up predatory incursions into the property of the church.' Theodor Wiedemann, *Geschichte der Reformation und Gegenreformation im Lande unter der Enns* (5 vols, Vienna, 1879–86), I. p. 75.

apparent opportunities, an organized Protestant Church was never established in Lower Austria.[11] On the one hand, it can be suggested that the nobility were unable to reach agreement on its doctrine as they became involved in the debates which were dividing Lutherans throughout the Empire by the 1570s. On the other hand, it seems unlikely that the nobility would have been willing to surrender their authority to a central church administration. In the 1620s there was little reaction against Ferdinand II's edicts which banished all Protestant preachers and thus administered the death blow to most Protestant communities. This could be interpreted as a lack of commitment by the nobility to the Protestant cause. However, in 1627 as Ferdinand II began this direct onslaught on Protestantism, the Lutheran nobility had been effectively silenced by the defeat of the rebellion of Protestant Habsburg subjects in 1620, had lost their most effective leaders in this defeat and, in any case, they themselves did not lose the right to continue to worship according to the Confession of Augsburg.[12] Their insistence on their political privilege should not be used to deny the conviction which marked the Lutheranism of many members of the noble Estates. Yet, whatever the reasons behind their original conversion, it had a profound effect on Catholic life in Lower Austria.

The political power of the Lower Austria nobility and their allegiance to Protestantism had united to greatest effect in 1568 when Lutheranism was officially tolerated by Emperor Maximilian II, in exchange for a massive tax for the war in the east. This *Concession*, confirmed by the *Assecuration* of 1571, granted to the members of the noble Estates the right to worship according to the Confession of Augsburg 'in all their castles, houses and possessions (except the princely towns and markets) for themselves, their families and their dependants; in the country however also in their churches for their subjects'.[13] The *Concession* was confirmed by successive Emperors, including the arch-Counter-Reformer Ferdinand II in 1620, and was even extended by Matthias as he sought support in his quarrel with

---

11   Victor Bibl, 'Die Organisation des evangelischen Kirchenwesens im Erzherzogtum Österreich unter der Enns von der Ertheilung der Religions-Concession bis zu Kaiser Maximilians II. Tode (1568–1576)', *Archiv für Österreichische Geschichte*, 87 (1899), 113–228; Gustav Reingrabner, 'Zur Geschichte der flacianischen Bewegung im Lande unter der Enns', *Jahrbuch für Landeskunde von Niederösterreich*, 54/55 (1990), 265–301.
12   See the excellent but unpublished thesis, Robert Douglas Chesler 'Crown, lords and God: the establishment of secular authority and the pacification of Lower Austria, 1618–1648' (dissertation, Princeton, 1979), pp. 230ff.
13   *Religions-Assecuration*, 11 Jan 1571, Wiedemann, *Geschichte der Reformation und Gegenreformation*, I. p. 367.

his brother Rudolf II in 1609.[14] With the *Concession* a Lutheran presence became legal in Lower Austria. The Lutheran nobility were, for example, even able to call on the Catholic Emperor to support them against the Flacians amongst the Lutheran preachers who were pursuing an independent radical line unacceptable to the nobility.[15]

The Bishop of Passau had immediately objected that the *Concession* would have a dramatic effect on spiritual life in Lower Austria by depriving many souls of the true Catholic Church.[16] Indeed it became the main obstacle to the recatholicization programme which was instituted by the Episcopal authorities working alongside the representatives of the Emperor in Vienna. From 1568 until 1627 while these Catholic allies were working to restore the Catholic Church, the Protestant nobility were legally permitted to hold Protestant services in their castles and homes, and to ensure that there was also Lutheran provision for their subjects. The work of these Catholic reformers was therefore limited to parishes controlled by other authorities – parishes directly under the Emperor or the Bishop, the Imperial towns and markets and the parishes incorporated into the slowly reviving monasteries.

This influence of the nobility over the affairs of the parish centred on the right of patronage which was attached to each church individually.[17] The most common form of patronage in Lower Austria was tied to the land and therefore transferred with the land when it passed into other hands, although the right of patronage itself could not be sold. It represented the privileges received by the benefactor in exchange for the

---

[14] In 1609 it was extended by Archduke Matthias to include the fourth Estate of Imperial towns and markets. On the granting of the *Concession* to the second and third Estates by Ferdinand II see Chesler, 'Crown, lords and God', pp. 143ff.

[15] Wiedemann, *Geschichte der Reformation und Gegenreformation*, I. pp. 426–7.

[16] Ibid., pp. 379–80. This objection would be frequently repeated as the practical implications of the *Concession* became clear and in particular when it was extended by Matthias in 1609: Diözesanarchiv Vienna (hereafter DAW), Reformation/Gegenreformation, 1585–1630, Protest des Passauer Bishofs Erzh. Leopold gegen den geplanten Majestätsbrief, 1609.

[17] The discussion of patronage in Lower Austria which follows owes much to the work of Helmut Feigl, see his *Die Entwicklung des Pfarrnetzes in Niederösterreich* (St Pölten and Vienna, 1985), 'Entwicklung und Auswirkungen des Patronatsrechtes in Niederösterreich', *Jahrbuch für Landeskunde von Niederösterreich*, 43 (1977), 81–114; 'Zur Entstehung des Pfarrnetzes in Österreich unter der Enns im Zeitalter der Babenberger', *Jahrbuch für Landeskunde von Niederösterreich*, 42 (1976), 52–69; and *Die niederösterreichische Grundherrschaft vom ausgehenden Mittelalter bis zu den theresianischjosephinischen Reformen* (Vienna, 1964), see also Ludwig Wahrmund, *Das Kirchenpatronatsrecht und seine Entwicklung in Österreich* (2 vols, Vienna, 1894–96) and Gustav Reingrabner, 'Parochie zwischen Patronat und Gemeinde. Anmerkungen zur Geschichte der evangelischen Pfarren in Niederösterreich während des Reformationszeitalters', *Jahrbuch für Landeskunde von Niederösterreich*, 40 (1974), 108–38.

original donation of the church living. When this patronage was in the hands of the local landowner it usually covered his 'subjects' as stated in the *Concession*. The central right of the patron was in the presentation of a priest to the living. In theory the candidate was selected by the patron but had to be approved by the episcopal authority and installed by the bishop in the *Spiritualia* and by the patron in the *Temporalia*. The bishop's rights in this, however, had been ignored when the *Concession* was granted and continued to be ignored, despite repeated protests from the Bishop of Passau. The nobility denied the jurisdiction of the ecclesiastical authorities over them, although their rejection of the authority of the prince was less direct. When ordered by the Passau Official as representative of the Bishop of Passau to halt the preaching in the chapel at Forsthof which was attended by citizens of the princely town of Stein, Freiherr von Althan responded that the Official lacked the authority to make this order: the Bishop himself could not order this and neither Emperor nor Archduke could force their will on him in this matter.[18] In some cases the preacher was installed by his supporting noble before the former priest had left; in other instances, however, the clergyman already exhibited many Protestant characteristics in his services – such as use of the lay chalice – and now simply formally admitted his Protestantism. Many nobles also used their contacts with Protestants elsewhere in the Empire to find preachers. Technically these preachers were under the discipline of the Passau Consistory in Vienna, but this was similarly ignored. During the 1570s it had seemed that a full Lutheran system of discipline might be established but, when this failed, the preachers remained answerable only to the local nobility who had appointed them, for there was no alternative ecclesiastical administrative structure.

However, secular involvement in the parish was not limited simply to the presentation; it included regulation of the temporal affairs of the parish. The *Vogt* (bailiff) who was often also the patron had the right, for example, to control the sale of church lands and to examine church accounts. He could also demand financial aid when a change in his situation required it. In turn, however, he was required to maintain the living of the priest at the necessary standard, particularly after disasters such as war, fire or earthquakes. With the support of the nobleman the church building was converted to Lutheran needs, with the traditional rights of the patron such as burial within the church and preferential seating retained.[19] The nobility were accused of exploiting the income

---

18 Wiedemann, *Geschichte der Reformation und Gegenreformation*, III. p. 45.
19 Gustav Reingrabner, 'Eine Kirche ohne Strukturen. Reformatorisches Kirchenwesen in den habsburgischen Erbländern. Konsequenzen für die Gestaltung kirchlicher Räume'

of the parish to their own ends, or even effecting the wholesale transfer of church property into their own hands. Church vessels were, however, not always simply sold off for profit: when the lands of the Eitzing family were confiscated for their part in the rebellion of 1620, the possessions of the parish which they had earlier confiscated were returned to the hands of the new Catholic incumbent.[20] Lutheran preachers in possession of the parish were also in possession of the rights of income. Additionally, however, as the preacher was dependent solely on the local nobleman, the preacher and his living were often viewed as part of the local estate and the preacher increasingly became dependent on a salary instead of the income of the original donation. In the light of such redistribution of parish income, edicts of restitution were considered essential to the revival of Catholic parish life. Indeed, when brought back under episcopal authority many parishes became involved in long-drawn-out disputes over the details of their original foundation, and in the meantime they often remained poorly endowed and as a result were united with neighbouring parishes or even left vacant.

Despite the defeat represented by the *Concession*, from the 1570s there was also a new vitality in the Catholic camp in Vienna. Influential figures such as Archdukes Ernst and Matthias, Rudolf II's brothers and his representatives in Vienna, several leading councillors and prelates and from 1580, the Passau Official, Melchior Khlesl, were determined to return Lower Austria to the Catholic fold. In 1582 Khlesl, for example, issued an instruction for improved standards of performance and behaviour by the parish clergy in his Officialdom.[21] These Catholic reform plans entered into a highly complex framework, facing for example ambivalent support from Prague and antagonism between Catholic parties within the apparent alliance. Above all, the position of the nobility based on the *Concession* remained impregnable. There was still no attempt to eradicate all Lutheranism in the province. Yet while removal of the *Concession* was deemed impossible, a strategy was devised to reduce all Lutheranism to the strictest possible definition of its terms. There was legal justification for an attack on Lutheranism in the parishes incorporated in the monasteries, in the princely towns and in the so-called Imperial parishes to which the Emperor nominated

---

in Klaus Raschzok und Reiner Sörries (eds), *Geschichte des protestantischen Kirchenbaues Festschrift für Peter Poscharsky* (Erlangen, 1994), p. 155.

[20] Niederösterreichisches Landesarchiv, Vienna: Klosterrat, Obermarkersdorf.

[21] Rona Johnston, 'The implementation of Tridentine reform: the Passau Official and the parish clergy in Lower Austria, 1563–1637', in Andrew Pettegree (ed.), *The Reformation of the Parishes. The Ministry and the Reformation in Town and Country*, (Manchester, 1993), pp. 220–1.

directly, an attack which was led by the *Klosterrat*, the Monastery Commission, which worked for the restoration of Catholicism on a Habsburg agenda.[22] Thus in 1602 a commission comprising the Abbot of Altenburg and the Rural Dean of Krems visited Dürnstein and ordered the removal of the magistrate who supported and furthered Lutheran practices among the citizens against the 'Reformation', the end to attendance at the services of the preacher in neighbouring Weissenkirchen, the closure of the Lutheran school and end to the teaching of the Lutheran Catechism and that the keys of the church should be surrendered.[23] This limited assault was at the heart of the first phase of the recatholicization process.

The picture so far has been of a large number of parishes becoming independent of episcopal jurisdiction while the Counter-Reformation was implemented in all others: that the pastor in the parish church and the preacher employed by the noble for services for his family and servants formed the official Lutheran presence in Lower Austria while the Catholic Church could be restored in parishes not controlled by the nobility. It had been specifically stated in the *Concession* that neither Catholics nor Lutherans were to harm the other party, with particular stress laid on the freedom of worship and protection of church possessions by both sides.[24]

The lines of demarcation between the two parties were not so clearly drawn. Subjects of Protestant lords who were members of parishes where the patronage remained in Catholic hands were forbidden from attending services in their own parish church. The Lutheran nobility were often eager to exploit the weakened Catholic presence in areas covered by the *Concession*. For example, the parish of Senning was in the patronage of the parish priest of Stockerau. By 1582 the priest of Stockerau had appointed a priest to the parish after the death of the former incumbent on the request of the parish whom the priest considered to be 'otherwise obedient parishioners'.[25] The local Steward had, however, examined this new priest on behalf of his master and ordered him not to say the mass but to preach the Confession of Augsburg or leave the parish. The priest of Stockerau ordered him to remain, the

22   On the Monastery Commission see Joseph F. Patrouch, 'The investiture controversy revisited: religious reform, Emperor Maximilian II, and the *Klosterrat*', *Austrian History Yearbook*, 25 (1994), 59–77; Röhrig, 'Protestantismus und Gegenreformation', pp. 135 ff, Wiedemann, *Geschichte der Reformation und Gegenreformation*, I. pp. 195ff.

23   Wiedemann, *Geschichte der Reformation und Gegenreformation*, III. p. 44.

24   Ibid., I. p. 367.

25   Ibid., III. pp. 458–9.

Steward threatened to throw his possessions out of the parish house if he did not remove himself. Spitz saw a constant battle between the existing Catholic patron, the Bavarian monastery of Niederalteich, and the local nobility and converted Protestant community.[26] While the monastery continued to supply Catholic priests – including one who, following a growing tradition, surrendered his vows, married, and squandered the parish income – Kuefstein appointed a Protestant house preacher and challenged Niederalteich's right of patronage. When this failed he built a new rival church. With this typical confusion of various authorities and their rights over the various parishes – who was feudal lord and what were his traditional privileges, who held the right of patronage, who was responsible for upkeep of the church and supervision of the priest – claims were made by various parties which could take years to resolve by legal means. The result was a long list of local disputes over the confessional basis of the worship provided and this stemmed directly from contention over authority over the parish, and who was to ensure the provision of this worship.

The possessions of vacant parishes were often seen as fair game and, in particular, the decline of the rich medieval monastic houses provided much opportunity. It was claimed, for example, that Hanns Wilhelm von Zelking had misappropriated the parish of Matzleinsdorf, belonging to the Abbey of Melk. He had seized the church keys and refused to open the church, even for a burial service. He had also taken control of the sacristy and changed the locks. The annual pilgrimage to the church was refused admittance for mass, and no services at all were being held in the church.[27] In 1610 Hanns von Kollonitsch was ordered to return the keys of the parish church of Kronberg after he had claimed the right to remove the parish priest and had retained the chalice 'with the result that many hundreds people at this holy time (Christmas 1610) leave the parish and must attend the preachers for their so-called ministry and take their sacraments'.[28] Catholic parish priests complained to the Passau Official that not only were their parishioners encouraged in their disobedience, but their subsistence was threatened by the lack of a regular income. In 1590 the priest of Haselbach resigned from the parish after numerous complaints that he could not support himself following the inroads of Wolf von Stein into the parish income. The priest claimed that he would be better off begging from door to door and expressed

---

[26] Ibid., III. pp. 20–1.
[27] Ibid., I. p. 556. After 1627 the procession from Melk was successfully reinstituted. Wiedemann, ibid., I. p. 609.
[28] Ibid., III. p. 356.

himself pleased that he could leave the parish with his own skin and hair, these alone having not yet been seized by von Stein.[29]

As long as there was opposition to reformed Catholic practices and to the men who represented them, neighbouring Lutheran services in the parish or the castle provided an attractive, although illegal, alternative. In 1581 the new Catholic priest in Waidhofen an der Thaya complained to Vienna that the townspeople were going instead to hear the preacher maintained by the Puchheim family although their castle had neither church nor chapel. Although Puchheim was repeatedly ordered to remove the preacher, he successfully defended himself by citing the *Concession* and the preacher remained.[30] If the parishioners did not like what they were offered in one rural church they could simply go to a neighbouring parish for the Lutheran alternative. Often the visit to the preacher some distance away would be made for a baptism or marriage, rites which were more deeply ingrained in the lay mind than the regular Sunday attendance which both Lutheran and Catholic authorities sought. Even while the towns and markets were being forcibly reconverted, all too often a legal Lutheran alternative remained available. The most dramatic example was found in Hernals and Inzersdorf to which the citizens of Vienna flocked. This *Auslauf* became a central concern of the Catholic reformers. Although declared illegal, it happened on such a wide scale that it proved impossible to prevent. Hernals, for example, despite various attempts to have it closed, flourished repeatedly and was only finally abandoned by the Lutherans when it was removed from the Jörger family after 1620, on the grounds of rebellion, and transferred to the Cathedral Chapter of Vienna; the attempt by Archduke Matthias to stop Lutheran worship at Inzersdorf was the spark which set off the dispute with the noble Estates over the oath of allegiance in 1609. It is not surprising, therefore, that the edicts issued by Ferdinand II after 1627 included the instruction not to attend services without official permission anywhere other than in the parishioner's own parish. Even when all Protestant preachers had been banished from Lower Austria, services in neighbouring Protestant Hungary still provided an alternative for some.[31]

While the process of recatholicization was fragmentary, the task seemed unending and frustrating to even the most enthusiastic of Catholic reformers. When Melchior Khlesl finally accepted the unpopular position of Bishop of Vienna in 1598, he declared that the only advantage

---

[29]   Ibid., II. p. 591.
[30]   Ibid., II. p. 574.
[31]   DAW, Reformation/Gegenreformation, bis 1650, Kirchberg to Passau, on attendance of members of parish of Dornbach at services in Pressburg.

was the excuse to leave the service of the Bishop of Passau.[32] The strength and effectiveness of the Protestant noble party were summed up in a letter from the *Statthalter* for Lower Austria to Rudolf II in Prague in 1599. He complained that,

> in many ways the Estates extend the *Concession* too far, in the name of the Confession of Augsburg they believe and do just what they want, that by means of their preachers they can deprive parish churches and old Catholic donations belonging to the Imperial estates and towns, that they use ecclesiastical possessions donated to Catholic priests for the maintenance of the preachers, by placing preachers in their markets and villages they lead the parishioners away from their proper parish and from Catholic ministry, with the result that for a whole year a parish priest will see none or only a few of the subjects in his church and possesses simply the title parish priest and an empty church, additionally that under the pretence of the *Vogtei* they withdraw the best income from the priest, or will not pass it on as is right, unless they give communion in both kinds, they draw to themselves citizens and subjects from His Majesty's and from the Catholic estates towns and parishes, allow them constant free access to their non-Catholic services, with the result that the Catholic religion in the countryside could be completely exterminated.[33]

The Lower Austrian nobility never lost the right to abide by the Confession of Augsburg, as was confirmed in the Peace of Westphalia in 1648, and continued to dominate rural religious life. How then was it possible to reintroduce Catholicism among the rural laity? Two developments are apparent. First, the nobility gradually returned to the Catholic Church. There had always been a minority of members of the noble Estates who had retained their Catholic faith, and in some cases they attempted to preserve that faith among their subjects as well, encouraging men such as Khlesl to preach and using their patronage over the local parish to try to maintain Catholic worship. As has recently been demonstrated, the numbers of Catholic and Lutheran nobility gradually changed in favour of the Catholic party under Rudolf II and Matthias, in particular among the leading members of the nobility.[34] A Catholic party began to emerge within the noble Estates as a

---

[32]   Melchior Khlesl to Archduke Matthias, 1595, printed in J. von Hammer-Purgstall, *Khlesl's, des Cardinals, Directors des geheimen Cabinetes Kaisers Mathias Leben* (4 vols, Vienna, 1847–51), I, p. 214.

[33]   The letter was sent to Rudolf II at the same time as a Protestant embassy complaining about the fining of several Protestant nobles for overstepping the terms of the *Concession* in 1599. Wiedemann, *Geschichte der Reformation und Gegenreformation*, I. p. 504.

[34]   Karin MacHardy, 'Der Einfluss von Status, Konfession und Besitz auf das politische Verhalten des niederösterreichischen Ritterstandes 1580–1620', in Grete Klingenstein

counterweight to the Lutheran majority. As the actively Catholic character of the Habsburg state emerged, many nobles converted.[35] In all official functions in which the nobility were dependent on the Habsburgs, such as land grants and state appointments, Catholics were favoured and promotion into and within the noble Estates was reserved by the Imperial authorities for Catholics.

The second development which aided the recatholicization process was the removal of the subjects of Lutheran nobles from noble protection as the authority of the Habsburgs was strengthened and exerted. The biggest single blow to the Lutheran nobility was the confiscation after 1620 of the lands of those Lutheran nobles who had joined the Protestant Bohemian and Upper Austrian rebels and who had mainly been leading figures in the Lutheran noble party.[36] These lands were passed into Catholic hands only, for now loyalty was clearly equated with Catholicism. Thus in the parish church in the town of Horn where, under the leadership of the Puchheim family, the Protestant nobility had often rallied and where one of the most impressive Protestant churches was built in the 1590s, the rights of patronage were given to the Jesuits and the *Vogtei* to Vincenz Muschinger who bought the confiscated Puchheim lands and promised he would not countenance non-Catholic practices.[37] The patronage rights in these lands were in some cases retained by the Emperor, to be added to the Imperial parishes to which he already presented directly and which had been the first to feel the full force of the Counter-Reformation.

After the defeat and humiliation of the rebellious Protestant subjects in the other directly ruled Habsburg lands and at the height of Imperial success in the Thirty Years War, the erosion of the *Concession* itself began. All Protestant preachers and schoolmasters in Lower Austria –

---

and Heinrich Lutz, (eds), *Spezialforschung und 'Gesamtgeschichte' Beispiele und Methodenfragen zur Geschichte der frühen Neuzeit* (Vienna, 1981), pp. 56–83 and 'The Rise of Absolutism and Noble Rebellion in Early Modern Habsburg Austria, 1570–1620', *Comparative Studies in Society and History*, 34 (1992), 411–27, also Thomas Winkelbauer, 'Krise der Aristokratie? Zum Strukturwandel des Adels in den böhmischen und niederösterreichischen Ländern im 16. und 17. Jahrhundert', *Mitteilungen des Instituts für österreichische Geschichtsforschung*, 100 (1992), 328–53.

[35]   Chesler, 'Crown, lords and God', pp. 238–59.

[36]   Ignaz Hübel, 'Die 1620 in Nieder- und Oberösterreich politisch krompromittierten Protestanten', *Jahrbuch der Gesellschaft für Geschichter des Protestantismus in Österreich*, 58–60 (1937–39); Chesler, 'Crown, lords and God', pp. 268–71; Winkelbauer, 'Krise der Aristokratie', pp. 348 ff.

[37]   Reingrabner, 'Die Reformation in Horn', pp. 57–61. It was, however, not a straightforward transfer: the Jesuits eventually had to make legal claim for the church possessions previously alienated by the Puchheim family, see Wiedemann, *Geschichte der Reformation und Gegenreformation*, II. p. 554.

who were usually those supported by the nobility – were banished from Habsburg lands, on the apparently spurious grounds that they were Calvinist rather than Lutheran. The nobility could, in theory, still use the Confession of Augsburg, but they had no ordained ministers to take services. Some Lutheran nobles encouraged their subjects to attend private meetings where Lutheran sermons were read by lay men, and even women.[38] The first Mandate was therefore followed by an edict ordering that no 'non-Catholic books and sermons' be read and requiring attendance at Catholic services only. And finally, all patrons were ordered to present Catholic priests in their patronage. Although this was a direct contradiction of their interpretation of the *Concession*, the willingness of the nobility to do so was dramatic. They rapidly signed the required promise to present Catholic priests and the demand for suitable candidates received by the episcopal authority could not be met. Thus, for example, in 1629 the Lutheran Wilhelm von Hardegg presented Niclaus Pranser to the parishes of Hardegg and Riegersburg where the family had previously supported Lutheran preachers.[39] All Habsburg subjects, including those under Protestant lords, were then required to attend their local church for confession and communion. This time there was no longer an alternative Lutheran service near at hand within Lower Austria.

It must be noted, however, that the reintroduction of Catholicism in these parishes did not simply return them to episcopal authority and end noble control of parish affairs. The right of patronage was retained and exercised by the landowners, although now in favour of capable Catholic priests only. It was a situation typical of the development of Habsburg authority: traditional rights were not denied, but were exercised along the lines advocated by the increasingly effective princely power. Assuring this alignment of Catholic patron and Catholic parish involved in some cases a new assignment of the patronage and was in such instances often tied to the furthering of the interests of the Habsburg-friendly nobility: in 1620 the parishes of Ebenthal and Dürnkrut were confiscated from Erasmus von Landau; the Emperor initially retained the patronage and instructed the Official to provide capable priests for the two parishes. The *Vogtei* of these parishes was granted to Rudolph

---

[38] On 19 February 1629 Ferdinand II complained to the Bishop of Vienna and to the Passau Official that although the forced reconversion had been largely successful in the towns and markets, the rural districts were still clinging to Lutheran ways, in many cases encouraged by the local Lutheran nobility. This made the need for capable parish clergy in the countryside even greater. Wiedemann, *Geschichte der Reformation und Gegenreformation*, I. p. 621.

[39] Ibid., III. p. 141.

von Teufenbach, with orders to support only Catholic worship; Ebenthal was returned to the previously disputed patronage of the monastery of Mauerbach.[40]

By 1600 the enthusiasm of the Liechtenstein family for a Lutheran presence in Lower Austria had been redirected and the leading members of the family became very active supporters of the Catholic cause in Lower Austria. As Maximilian von Liechtenstein acknowledged in 1600, 'after recognising the Catholic truth, I devoted myself in all means and ways to that end of how I could also cause and move the subjects entrusted to me by God to that understanding'.[41] He invited the Bishop of Vienna to preach and talk to his subjects, and to find capable parish priests for him. He himself continued to press for the conversions of his subjects, and the obdurate were banished from the Liechtenstein lands.[42] Following his conversion in 1602 Gundacker von Liechtenstein instructed that all children should be examined by the priest on the articles of the Catholic faith and that all his subjects should take confession and communion. At the same time he listed as offences such moral concerns as gambling, drunkenness and swearing, and outlined in detail the dues payable by the peasants and services they owed him.[43] This is a clear example of the social disciplining and political control which identify confessionalization, but it was forming at the level of the noble estate.

In 1612 Maximilian von Liechtenstein warned his subjects that they were to obey their parish priests, particularly in attending church services, as they would obey him as their temporal overlord.[44] Yet the parish was not to be simply passed back into episcopal hands which would ensure the provision of a Catholic priest who would in turn create true allegiance to the Roman Catholic Church among his parishioners. This episcopal authority had been so weakened by the inroads of neglect and Protestantism that even the provision of competent priests able to carry out the set daily duties was often beyond its ability, let

---

[40]   Ibid., pp. 414–15.

[41]   Ibid., I. pp. 509–10.

[42]   See the letter to Monastery Commission from Maximilian von Liechtenstein, 1600 cited in Wiedemann, *Geschichte der Reformation und Gegenreformation*, I. pp. 509–10.

[43]   Thomas Winkelbauer, 'Sozialdisziplinierung und Konfessionalisierung durch Grundherren in den österreichischen und böhmischen Ländern im 16. und 17. Jahrhundert', *Zeitschrift für historische Forschung*, 19 (1992), 333–4, also James Van Horn Melton, 'The nobility in the Bohemian and Austrian Lands, 1620–1780' in H. M. Scott (ed.), *The European Nobilities in the Seventeenth and Eighteenth Centuries*, II. *Northern, Central and Eastern Europe* (London and New York, 1995), p. 133.

[44]   7 March 1612, *Pastoralschreiben* from Maximilian von Liechtenstein, Wiedemann, *Geschichte der Reformation und Gegenreformation*, III. p. 273.

alone the work of reconversion. While acknowledging the authority of
the Bishop of Passau over the parishes, the Liechtenstein family repeatedly appeared frustrated at the failure of the Church administrative
structure to support these new converts. The family was often in contact with the Passau Official in Vienna urging and encouraging the next
moves, while repeatedly disclaiming any attempt to usurp episcopal
authority. The teaching of the catechism, which had been acknowledged
at Trent as a central requirement for creating understanding of the
Catholic faith, was repeatedly advocated in letters to the Official and
was eventually followed by a general instruction from the Official for
all parishes to ensure that the catechism was taught to both children
and adult converts.[45] Gundacker von Liechtenstein wrote to his parish
priests stressing the importance of repentance for the souls of his parishioners and indicating how this should be taught – in the church, the
school and each household through instruction and prayer – although
he was also careful to state that this was only a suggestion as he had no
authority in spiritual affairs.[46] In 1632 in frustration at the continued
lack of understanding of the Catholic rites and obedience to these rites
other than at Easter when confession and communion were compulsory, Maximilian von Liechtenstein decided to ask the Jesuits in Vienna
to send two men to lead his subjects to a 'true Christian life' and to
teach them the catechism and articles of belief.[47] The active role the
Liechtenstein family had adopted in parish affairs when Lutheran, was
retained after their conversion and as a result the nature of Catholic
provision in the parishes was also at this time largely at their behest.

The parish could not function as a unit controlled from Vienna and
distinct from local events, jurisdictions and traditions. The new limita-
tions on the powers of patronage did not simply remove local secular
influence over the affairs of the parish or the person of the priest; the
sphere of control of the local authorities still extended into aspects of
the life of the parish priest beyond his appointment. Bringing all parish
affairs into sympathetic hands became the primary concern of successive representatives of the Bishop of Passau. In 1633 Karl von Kirchberg
complained that the insubordination of the parish clergy to the orders
of the Consistory and in particular the continuing practice of concubinage

---

[45] DAW, Konsistorialakten, Katechetik bis 1784, Liechtenstein to Kirchberg, 19
February 1629, see also DAW, Konsistorialakten, Katechetik, Gundacker von Liechtenstein to Kirchberg, 30 August 1632.
[46] DAW, Reformation/Gegenreformation, 27 May 1630, Gundacker von Liechtenstein to parish clergy.
[47] DAW, Reformation/Gegenreformation, 1630–99, 3 April 1632, Maximilian von
Liechtenstein to Karl von Kirchberg.

was actively supported by local authorities who denied his jurisdiction.[48] Yet the Official required the assistance of this secular arm in the face of resistance from the priest and his parish. In the eyes of the Church the secular authorities were bound to assist the spiritual authorities; the former had, however, no right to question the decisions and judgement of the ecclesiastical bodies; their role was executive only. Such opposition continued to involve von Kirchberg in the long-drawn-out litigation to establish his rights which had long been a feature of Passau's attempts to justify its actions. In 1633, he requested that Ferdinand II issue a *Patent* to instruct the local authorities to give assistance to the Official in achieving the desired standards among the clergy.[49]

Reformed Catholicism as defined at Trent had to be incorporated into existing interests in the localities. Thus the confessional allegiances which were adopted by the nobility were used as part of the growing stress on seigniorial rights which characterized their position on their estates in the seventeenth century; in the same way princely authority identified its distinctively Catholic nature with the increase in political and social control. At the same time the system of lay belief was channelled into that outward display of piety which came to characterize the hereditary lands. Lower Austria provides few of the tales of repression, defiance, hardship, martyrdom and exile which characterize the process in neighbouring Bohemia, Moravia, Upper Austria and Inner Austria. But this apparent uneventfulness provides an important clue to the nature of recatholicization in Lower Austria. There is no single event or date to answer the question raised at the beginning of this essay: when did the Counter-Reformation in Lower Austria take place? It was a long-drawn-out and many faceted process which eventually saw the gradual creation of a dominant reformed Catholic ethos at all levels of society and in all areas of the province. After 50 years at the heart of the work of the Catholic Reformation in Lower Austria, in 1628 the Bishop of Vienna recommended: 'if one just leaves the parents without churches and schools in the land, then if not they, then their children will become Catholic, their descendants will remain in the

---

[48]   DAW, Reformation/Gegenreformation, 1630–99, Kirchberg to Ferdinand II, 15 February 1633. Von Kirchberg was defending the jurisdiction of his office; he also claimed the landowners diverted the law into their own hands by sentencing the clergy themselves.

[49]   The request was met positively and the Lower Austrian *Regierung* was instructed to draft the requested *Patent*, DAW, Reformation/Gegenreformation, 1630–99, Kirchberg to Ferdinand II, 15 February 1633; Kirchberg intervened to urge the processing of this *Patent* for he clearly recognized its urgency for the effectiveness of his work: DAW, Reformation/Gegenreformation, 1630–99, Kirchberg to Regierung, s.d.

country, money and trade will not be removed from the country and the prince will not be so hated everywhere'.[50] Yet while successive Emperors had never pushed their hand in the later sixteenth and first decades of the seventeenth centuries, neither were the nobility willing or able to defend the Lutheran cause after 1620. Neither side was defeated which made possible their union in the Habsburg state and under the Catholic banner. It was a staunchly Catholic alliance into which provision in the parishes was drawn.

---

[50] 12 February 1628, cited in Wiedemann, *Geschichte der Reformation und Gegenreformation*, I. p. 616.

Index